The Exemplary Presidency

The Exemplary Presidency

Franklin D. Roosevelt and
the American Political Tradition

Philip Abbott

The University of Massachusetts Press
Amherst

To Janet and Ralph Nase

Copyright © 1990 by
The University of Massachusetts Press
All rights reserved
Printed in the United States of America
LC 89–20247
ISBN 0–87023–706–3 (cloth); 709–8 (pbk.)

Designed by Edith Kearney
Set in Linotron Bodoni Book by Keystone Typesetting, Inc.
Printed and bound by Thomson-Shore, Inc.

Library of Congress Cataloging-in-Publication Data

Abbott, Philip.
     The exemplary presidency : Franklin D. Roosevelt and the American
political tradition / Philip Abbott.
          p.   cm.
     Includes bibliographical references.
     ISBN 0–87023–706–3 (alk. paper).—ISBN 0–87023–709–8 (pbk.: alk. paper)
     1. Roosevelt, Franklin D. (Franklin Delano), 1882–1945.
     2. Presidents—United States—History. 3. United States—Politics
and government—1933–1945. 4. United States—Politics and
government. I. Title.
E807.A68   1990
973.917′092—dc20   89–20247
                                                            CIP

British Library Cataloguing in Publication data are available.

Not being always able to follow others exactly, nor to attain to the excellence of those he imitates, a prudent man should always follow in the path trodden by great men and imitate those who are most excellent, so that if he does not attain their greatness, at any rate he will get some tinge of it. He will do as prudent archers, who when the place they wish to hit is too far off, knowing how far their bow will carry, aim at a spot much higher than the one they wish to hit, not in order to reach this height with their arrow, but by help of this high aim hit the spot they wish to.

Machiavelli, The Prince

Contents

Preface

One of the explanations James Bryce offered for his assertion that "great men are not chosen presidents" was that "brilliant intellectual gifts" were not only not valued by the American citizenry but that the office itself only required "firmness, common sense and most of all, honesty." "Eloquence," "imagination," "profundity of thought" were valuable assets, of course, but no more necessary for the successful execution of the demands of the office than they were to the chairman of a commercial company or to the manager of a subway. It is the argument of this book that Bryce, for all his insight, was wrong on this point and that students of the presidency, as well as students of American political thought, who seem to have accepted Bryce's statement, are wrong as well. Americans do value brilliance of thought in their presidents but our concept of profundity has escaped them.

Certainly Franklin Delano Roosevelt would appear to confirm Bryce's observation. FDR may be credited with holding the nation together during the catastrophe of the Great Depression, patching together a welfare state American-style, and bringing a reluctant citizenry to support the embattled nations of Europe. But the country squire interpretation of Roosevelt, first stated by Walter Lippmann in 1932 when he described him as a "pleasant man" who "would very much like to be President," still heavily influences the assessment of Roosevelt's presidency.

In general support of the approach put forth in this book, I would like to offer commentary from two very disparate observers, Niccolo Machiavelli and the staff of Walt Disney World. In *The Prince* Machiavelli prefaces his discussion of the "exalted instances" in which men found new dominions by noting that "men walk almost always in the paths trodden by others, proceeding in their acts by imitation." If copy he must, advises Machiavelli, "a prudent man should always follow in the path trodden by great men and imitate those who are most excellent." If in the imitative act he does not attain their greatness, "at any rate he will get some tinge of it." At Disney World one of the most popular exhibits is "The Hall of the Presidents." Each president is presented before the audience in robotic replica. Sitting in the middle of a semicircle is Abraham Lincoln who is programmed for more movement than any other president (sixty-five body movements and seventeen facial expressions) and is the only president awarded the gift of electronic speech. After each president is introduced and nods to the audience, Lincoln rises and gives a brief address. The staff at Disney World did not program the Lincoln robot to deliver the Gettysburg Address or the Second Inaugural but created instead their own speech, a composite called the "best of Lincoln." When the address is over, the other presidents give their approval, a chorus of the "Battle Hymn of the Republic" is played, and audiences, always visibly moved, are led to an adjacent souvenir shop.

Both Machiavelli and the Disney World staff can tell us much about the American presidency as an institution that is in a fundamental sense exemplary. Presidents cannot be programmed to follow in the paths of others, as Machiavelli well knew. But as the Disney staff appreciated, Americans admire and respond to exemplary activity. This book examines how one president followed Machiavellian advice. I hope to show how complex this process of imitation can be and, contrary to Bryce, how much eloquence and profundity it requires. For the "prudent archer" of which Machiavelli speaks, even when aiming high to reach a difficult target, inevitably selects a model that contains its own liabilities, both in terms of the imitator and in terms of the consequences the choice can produce for the polity of which he is a citizen.

Support for this project was provided by the Earhart Foundation. Portions of chapter one appeared in the *Presidential Studies Quarterly* and portions of chapter eight were presented as a paper at the 1988 Midwest Political Science Convention. I am very grateful to the following individuals who provided comments on all or part of the book: Irwin Hargrove, Cal Jillison, Michael P. Riccards, R. Gordon Hoxie, and Kenneth Thompson. Bruce Wilcox has been a supportive editor whose advice has been warmly appreciated. Naturally, all material is the exclusive responsibility of the author. As always, Patricia Abbott has been an exemplary counsel. As my son and daughter, Josh and Meg, have come of age, they too have become valued daily editors.

Philip Abbott
Grosse Pointe Woods, 1989

The Exemplary Presidency

1

Exemplary Governance

On December 3, 1925, the *New York Evening World* published a book review of Claude Bowers's *Jefferson and Hamilton* by a New York politician and former unsuccessful Democratic candidate for the vice-presidency. The reviewer was Franklin D. Roosevelt. It was the first and only book review he would write. Roosevelt gave the book unqualified praise, describing Bowers's effort as "thrilling," a "supreme contribution to current thought" that should be studied in "newspaper editorial rooms as well as in the homes and schools of America." The future president admitted that his reaction was influenced in part by "personal experiences." A year ago he had sent a letter to hundreds of Democratic leaders throughout the country and referred to "the difference between the Jeffersonian and Hamiltonian ideals for a method of government" and suggested their "fundamental differences could be applied to present day policies." The response had been less than enthusiastic. Many editors "launched sneers at the mere suggestion that Jeffersonianism could, in any remote manner, bear upon the America of 1925." Roosevelt confessed to "still boil[ing] inwardly when I think of these smug writers." He also admitted to being "fed up with the romantic cult which . . . surrounded the name of Alexander Hamilton." He himself had "longed to write this very book." Now having read the work that came from the "delightful pen" of Bowers, he "felt like saying 'At Last.'"[1]

"Hamiltons we have today"

What had a future president—whom Herbert Hoover would later complain had no political philosophy (he is "a chameleon on plaid")[2]—seen in this popular history? Bowers, whose talent for dramatic historical reconstruction never reached higher levels than in *Jefferson and Hamil-*

ton, had described a capital on the verge of a coup d'etat. At every dinner party he saw the arrogance of aristocratic privilege in dress and manners, every whispered conversation led either to a discussion of the timing of a return to monarchy or to schemes to make money from inside information. The contest between Hamilton and Jefferson became a contest for the soul of the Republic with Jefferson nearly defeated at every step, opposed by powerful allies of the Treasury secretary and confronted by an indifferent Washington. Then Jefferson, portrayed by Bowers as a Westerner and a man of philosophical, peaceful bent with profound domestic yearnings, awakes a sleeping people through a republican press and a new political party. It was indeed a thrilling story and one that seemed to vindicate FDR's call to party leaders for a return to Jefferson. Herbert Croly after all had referred to Roosevelt's circular as the "Great Jefferson Joke": "A political party which, when asked to deal with difficult and novel political and economic problems, always answers by shouting, 'Hurrah for Jefferson,' belongs to musical comedy rather than to the sinister and tragic drama of politics."[3]

Roosevelt seemed fascinated by both figures in the Bowers drama. Hamilton was a "romantic and fascinating figure, albeit in his true character of aristocrat." Jefferson was the "calm philosopher" but also "the consummate politician" and the "savior of the deeper ideals of the revolution." The latter had faced a "colossal task." He could "count only on the scattered raw material of the working classes, difficult to reach, more difficult to organize." But perhaps most significant of all in this short review was FDR's belief that the period 1790–1800 was the most crucial period in American history, as important "in every way" as the Civil War. The future president contended that he had a "breathless feeling" when he had completed the book. He saw "a picture of escape after escape which this Nation passed through in those ten years; a picture of what might have been if the Republic had been finally organized as Alexander Hamilton had sought." FDR wondered with "breathless feeling, too" if 125 years later "the same contending forces are not again mobilizing." "Hamiltons we have today," he closed, but "Is there a Jefferson on the horizon?"[4]

Was Roosevelt's review a minor strategic gambit of an ambitious politician in medical exile? FDR always professed puzzlement when asked directly about his own political philosophy. He was a "Christian and a Democrat." As I shall discuss, both critics and supporters tended to accept this self-assessment. The portrayal of Roosevelt as either a pragmatist or an opportunist may reflect the two poles around which assessments of the New Deal gravitate ideologically, but both portraits tacitly or directly deny this president philosophical insight.

Yet the fact remains that FDR spoke and acted in the language of Jefferson as well as of other presidents. Lincoln would be called up sporadically for the depression emergency and then more consistently for the war effort. Jacksonian populism emerged briefly in 1936. But it was through the language of Jefferson that the bulk of the New Deal would be justified. Jeffersonianism was an ingenious choice. Even though, as I shall argue, it was born of necessity, the model of Jefferson provided the New Deal with both a durability and possibilities not even always perceived by its adherents. This is not to say that the philosophical base of the New Deal in Jeffersonian republicanism was not without significant strains, strains that later would damage the programs of the New Deal itself. There is most obviously the strain of justifying a society partially planned from the center on the basis of an antistatist, local, and agrarian philosophy. There is also the difficulty of creating a stable alloy with Lincolnesque and Jacksonian perspectives. Parallel use of Jefferson and Lincoln in 1933 might appear absurd, but emergency powers can be justified in the name of restoration. By 1936–37 it was clear that a risorgimento required other symbols. By 1940 a marriage of statist and antistatist perspectives was struck. The war, with all the emergency powers and martial rhetoric that Lincolnesque theory offered, could be justified in terms of Jeffersonian republican principles.

There are also the strains emanating from the New Dealers themselves. For the most part the Brains Trust and agency heads had little sympathy for republicanism. Jefferson smelled of old—and lost—battles of the New Freedom and the New Nationalism. The New Dealers wanted to plan. If they had to plan in the name of Jefferson they would do so; they would plan in the name of anybody. But they were constantly worried about FDR's congenital "orthodoxy," about his coming under the sway of Rasputinian advisers, about his excessive concern with "political" considerations.[5]

It is this struggle between the perspectives of the New Deal apparatchik and FDR himself that partially explains the widespread belief that the New Deal simply had no philosophical basis. There are, of course, other reasons. Disappointment with the "reformist" scope of the New Deal had produced a deep resentment not only among the left but among liberals as well. Why, asks Howard Zinn, did FDR simply ignore Marxism when it was "in the air all around him?" Was there, asks James Mac-Gregor Burns of FDR, "no hard center, no core personality, no final

commitment to this man?"[6] Even supporters of the New Deal have emphasized its and FDR's antipathy to theory. Roosevelt experimented freely
without commitment to any "rigid ideology" is part of Arthur Schlesinger's famous assessment. He might hire ideologues, "bold and imaginative
subordinates," but only to have them "balance the right and the left." In
Louis Hartz's analysis there is an appreciation for American political
culture as an explanation for the apparent absence of a New Deal theory.
Without a strong left FDR never was forced to fully articulate his "middle
way."[7]

While all these assessments capture important aspects of the New
Deal, they all also miss the ferocious theorizing that characterized the
1932 campaign as well as the concerted theoretical efforts to construct the
welfare state and win a war. That FDR did not make use of the Marxism
that was in the air around him because he developed another theoretical
perspective that might be as rich and productive as Marxism (as well as
more appropriate to American culture) is a point that Zinn is not able to
appreciate. That FDR made strategic errors and missed opportunities, as
Burns argues, may be as much the result of Roosevelt's theoretical
perspective as his opportunism. If he refused to accept Keynesianism and
its "rigamarole of figures," does that refusal establish that FDR was an
"intellectual failure"?[8] Most important, the Rooseveltian middle way
explored and celebrated by Schlesinger leaves unanswered the question
of how the New Deal furrowed that field. Experimentation is Schlesinger's
answer; but as his critics have noted, caution and restraint as often
characterized the New Deal.

"Leadership . . . is interpretation"

If participants as well as students of the New Deal have missed the central
aspect of the presidency of FDR so have presidential scholars as well. The
American presidency as a subfield has benefited from a variety of approaches. A legal-historical perspective focuses upon the conditions of
legal grants and interpretations of presidential authority.[9] Institutional
studies examine the organizational structure of the presidency as the
major determinant of policy.[10] Power approaches emphasize the role of
more informal sources of presidential authority, including the sources and
impact of prestige and political skills of individual presidents.[11] A
psychological perspective studies the personal values and biographical
backgrounds of presidents with special emphasis upon the nonrational
bases of decision making.[12] Policy approaches focus upon the outcomes

of presidential decisions.[13] These perspectives are not mutually exclusive. For instance, Richard Neustadt's *Presidential Power* presents a view of the presidency based upon the personal use of power, but Neustadt's analysis is based upon an assessment of institutional constraints. Thus while there is a degree of competitiveness among these committed to different approaches to the study of the American presidency, especially in terms of the susceptibility to various approaches to quantitative analysis, the identification of primary independent variables and normative implications, each approach can potentially contribute to the rest in terms of the advancement of generalized knowledge of the presidency.[14]

There is however, an additional approach to the study of the presidency that can supplement existing perspectives. Rarely has the presidency been studied as a structure for the creation of political philosophy. Some possible reasons for this absence are discussed below, but there are some initial presumptions for considering the presidency from this perspective. First, presidential statements are widely cited as models of American political thought.[15] Of course, early presidents (Adams, Jefferson, and Madison) have been recognized for making major contributions to American political philosophy. But despite Richard Hofstadter's thesis that a radical separation of power and intellect occurred early in the republic, Lincoln, Theodore Roosevelt, Wilson, Franklin Roosevelt, and Hoover have offered significant reinterpretations of American political principles while in office. Such attempts, I would argue, have also continued in the modern era of the presidency. Second, several of the roles assumed by presidents place the president in the position to articulate a political philosophy. The ceremonial and agenda-setting roles of the president require the formulation of broad political principles. While these tasks may be completed through the simple (or even cynical) recitation of political symbols, the number of occasions in which a creative rendering is offered is not uncommon. Third, presidents do speak in the language of political philosophy, although often of a unique kind. The search for principles to guide political action, the articulation of a moral dimension to political policy, the attempt to find historical justification for decisions characterize at least the form of major presidential statements. Moreover, the self-consciousness of presidents themselves of this role has led to the use of the previous chief executives as exemplars for policy initiatives.

A few recent studies suggest the promise of approaching the American president as political philosopher. Kenneth Thompson has recommended that the presidency be seen as a source of political philosophy.

He argues that the *Federalist Papers* have provided a structure for the creation of a "public philosophy" in the presidency, that "it is no accident that past discussions of public philosophy have been linked with elaborate accounts of particular presidencies. . . . It is the president who sets the tone, helps shape moods and expectations, fails to provide a framework for public understanding."[16] He outlines in general terms the points at which the presidency can articulate a political philosophy. These include moral example, diagnosis of decline in public commitment, application of principles like human rights. Robert Bellah's well-known article on "civil religion" in America in which he argues that presidents have explored America's conception of a special historical mission in the world, one that is not explicitly Christian but that employs Christian concepts, is the starting point for Dante Germino's provocative analysis of presidential inaugural addresses. Germino concludes that presidential speech is "of a special kind" because of its "anchorage" in "the American public philosophy."[17] In a more critical spirit James Ceaser and his colleagues have focused upon what they see as the heightened role of presidential speech-making in the policy process. They argue that "popular or mass rhetoric . . . now serves as one of the principal tools in attempting to govern the nation.[18]

Despite these efforts, an approach that examines the normative contributions of presidents has not emerged for the following reasons: (1) the Vietnam and Watergate experiences may have created a certain caution or even moral objection to a further examination of a presidency from a perspective that may resurrect images of an "imperial presidency"; (2) most approaches to the presidency tend to be case-study specific and hence overlook the longitudinal aspects necessary to this perspective; (3) both political and policy approaches assume a pluralistic model of politics that tends to treat public principles as disguised objectives of interests; (4) major studies that do take presidential statements as a basis for policy use a psychoanalytic framework, which by its nature demythologizes publicly stated objectives; (5) there is a tendency among students of political theory to seek more formal and abstract presentations and to implicitly accept a sharp distinction between the worlds of intellect and of action.

There is an additional reason for the general lack of development in the consideration of the president as political philosopher. As Louis Hartz has noted, the absence of a feudal tradition has created a tradition of political thought in America that is nearly uniformly liberal in a general sense.[19] Hartz argues, as we have noted, that Franklin Roosevelt largely avoided philosophical discussion of the nature of private property in the New Deal because of the lack of either a socialist or a traditional conservative vocabulary of politics in America. But Hartz's truth also conceals an important aspect of the normative role of the presidency. For when the American president speaks in the language of political philosophy and appears only to be reiterating received opinion, he may also be engaged in major attempts to reinterpret and redefine the basic tenets of this liberal tradition.

An approach to the president as political theorist must first include the question, "How do presidents speak?" with a view toward determining if there is indeed such a thing as presidential discourse in a philosophical sense. American political culture does indeed place severe restrictions on a president's speech. Not only are there entire vocabularies of politics unavailable to a president, but there are cultural beliefs, deeply held, that are radically inconsistent. Moreover, suspicion of elites and political authority in general as well as the creedal acceptance of individualism often requires a president to justify not only his administration but government itself.[20] Yet at the same time, it is just as important to note that there has been a remarkable consistency in American political beliefs. The American consensus has suffered some severe shocks but has historically been remarkably stable.[21] While attachment to some values over others has varied, differences over time have not been great nor has general support fallen below consensus levels. There is then available to a president a history of common discourse, albeit limited, from which to draw upon while attempting to provide foundations for dealing with political problems. Bellah's outline of a tradition of inaugural discourse illustrates this consequence of culture stability as do both Thompson's and Germino's assertions that presidents speak a common language of public philosophy.

But are there features of presidential discourse more specific than the attempt to apply generalized cultural beliefs to political problems? An analysis of the history of presidential thought reveals the persistent use of approaches to political problems that are more concrete than the continued reaffirmation of American beliefs. It is common for presidents to cite other presidents. Often this practice illustrates nothing more than an exercise in simple rhetorical legitimacy. Presidents are admired men and aspirants hope to establish some basic association with past leaders. But the citation of past presidents and the analysis of their policies can also suggest the exploration of potential policy alternatives in the context of American political culture.

The use of past presidents as exemplars for current policy initiatives serves a variety of functions. First, it links cultural beliefs to potential common courses of action. A threat to national unity is given an immediacy and focus if a leader can associate the current crisis with the actions of a Lincoln or a Wilson. As I shall discuss shortly, FDR used the circumstances of war and the ways both Lincoln and Wilson responded to crisis to outline his plans for dealing with the depression.

Second, the use of a past president as exemplar provides a president with an expression of an ideal behavior to be imitated. The use of the "patriot-hero" forms a central aspect of American political thought.[22] Republican political thought developed a complex (if circular) argument concerning the value of "patriot-heroes." The high value placed upon public-regarding behavior in classical republicanism required imitative models for both citizens and leaders. Only a citizenry with a knowledge of the public virtues could recognize ideal behavior, and the values of the patriot-hero would be molded by those who would potentially bestow public honors. Thus it would be in the self-interest of ambitious men to seek out and study the achievements of revered figures. Gary Wills writes about the frantic attempts of Americans to place Washington in the pantheon of biblical founders and ancient republican military figures. Jefferson was frequently compared to Hampden and Sydney, the martyred heroes of the English Civil War.[23] To a certain extent vestiges of republican thought on this question remain in presidential discourse although they are overlaid with more recent, individualistic models of leadership.

This imitative aspect of presidential discourse has been applied by presidents themselves. Washington's favorite play was Addison's *Cato*, a work that emphasized the imitative powers of heroic figures on character and conduct.[24] Wills assigns a kind of psychological methodology to the early presidents. By studying the conduct of the ancient republicans one could internalize portions of their character: "Men like Jefferson had a sense of moving deeper and deeper into the tunnel of time until they came out the other side, where reason and freedom were at home under the Mediterranean sun."[25] The imitative aspect in presidential talk is directed less toward specific policies than toward characteristics of leadership. Presidents today may be less concerned with the special combination of strength of character and asceticism of the republican hero, but they are still noticeably reflective in regard to leadership models. Wilson emphasized the persuasive nature of democratic leadership, Theodore Roosevelt complained about the paucity of strong leadership figures in American culture, Carter is reported to have been influenced by Barber's typologies, Nixon's post-presidential writing shows an obsessive preoccupation with world leaders.[26]

Probably the modern president who most consciously revised this psychological process was Woodrow Wilson. In *Leaders of Men* Wilson argued that a leader must through empathetic understanding reach into the "minds and purposes of groups and masses of men." Wilson in this essay argued that even the most demanding leaders, men like Savanarola and Calvin, governed by a process of "analysis of character." The task of the prospective leader then was to apply the insights of past successful leaders who had mastered this technique. To know as a leader was for Wilson a skill different from knowing in either a personal or a conventional intellectual sense. One could not—indeed should not—attempt to "pierce the hearts of individual men" nor think "thoughts born out of time."[27]

The vocabulary today is indeed noticeably different; leadership "styles" convey a managerial paradigm as well as a different sort of approach to the self-reflection described by Wills. But whether presidents think in terms of Cato's virtues or Barber's "charactological traits"[28] their speech in part is a reflection upon their reflections of past leaders.

At a more specific level the citation of previous presidents conveys the kind of leadership a president hopes to promote. Washington, the founding president, has for some time been a vague and ubiquitous figure, but this had not only been the case. Washington was originally regarded as the partisan symbol of the Federalists until Jefferson began to use the first president as a leadership symbol of national unity.[29] During the tumultuous years before the Civil War, Washington was used by both Northern and Southern politicians when Lincoln claimed him for the Republican cause in his famous Cooper Union speech.[30] More recently William Leuchtenburg has shown how the symbol of FDR has been transformed from a partisan referent to a more general figure of strong executive action and innovative policy-making.[31]

Most important, presidential exemplars function in presidential discourse as a way of reading American political culture. In a sense, presidents engage in an activity that bears some similarities to hermeneutical understanding.[32] The interaction between the text and the reader and the different historical circumstances of each does seem to be a feature of presidential speech. This is not to say that the primary goal of a presidential understanding of exemplars is directly one of discovering the truth of a text, or that the effects are not frequently very partial and the results inchoate. But Lincoln's persistent reading of the founding fathers, Wilson's reflections on the American political system, Hoover's examination of American individualism, and other interpretive efforts of presidents do have a hermeneutic quality to them. One can even take what many might regard as an unlikely source, Calvin Coolidge, to detect an attempt to understand current events through systematic understanding of the texts that form the basis of our culture. Speaking in 1919 at commencement exercises at Amherst, Coolidge spoke of the returning soldiers who were "defending their ideals, and those ideals came from the classics."

This is preeminently true of the culture of Greece and Rome. Patriotism with them was predominant. Their heroes were those who sacrificed themselves for their country. . . . Their poets sang of the glory of dying for one's native land. The orations of Demosthenes and Cicero are pitched in the same high strain. The philosophy of Plato and Aristotle and the Greek and Latin classics were the foundation of the Renaissance. The revival of learning was the revival of Athens and Sparta and the Imperial City. Modern science is their product. To be included with the classics are modern history and literature, the philosophers, the orators, the statesmen, the poets—Milton and Shakespeare, Lowell and Whittier, the Farewell Address, the Reply to Hayne, the speech at Gettysberg— it is all these and more that I mean by the classics. They give not only power to the intellect, but direct its course of action.[33]

Coolidge's linkage of the great texts of ancient Greece and Rome with those of Washington and Lincoln may seem incongruous for a New Era politician presiding over a society given over to commercialism, but Coolidge's remarks are designed to remind his audiences that the "great captains of industry who have aroused the wonder of the world by their financial success would not have been captains at all had it not been for the generations of liberal culture in the past and the existence all about them of a society permeated, inspired, and led by the liberal culture of the present."[34]

This function, of course, needs to be revised considerably in terms of traditional hermeneutic activity. Presidents as well as presidential aspirants are foremost regime actors. Their everyday concerns center around personal career goals and the resolution of pressing political problems. Yet in a constitutional democratic regime the pursuit of these activities requires at various points some deeper understanding of the nature of the regime in which they operate as well as the ability to convey that understanding to the citizenry. In this respect the tradition of presidential discourse is a means by which presidents can hope to achieve some measure of self-understanding. If they can understand what Jefferson or Lincoln meant they may be able to understand what each means to Americans in general. To the extent to which a Jeffersonian ideal can help formulate or justify a particular policy the hermeneutic circle is at least temporarily closed. When other candidates challenge his interpretation, when the press and other elites respond critically, when certain propositions are not even remotely understood by the population or openly rejected, the circle is not completed. Added to this process, which admittedly rarely works successfully for long, are the endless series of responses to new unanticipated events.

Whether a president or a candidate is seeking to employ a presidential exemplar in a policy, imitative, or general hermeneutic sense, or in some combination, there arises special sets of problems. While the list of most admired presidents is relatively stable, popular attachment to these figures is often extremely general and unfocused. Washington may be a symbol of national unity, but the linkage of a policy alternative to the first president by itself is unlikely to elicit any additional support or understanding. There are also basic generational discontinuities in attachment to various presidents as leadership symbols or policy referents. Jimmy Carter began his 1976 campaign with frequent references to FDR but soon found that the identification was not an asset and largely dropped references to 1976 as a replay of the 1932 election.[35] If some presidents have mass support that is too generalized, others are of limited use because of their strong partisan identification. FDR found that the use of Wilson had limited utility in 1928 and engaged in massive efforts to transform first Jefferson and then Lincoln to a symbol of the "new" Democratic Party.[36] Other presidents do evoke a certain specific response but the substance of their image is relatively limited. Harry Truman, for instance, is fondly cited by both Democrats and Republicans but for the relatively simple purpose of establishing a folksy combativeness and foreign policy agressiveness. Still other presidents have left a symbolic legacy that is ambiguous. Moreover, journeymen presidents do not form the stuff for presidential discourse. There are also a whole group of presidents whose impact is so negative that they have functioned as reverse imitation symbols. Grant, Harding, and Nixon are models for corruption; Van Buren and Carter for indecision; Wilson, Hoover, and Johnson for policy failures.

"The ruling passion of the noblest minds"

There is a sense then that the study of a single presidency from the standpoint of exemplars is the study of the history of the American presidency itself. For any president carries with him the successes and failures of past presidents as burdens to be borne, or as opportunities to be explored, or, as often, both. The focus of this book on the Roosevelt years will, I think, confirm this point. But there is a sense in which a study of the FDR presidency offers a unique opportunity. Roosevelt managed to use more presidential exemplars than any other president, to use them more successfully (at least in the short run) and more imaginatively than any other president. He was truly the "exemplary president." The "shadow of FDR," to use Leuchtenburg's phrase, is long indeed and it remains to be seen, although some speculations will be offered in conclusion, whether Roosevelt's legacy rests in part with the creation of himself as an additional exemplar or whether the New Deal has now been deconstructed into Hamiltonian, Jeffersonian, Jacksonian, and Lincolnian pieces.

To the extent that presidents use past presidents as exemplars, their choices are relatively limited. The potentially most effective exemplars are presidents whose general philosophy and policies represent or can be reinterpreted to represent basic dispositions in American political culture. Thus even if the identification of a president and a policy alternative is a relatively weak one, the exemplar can serve as a kind of crystalization of a generally felt belief. The most commonly used exemplars in modern presidential discourse function in this manner.

Who are these exemplars? If there is a single one that most naturally reflects the fundamental dispositions of American political culture, it is that of Thomas Jefferson. The set of principles that have come to be known as Jeffersonian consists of beliefs that seem to have an enduring cultural adherence. Jefferson's elucidation of what has come to be called American exceptionalism—the belief that certain features in our history make America a sui generis in which parallels to European societies are largely irrelevant—is not only a source of patriotic expression but a philosophical premise that marks off the importation of a whole range of policy alternatives. There is also Jefferson's general antistatism and his preference for decentralization that provides a structural alternative to the liberal distrust of central political authority. Jeffersonianism as well offers a theory of political economy that is agrarian. Of course, major portions of Jefferson's theories are contestable. Was Jefferson a Lockean liberal? How strong are communitarian elements in his theory? The protean character of Jeffersonianism has permitted various groups, local elites, civil libertarians, farming interests, even the Communist Party in its popular front period, to claim this president as a source of authority.[37]

Yet however a particular aspect of Jefferson might be emphasized as an exemplar for reform, Jefferson functions most readily as a model for reenforcing American cultural beliefs. In fact the famous words of Jefferson's first inaugural, "We are all federalists, we are all republicans," can be applied to the subsequent presidential uses of his political theory. The gap between Jeffersonian ideal and reality might be enormous, but the belief in decentralization, limited government, and frugality are often tenets that favor those who currently hold onto the pieces of power that make up the American system. No American political theorist understood this ideological aspect of Jeffersonianism better than Herbert Croly, who spoke of the need to emancipate ourselves from "Jeffersonian bondage." But America could no more abandon Jefferson than abandon Locke, and thus while interpretations of Jefferson often have a utopian element they as often have an ideological one. The Southern secessionists, although uncomfortable with Jeffersonian democracy, rallied behind the symbol as did Lincoln, who claimed "All honor to Jefferson" even as he created his own exemplar that owed little to the tenets of decentralization. Wilson defeated Theodore Roosevelt with Jefferson although both he and his opponent struggled to move America in other directions. And the subject of our focus, the New Deal presidency, involved still another appropriation that pushed imaginatively but sometimes hypocritically at the edges of Jeffersonian beliefs.

But in the early days of the republic the Jeffersonian creed, self-consciously defined as consisting of the texts of Sidney and Locke and the Declaration, the Virginia Report, and somewhat begrudgingly the Federalist Papers, was an ideology in opposition. The first operational exemplar was aggressively Federalist in nature. Washington might be claimed by Republican and Federalist alike, but both parties recognized the influence of Hamilton on the first president. In 1825 Madison had recommended the addition of the Farewell Address, redrafted by Hamilton himself, to the creed of the University of Virginia on the grounds that it "may help down what might be less easily swallowed."[38] Hamilton never became president but his vision, clothed with the legitimacy of Washington, became a clear alternative exemplar to the Virginia opposition.

Hamilton was a nationalist, an avowed antidemocrat (critics charged not without some evidence that he was antirepublican as well), a supporter of industry and state financial planning, an imperialist in the eighteenth-century meaning of the term. Clearly in a more volatile revolutionary situation he could have been hanged as a counterrevolutionary or could have installed himself as the leader of a white terror. The Constitution was for him only possibly a choice as a second best regime, and one mark of his genius as a politician was that he was able ideologically to come to terms with it. An early sympathetic biographer concluded candidly that having been "unable to introduce a class influence into the Constitution by limiting suffrage" he hoped to "array property on the side of the Government . . . to insure to the property of the country a powerful influence upon the Government."[39]

But no institution of the new regime excited Hamilton's ideological imagination more than the presidency. For hours Hamilton spoke to a stunned constitutional convention of the need for what in America was a radical nationalism that included a president elected for life with an absolute veto over legislation. Stung by the manner in which the delegates largely ignored his plan, he left the meetings in June returning only to sign the document. Yet during the ratification controversy he played upon the theme of the republican hero to silence opposition to the presidency. In general terms, Madison had insisted that the Constitution was not a departure from republicanism. Only "republican remedies" were employed to cure "republican defects." But it was Hamilton who performed the ideological tour de force by using republican concepts to justify the proposed presidency.

Publius dismissed the comparison between the president and monarchy by reviewing the powers of the president in relation to the Crown and governor of New York. In nearly all cases the governorship is portrayed as a more powerful office than the presidency. There is no "diadem sparkling" on the president's brow, no "imperial purple flowing in his train."[40] To the extent that a resemblance of the president to a monarch was effectively repudiated, the antifederalist republican was left to argue the specifics of executive power. In all instances Hamilton employed republican arguments to defend the presidency. The electoral college was justified on the grounds that it was designed to avoid "cabal, intrigue and corruption," "these deadly adversaries of republican government." The college would guarantee that "the station be filled by characters preeminent for ability and virtue." In no. 70 he chides republicans for relying upon temporary dictators. He reviews the history of plural executives in Roman history. "Republican jealousy" requires a single, not plural executive. A plural executive deprives the people of the "two greatest securities" against the abuse of executive power: accountability and easy discovery of misconduct. The absence of a provision against reeligibility (an omission about which Jefferson complained) is defended both on the general grounds of suspicion of executive power as well as for providing space for the emergence of the republican hero. "The love of fame, the ruling passion of the noblest minds," can prompt "a man to plan and undertake extensive and arduous enterprises for the public benefit." A wise republican will allow these great men to complete these undertakings, lest "the most that can be expected from the generality of men . . . is the negative merit of not doing harm, instead of the positive merit of doing good." Hamilton is always ready to harness the ambition of the republican hero to the public good. He complains that a reeligibility restriction would leave a dozen men "who had credit enough to raise themselves to the seat of the supreme magistracy wandering among the people like discontented ghosts. . . ."[41]

Washington, despite the complaints of both Hamilton and Jefferson, did much to operationalize this model. Through his actions against Indians and rebellious farmers at home and his policies toward intrigue and conflict abroad, Washington developed the concept of executive privilege, personal diplomacy, and executive actions independent of congressional approval. When he left office in 1797 Washington had created the "federalist model" of the presidency based upon "mass appeal, often regardless of public policy positions; strong assertion of executive authority, especially in foreign affairs; general disregard of political parties; preoccupation with official pomp and protocol as a way of protecting and buttressing the incumbent; a conservative economic and social orientation; and an aloofness toward legislative controversies except where they infringe on the executive."[42]

No exemplary president has been canonized as quickly and completely as Washington, who became—as Hamilton had prophesied for the presidency in general and as Jefferson shrewdly recognized—*the* republican hero. But behind the mantle of legitimacy created by Washington and his hagiographers stands the discontented ghost of Hamilton. Conservative sympathizers have always preferred to see Hamilton in Nietzchean rather than in republican terms, and their characterization does express the yearnings for the creation of order in a country frequently anarchist in instinct. Whether Hamilton was prime minister or used effectively by an astute Washington matters not in exemplary terms. The now hoary insight reached early in American history by John Fiske ("As in philosophy all men must be Aristotleans or Platonists, in American politics all men must be disciples of Jefferson or Hamilton") shows the historical power of the exemplar.

A variation of the Jeffersonian-Hamiltonian exemplary struggle emerged in the 1820s. Jacksonian democrats appropriated a somewhat tarnished Jeffersonian exemplar with phenomenal success. "So tight" were the Jacksonian symbols of Jefferson, democracy, and the Democratic Party, argues Merrill Peterson, that "one scarcely existed in the public mind apart from the others and attempts to disengage them met with fleeting success." Democratic politicians developed with great skill the tactic of answering opponents "by squirting Jefferson's opinions in their eyes."[43]

But in the process of employing the Jeffersonian exemplar, the Jacksonians created one of their own. Differences in current historical interpretation of the movement can help illustrate this point. Arthur Schlesinger's *The Age of Jackson* saw Jackson's presidency as a significant enlargement of the political system in terms of participation of both urban and farming populations.[44] Jackson's presidency was interpreted as a struggle against Eastern capitalist elites. More recent historiography has emphasized the entrepreneurial essence of Jacksonianism and has seen the struggles of the period as primarily ones between established capital and more newly organized commercial interests.[45]

In a sense both major interpretations reveal directions in which the Jacksonian exemplar can be directed. For Jacksonianism is foremost an antielitist theory, again illustrating the role of presidential exemplars in articulating basic facets in American political culture. Pushed in one direction the exemplar becomes a populist model for the reassertion of fundamental rights by the "common man" against established elites. FDR used Jacksonianism in this fashion especially in his second term. The "princes of property" would "gang up" against the people's liberties as they sought the "restoration of their selfish power."[46] As powerful as this exemplar can be under certain circumstances, Roosevelt found that it was not strong enough to combat the constitutional crisis he precipitated in 1938. Moreover, Jacksonianism is theoretically neutral in its antipathy toward elites and as such can be used effectively to attack governmental and cultural elites in the name of liberty and local autonomy. Thus the "forgotten man" of FDR was reinterpreted by Nixon as the "silent majority."[47] Ronald Reagan has, of course, used this version of "conservative" Jacksonianism with great success, sometimes to the consternation of traditional Republicans.

Recent scholarship has also discovered another thematic element in Jacksonianism that subsequent presidents have employed. Whether the historical Jacksonians were populist democrats or petit bourgeois capitalists, their language was very much encased in the republican paradigm.[48] Jackson was portrayed—and portrayed himself—as a simple republican hero presiding over "plain, honest men," a "simple stable economy," and a "wise and frugal government." The Jacksonians, in short, justified their policies in terms of restoration of old and challenged republican virtues. That Jacksonians had created a paradox, as Marvin Meyers contends, by clearing a path for the triumph of laissez-faire capitalism through the language of restoring a chaste republican order may reveal less a ruse on the part of political and economic elites than an implementation of two divergent but deeply held American cultural beliefs, the desire for increasing material happiness together with republican community.

In any case, historically the task of modernizing elites has not been an easy one in America. In the Jeffersonian exemplar the enemies are the Hamiltonians, those who would use the government to promote a centralized commercial republic. In the Jacksonian model in the populist version, Eastern capitalists are the aristocrats. In the entrepreneurial statement political elites are "the money power" who "hope to grow rich without labor."[49]

Not until Lincoln had a president had available an exemplar that explicitly and directly outlined a set of justifications for centralized authority. Borrowing upon portions of the Hamilton-Washington exemplar, especially as filtered through Whig theory, Lincoln created an exemplar that is probably the most complex and inventive in American political discourse. Composed of his reading of the founding fathers as well as a dark, forbidding theology, Lincoln created a language unknown to American politics save perhaps in some of the sternest Puritan sermons.[50] Briefly put, Lincoln asserted that there is a core set of beliefs that define us as Americans; when this core set is challenged, all the force of political authority must be brought to bear to enforce it or Americans will risk retribution by straying from the providential course laid out for them. Not only had he expressly defined the limits of pluralism and private right, Lincoln provided the rationale for centralized authority to act without restriction in putative emergencies. Lincoln's vision of American exceptionalism has a deep mythic content far removed from Jefferson's articulation.[51] His language is a martial one in which political conflicts are envisioned as fractions that cannot be accepted. Lincoln as presidential exemplar offers a model so deeply expressive of national emergency that the charge of Hamiltonianism is often difficult to make effectively.

Many presidents have viewed the Lincoln exemplar enviously. Theodore Roosevelt was the first president to see its broader implications. He had openly derided the Jeffersonian vision of America and had come to realize the liabilities of some versions of Hamiltonianism. Lincoln, on the other hand, was the model "radical conservative." But Roosevelt knew that the Lincoln exemplar required a genuine crisis for implementation, a circumstance that he admitted he could not find.[52] The president who has most effectively employed the Lincoln exemplar is FDR. Roosevelt had during the 1932 campaign selectively talked in Lincolnian terms, but only with his first inaugural address was the full weight of this model presented; and it was not until the world crisis in 1939 that FDR turned systematically toward Lincoln.

Do these exemplars exhaust the possibilities of presidential discourse? There is, of course, the possibility that future presidents may be able to recover symbolic aspects of other presidents not yet explored or to combine exemplars in new ways. Certainly Franklin Roosevelt's administrations seem to represent an additional exemplar. Roosevelt's transformation of Jefferson laid the foundation for the American welfare state, and in some future period of severe economic crisis a president could certainly build upon the theoretical work of the New Deal to help justify new initiatives. But it must be remembered that presidential exemplars are a reflection of the contours of American political culture. To the extent to which the Roosevelt model imaginatively but expediently pushed against the American consensus, as an exemplar it is subject to deconstruction. Reagan's willingness to use FDR as an exemplar in the name of fiscal restraint and the indispensability of a work ethic reveals not simply opportunism but an understanding of the cultural pieces from which the New Deal was constructed.

Presidential discourse is not the only—and in many periods, not even the most significant—source of the interpretation of American political culture. Nor are presidential exemplars the only foundation of presidential speech. But the four most enduring exemplars that we have examined, while all are well within the bounds of the liberal consensus, do provide the theoretical basis for a range of policy alternatives. Hamilton-Washington, Jefferson, Jackson (in both permutations), and Lincoln represent sophisticated models of politics that examine the limits and purposes of government as well as the ideational basis of political activity itself in America. The "Father of Our Country," the "Sage of Monticello," "Old Hickory," and the "Great Emancipator" each represent distinct styles of leadership that are embedded in the American cultural experience. One presents a model of a stable, if unequal, society. One offers a unique American version of the Enlightenment. Another boldly insists that successive generations have a right to recover their legacy that Americans are "born equal." And finally the fourth creates a vision of a demanding regime of sacrifice and discipline.

These exemplars allow presidents to explore the viability of the central tenets of the republic. As regime actors their own personal destinies require an understanding of the American political system as a system of beliefs. It is appropriate then that they should rely at least in part upon the philosophies of past regime actors who have undergone similar struggles. Commonly presidential talk is composed of conventional partisan use of political symbols with little purpose other than immediate political advantage. As frequently the use of presidential exemplars can be misplaced or inchoate. For each the choice of each of these exemplars is not without risk. Machiavellian fate often limits a president's choice and—as we shall see—each exemplar, however majestic, carries with it a well-developed critique. But on occasion elections can take on the aura of great hermeneutical struggles, presidential attempts to resolve problems and crises can involve the most imaginative and thorough examinations of the efforts of past leaders, ceremonial occasions can be moments in which the very essence of the American regime is pondered.

FDR understood, although often developmentally and often intermittently, the nature of the exemplary presidency. Through his efforts we can understand better this complex American invention.

2

The Story Teller and the Theorist

The general philosophical base of the New Deal was established in the 1932 campaign. Much attention has been given to 1936 and the "second" New Deal (a point I shall discuss shortly) and FDR's leftward movement. But the doors opened and the foundations laid in the first campaign were never fully discarded. As far as electoral politics permits, 1932 actually did offer a choice between philosophies of government as Hoover had insisted in Madison Square Garden in October. But even Hoover did not draw this conclusion until late in the campaign. He had preferred to use the scholar's tricks, castigating FDR for his inconsistencies, pointing with alarm to the governor's generalities, "educating" his opponent on the origins of the depression and the measures of his administration already in place. Roosevelt, according to Hoover, was a novice and a dilettante. The campaign involved a choice between the characters and experiences of two men.

Roosevelt for his part suffered from his share of vacillation. The Hoover administration was accused of being the "greatest spending Administration in peace times in all of our history." It had "piled bureau on bureau, commission on commission . . ." At the same time Hoover was condemned for the modesty of his relief efforts. FDR never did manage to develop a consistent position on tariffs. Finally he simply told advisers of two opposed positions to write a speech that would "weave together" the views. In Pittsburgh, Roosevelt parenthetically reminded the audience that "if starvation and dire need on the part of any of our citizens make necessary the appropriation of additional funds" he would "authorize the expenditure."[1] This speech was delivered, to state the obvious, at a moment when 13 million people were unemployed. Teachers and students were fainting in classrooms. Unemployed men, women, and children scavenged city dumps for garbage to eat. Hoover, on the other hand, could offer unabashed sympathy for those in distress: "No man with a spark of humanity can sit in my place without suffering from the picture of . . . the anxieties and hardships before him day and night. The people would be more than human if they were not to blame their condition upon the government in power." Job-like, Hoover would repeat that he suffered as he "understood the sufferings" and "worked to the limit of my strength to produce action that would really help them." In September he told a conference on relief that people "are not the authors of the misery which is upon the land. They are its victims."[2]

These and other instances in the campaign led Marriner Eccles to conclude that the speeches "often read like a giant misprint, in which Roosevelt and Hoover speak each other's lines."[3] Added to this is the fact that both the president and the governor seemed to agree on many issues. Both were largely silent on collective bargaining and other concerns of labor. Their positions on Prohibition were not that far apart. Hoover and the Republican platform leaned more to the drys, FDR and the Democrats to the wets. Hoover continued to see the Eighteenth Amendment as the experiment "noble in motive" he had described in 1928 but now implicitly, and still with sympathy with the aims of Prohibition, pushed across the GOP platform calling for state consideration. FDR made much of this "equivocation" early in the campaign. At Sea Girt he told an audience (in language comprehensible only in American politics) that he knew the "honest dry" would prefer the "honest wet" to the "shifty dry" as would the antiprohibitionist the "Four-square dry" to the "uncertain wet."[4] Both candidates opposed the return of the saloon. On foreign policy there was little discussion apart from the implications of tariffs and foreign debts. FDR had struggled with the League issue in 1924 and was not to challenge the Hearst position in this campaign. The real discussion related to the origins of the depression. Hoover repeatedly attempted to place the economic conditions in international context. Roosevelt, beginning with the nomination speech and then pursuing the theme with ever greater intensity, developed a nativist theory of the economic crisis.

But even granting the contortions of electoral politics and the similarities between Hoover and FDR, a genuine philosophical battle was being waged in 1932. It is sometimes missed because of the limits of discourse in American politics. But the campaign—and campaign it was on this point in a military-philosophical sense—was fought with the full knowledge of both the president and the governor over the heart and soul of Thomas Jefferson. Why Jefferson? To answer this question is to find the key to the 1932 campaign as well as to the triumphs and failures of the

New Deal. It also can illuminate the genius of FDR as a political theorist, a fact overlooked by nearly every student of the period.

"I could . . . tell you a thousand stories"

A single factor led inexorably to the centrality of reinterpreting Jefferson for the perils facing the nation in 1932 and this involves the character and careers of the candidates themselves. A world-weary view of 1932 sees a tragicomic display. On the one hand there is Herbert Hoover, a rigid technocrat who quietly labored under the Harding-Coolidge administrations and doggedly insisted upon preserving Manchester liberalism. Street vendors sold apples because there was believed to be a lucrative market in produce. Budgets must be balanced; relief projects must be "self-liquidating"; prosperity was simply a question of a return to confidence in business. On the other hand is FDR, the Harvard graduate and squire from Dutchess County who "very much wanted to be president." Stories abound concerning Roosevelt's obliviousness to theory. The most informative involves his response to a young reporter who asked, "What is your philosophy?" FDR seemed puzzled by the question. He finally responded, "Philosophy? I am a Christian and a Democrat."[5]

Roosevelt's self-description as a Christian and a Democrat may have told more about philosophical commitment than the story's point suggests. In any case, both FDR and Hoover were men of far greater experience and philosophy than the 1932 campaign as farce admits. It is certainly possible to explore the irony of the self-made Hoover defending the American system against the squire from Dutchess County. But the striking feature of the careers of both men is the eminent qualification of each for the American presidency. I speak not simply of the offices both men had held but their appreciation of the contours of American politics derived from their respective experiences that led them both in 1928 to pursue the Jeffersonian exemplar.

Roosevelt began his career as a progressive Democrat in a district that had elected only one Democrat since 1856. His early and well-publicized battle with Tamany not only endeared him to his Hudson Valley constituents but also placed him squarely in the national Wilson wing of a party. There is no evidence to indicate, however, that Roosevelt's admiration for Wilson was not genuine nor that his progressivism was not the product of natural sensibilities derived from family and class background. He believed in "clean" government, conservation, direct primaries and popular election of Senators, help for the downtrodden, women's suffrage, and internationalism. But Wilson's tragic failures placed FDR in the position of surviving during the period that can only be called the fag end of the Progressive Era.[6] He could not break the machines; he was left defending the League of Nations when it had become a liability; he ran for national office at the beginning of the long period of conservative Republican hegemony. As is generally the case in American politics the dominant party soon determines the agenda for the opposition. The ranks of progressive Wilsonian Democrats grew smaller and smaller. It has been noted that Roosevelt's illness was oddly fortuitous. FDR had been removed from politics during a period in which few progressives could survive the factionalism, recrimination, and resentment that follows the death of a reform movement and the electoral price that is necessarily paid. Roosevelt's advisers did not want him to run for governor of New York in 1928. This was not to be a good year for Democrats.[7] When run he did, the strategy in the initial stages was to develop a campaign heroic in its defeat so that FDR would have a base of support in 1932 or 1936. Louis Howe had initially advised the candidate to limit campaigning to a few radio addresses supporting Alfred E. Smith. Presumably a third replay of the Happy Warrior theme would keep Roosevelt politically alive.

The nomination speech began cautiously enough and along the lines of the Howe plan. FDR pledged to continue the work of Governor Smith. He featured pledges to farmers and reorganization of state government and of the criminal justice system. State ownership of public utility sites received the firmest commitment. Water power, the candidate promised, would "not pass from the hands of the people of the State." The next day at Binghamton, the themes of the campaign still inchoate, FDR devoted his speech evenly between governmental reorganization and religious prejudice. This short address contains four stories, one about the "four bears" (the jurisdictional division of brown, black, Alaskan, and grizzly across four departments), one about a Georgian who thought that if Smith were elected the children of Baptists would be declared illegitimate, one about a man of Irish descent running for office in Dutchess County. The punch line to the last story concerns a farmer who supported the local candidate and who explained that he was not against Irish Catholics, just Roman Catholics.

It would be unfair to make too much of an extemporaneous speech delivered in a small town, but it is worth noting that FDR found himself straddling a fine line in his stories regarding religious prejudice. The jokes were designed to show the ignorance that intolerance is based upon. Roosevelt went as far as to admonish the audience: "Yes you may laugh;

but they [the bigots] were not laughing. They thought it true; and they were honest, law-abiding citizens. They did not have the education, the contact, to know better. . . . Oh, I could go on," the candidate continued, "and tell you a thousand stories along that line."[8] He told one more. But the stories were designed to make the audience laugh—to show the absurdity of anti-Catholicism in the cause of toleration. The problem is that this kind of joke at one level slanders everyone. Farmers are portrayed as stupid, and the telling of the joke itself legitimizes the telling of others less "liberating." No doubt the circulars that FDR himself mentioned being passed around Binghamton contained some of this sort of material.

In any case, Roosevelt's position could not have been more forthright even while his method of presentation may have been less than appropriate to the kind of issue he was addressing. In the speech he had said that those who wrote and printed pamphlets of religious prejudice "ought to be put on the first boat and sent away from the United States." Republicans used the remark to assert that FDR had claimed that those who were reticent to vote for Smith because of his religion ought to be deported. Candidates for other offices from minority groups pleaded for silence on the bigotry question.

But Roosevelt tried again in Buffalo. He asked Samuel Rosenman to help prepare some material on labor. This was Rosenman's first effort at speech writer, and he details how FDR had simply said not to worry about a particular line but to "just put something together that we can look at in the morning."[9] When he looked at the draft the next day, FDR added two paragraphs. One opened the speech. It too was a story of sorts. "Somewhere in a pigeon-hole in a desk of the Republican leaders of New York State is a large envelope, soiled, worn, bearing a date that goes back twenty-five or thirty years. Printed in large letters on this old envelope are the words, 'Promises to labor.'" Nowhere in the envelope, Roosevelt, concluded, was there a single page bearing the title "Promises Kept."

The addition to the speech is a nicely crafted story but in itself represents the conventional campaign rhetoric that revolves around promises kept and promises delivered. What is instructive about the Roosevelt additions is the effort to call up the ghost of progressivism. FDR paralleled the issues facing the electorate in 1928 to his own experiences in the state Senate in 1911. Here too men of good will, men like Smith and Wagner, fought good fights. "Arrayed against us on the other side was the silent, powerful pressure of the old school of thought, which held the theory that when an employer hired a working man or a working woman, he became the master of the fate of the employee. . . ."[10] For their efforts in behalf of American workers, these young men were called "radicals," reds, and socialists. The speech closed with another Roosevelt addendum, another story about religious toleration. After reminding his audience that some people were "violating by written and spoken word" the Sixth Amendment to the Constitution, FDR urged his listeners to remember again.

I go back in my memory ten years ago—ten years ago this autumn. I go back to the days when I saw Chateau Thierry; I go back to the days when I was following up the advance of the American Army; I go back to a day in particular when several miles behind the actual line of contact between the two armies I passed through wheat fields, wheat fields with the ripened grain uncut; wheat fields in which there were patches, little patches of color, something in the wheat, and some of those patches wore a dark gray uniform and others of those patches wore an olive drab uniform. As we went through these fields there were American boys carrying stretchers, and on those stretchers were German boys and Austrian boys and American boys being carried to the rear, and somehow in those days people were not asking to what church those German boys or those American boys belonged. Somehow we got into our heads over there and we got into our heads back here that never again would there be any question of a man's religion in the United States of America.[11]

These two additions hardly make the campaign address at Buffalo a great speech, much less a coherent political theory. But they do illustrate the struggles and limitations Roosevelt found for himself in 1928 and how he moved to deal with them. At Jamestown he had joked that the country had had its "beauty sleep" under Harding and Coolidge and, more seriously, that "it may have been a good thing for us to quiet our nerves after the struggle of the Great War."[12] Campaign anecdotes, after some experimentation, were tied to the task of forcing audiences to remember the triumphs and the conflicts of another generation. Progressive politics was certainly not dead in the 1920s; FDR campaigned in large part on Governor Smith's record. But the movement was well past its salad days and it was this period that FDR attempted to evoke, first in recalling the republican ethos of the young New York progressives and then in sternly reminding his audience of battlefield equality and the price that it extracts. The two images were not entirely complementary. The battle against the "silent," "powerful" forces that would "own" a worker is broadly Jeffersonian. The conditions and terms of work must correspond to republican principles. Power must be dispersed in any sphere, especially since there are always aristocratic forces at work that would corrupt the spirit of republican equality. The scene at Chateau Thierry reflects upon soldierly sacrifice and its implications for citizenship. It suggests (FDR never lays out the complete argument, only asserting that "somehow we got it in our heads . . .") that there is an essence to citizenship that is discovered through a common cause and that lesser loyalties must self-evidently pale before it.

But that one implies a principled pluralism, and the other unity was not FDR's immediate concern. FDR was searching for some basis of support independent from the "happiness, prosperity, and security" etched in voters minds from a decade of Republican hegemony. To do so he dredged up two narratives appealing to voters' sentiments. These two experiences, reform and sacrifice, were still part of the American ethos and their antipodes worth remembering. In Rochester he raised the issue of Americanism and red-baiting again. When he had worked for a workers' compensation bill seventeen years ago he had been called a "Red" and he was certain that his current request to study old-age pensions would make him a "Bolshevik" once again. [13]

The remainder of the campaign would be devoted to these twin themes. Roosevelt began to replace the progressive label and refer to the "human functions" of government. Always he sought to outline his support for public programs on the simplest and broadest terms: "wheel-chair cripples," "little children who have been thrown on the mercy of the community" by the deaths of their fathers, widowed mothers, the blind. He defended the public development of water power by referring to his discussion as a "sermon." He was going to "preach from the Old Testament." His "text" was to be " 'Thou shalt not steal.' " [14] FDR portrayed the utility companies and their lawyers as "pirates" who would "steal" the "priceless heritage" of the people of New York State. Should the legislature block his efforts to create a state power authority he would submit the question to a referendum. In Queens he proposed an extensive parks program. The enemy here were owners of summer estates. But there were millions of citizens, the great rank and file of us, and particularly the children, who have no home of their own in the country and who long for a chance to obtain appreciation at first hand of the value of outdoor life. FDR piled number after number: Bear Mountain Park was visited by 4,875,000 people last year; 10,000 bathers had used one "two-by-four" park on Long Island every weekend last summer. More and more families were faced with "no trespass" signs. If, he concluded, public park development was socialistic, then "we are all socialists." [15]

The 1928 campaign did, as many observers have suggested, prefigure the philosophy of the New Deal outlined in 1932. But for the most part Roosevelt's attempts to offer an alternative to Republican hegemony were fragmented. He pushed up against the American consensus whenever he could by recalling the last threads of sentiment left from the earlier progressive formulation. He sought out a political formulation of public activities that would not require an overt theoretical structure. Even in these instances, even when he had narrowed the arena to crippled children and parks, he felt the necessity to confront charges of "radicalism."

The last major speech of the campaign did illustrate, however, how FDR finally hit upon a formulation that not only had the potential for electoral power but that also was broad and strong enough to carry New Deal reform on the back of the dead weight of American political culture. Of course it still took three years of depression for its success. The opening theme of the address at Yonkers, "Is Hoover human?" followed the general lines of previous speeches. Government programs could be justified in simple human terms. No other discussion need follow. Implied in the question as well was the implication that Hoover was a cold-hearted technocrat. But the speech went further. There was, he began, an interest today in the "philosophy of politics, in the theory of our government." Roosevelt took a quote from Hoover's *American Individualism:*

Acts and deeds leading to progress are born of the individual mind, not out of the mind of the crowd. The crowd only feels, it has no mind of its own which can plan. The crowd is credulous, it destroys, it hates and it dreams, but it never builds. It is one of the most profound of exact psychological truths that man in the mass does not think, but only feels. [16]

Hoover had meant to say that a polity is a delicate thing, that there is no sure way to produce leadership (it cannot be replenished "by selection like queen bees"), that a citizenry must rely on its own considered judgments and that a leader, as opposed to a demagogue, must govern on the basis of these collections of individual judgments. But Hoover in *American Individualism* as well as in his public addresses had always employed an implied argument that appeared invincible in a cultural sense, and it was at this suppressed premise that FDR aimed his attack. For Hoover had always presented an exceptionalist argument. He was an "individualist—an unashamed individualist" but always "also I am an *American* individualist."[17] This assertion that he was describing not an abstract body of principle but also intuiting principles especially American meant that opponents must question not only his premises but the premises of the American system. There are, he announced, five or six great philosophies in the world. There are Communism, Socialism, Syndicalism, Capitalism, and Autocracy. There is even Divine Right of Kings in some parts of the world. But, "there is Individualism in America." Who could not say, without the most careful equivocation, that he or she was not an American individualist? Roosevelt certainly would not. But what he did was to insert his own cultural premise. Who would say in America that he or she was not a democrat? Perhaps, intimated FDR, Hoover was saying just this such thing:

Now, Mr. Hoover's theory that the crowd, that is to say, 95 percent of all the voters who call themselves citizens, that the crowd is credulous, that it destroys, that it hates, that it dreams, but that it never builds, that it does not think, but only feels—that is in line with his training, the record and the methods of accomplishment of the Republican candidate for the Presidency. [18]

All this, FDR said (and he insisted that he was speaking as an "analyst and not as a candidate"), was another way of saying that "there exists at the top of our social system in this country a very limited group of highly able, highly educated people, through whom all progress in this land must originate." This "small group" was to do "all the thinking and all the originating." [19]

In a sense this was Hoover's philosophical view as well as his cultural weapon. Hoover had insisted that equality of opportunity would "free" individuals from the "frozen strata of social classes . . . to take that position in the community to which his intelligence, character, ability, and ambition entitle him." [20] In itself, and assuming that the strata of social classes were indeed unfrozen, Hoover's position is an interpretation of Jeffersonian philosophy in which the gems would be raked from the rubble. But Roosevelt had detected a Hamiltonian edge to Hoover's formulation. The crowd must be the average citizen and certainly the average citizen was self-governing. So FDR had hit upon his own American truth. There were no "crowds" in America. We are all capitalists, we are all individuals, was a truth that American Whiggery had discovered after Jackson, and FDR seemed to think that Hoover had forgotten this point. He reviewed once more his proposals for parks and water power, insisting that these ideas had come from "that urge from the bottom" that "may have been a dream as Mr. Hoover would call it. . . . It may have come from people who do not think, as Mr. Hoover says." Both the state and the national campaigns revolved around the issue of Hoover's belief "in the incapacity of the mass of average citizens either to think or to build."[21]

Roosevelt won the election by the slimmest of margins, although he ran ahead of Smith in New York State. Had the late effort to portray Hoover as a modern-day Hamilton been successful? Probably not in 1928. But four years later the evocations of progressive triumphs would be absent or perfunctory. FDR immediately and incessantly pursued the Jeffersonian position.

"Our individualism differs from all others"

Hoover's defeat in 1932 has overshadowed his success in 1928. While FDR was struggling to find some reconstruction of progressivism Hoover had already established one. Historians have expressed major disagreement over just what this synthesis was. The traditional view portrays Hoover as a typical New Era politician. He may have been smarter than Coolidge and cleaner than Harding, but these attributes made Hoover even less able to deal with the Great Depression. Hoover on this view was the technocratic progeny of the end of the Gilded Age. He was a man of dogma whose policies helped bring on the depression and whose policies failed to alleviate it. Thus Elliot A. Rosen writes: "Herbert Hoover was not a progressive. . . . his American system [was] intended to preserve individualism and nineteenth-century anti-statist, laissez-faire attitudes. His policies as Secretary of Commerce, then as President, contributed substantially and directly to the Great Depression."[22]

The case has also been made for Hoover as a progressive. He was after all a high official in the Wilson administration, a man who built his career on feeding people; he was a friend to labor. His nomination acceptance in 1928 promised the abolition of poverty in America. Martin L. Fausold insists that Hoover was "the more liberal and progressive candidate in 1928." His name had come "to mean food for the starving and medicine for the sick." Jane Addams, who had voted for Debs in 1920 and La Follette in 1924, supported Hoover for his position on collective bargaining, his farm policy, his "war" on poverty, his relief work, his promise to enforce prohibition without federal gunmen. For Joan Hoff Wilson "the great engineer and humanitarian still lived beneath the new mantle of the Great Depression president"; Hoover was a "forgotten progressive and a remembered conservative."[23]

Perhaps the most innovative assessment detects a certain originality in Hoover's political philosophy. William Appleman Williams has described Hoover as "the keystone in the arch that leads from Mark Hanna and Herbert Croly to such later figures as Nelson Rockefeller and Adolph Berle." Hoover came "very close to being . . . the first class-conscious corporation leader produced by the system." According to Williams, Hoover had abandoned the premises of a competitive early capitalism of primitive accumulation and proposed a cooperative system of labor and capital led by a "class-conscious industrial gentry."[24] Ellis W. Hawley has described Hoover's political thought in these terms as "corporatism." In Europe as well as in America the reaction against "destructive competition" led many liberals to search for a system that could promise stability and order. Hoover had accepted this critique and outlined and partially implemented a "social order organized around and regulated by functional groupings, which are held together and stabilized by responsible leadership, established principles of social equity and efficiency, and institutionalization of a 'natural' mutuality of interests." Hawley asserts that the dividing line between Hoover's new liberalism and FDR's New Deal is in part a disagreement in management theory: "The shift was not from laissez-faire to a managed economy, but rather from one attempt at management, that through informal private-public cooperation to other more formal and coercive yet also limited attempts. . . ."[25]

Was Hoover an antistatist liberal, a progressive, or a corporativist? The 1928 campaign was actually an addendum to a political theory worked out years earlier. Each set of interpreters of Hoover properly regards his *American Individualism* as the complete statement of his views. Yet an examination of this unusual little book suggests that Hoover's political theory does not quite fit any of these analyses. There are far too many attacks on entrepreneurs to allow for the first thesis; far too many concerns about the dangers of change to permit us to call Hoover an unalloyed progressive; and far too much emphasis on individualism to permit the description "corporativist" without severely expanding the definition of the term.

Three major concepts are elucidated throughout Hoover's essay. First is a presentation of a theory of American exceptionalism that is surprisingly Hegelian in formulation. But despite this unusual idealism, Hoover's understanding of America is unmistakably Jeffersonian. Any other formulation of Americanism than that of Jefferson is, for Hoover, logically really un-American. Here was the stick with which Hoover beat Smith in 1928 (although he did not even need to use it) and here was the weapon that FDR stole from him in 1932. In fact Hoover still thought he had the ultimate defense and it could be said that he brandished a weapon that was gone from his hand. But first to the Hegel-like presentation.

American Individualism begins with the proposition that the "war itself" was a "conflict of social philosophies." For Hoover the power of these ideas is inestimable. Hooverian imagery is apocalyptic. There had been "social explosions," forces "freed from restraint," "urgent forces" plunging societies into a "terrible furnace" resulting in nations "burned with revolutions." In his seven years of service overseas he had seen with his own eyes and had to contend with "economic degeneration," "social degeneration," and "political dislocation." For the most part America had thus far been spared from this caldron of contending political ideas and the "havoc they have unleashed." But the "storm of war" has to a certain extent reached American shores. The European conflict, and America's participation in it, had "left even with us . . . much unrest, much discontent with the surer forces of human advancement." But Americans must realize that there are "underlying forces in our American life" and that our political and economic structure were only the "products of our social philosophy." Ours was a "special social system" because we had developed a special set of ideas.[26]

Hoover thus made an extraordinary claim, one that carried the Jeffersonian enunciation of Americanism in both relativist and absolutist directions. It was relativist in the sense that individualism—the philosophical essence of Americanism—was culturally specific. "Our individualism differs from all others," claimed Hoover, who insisted "it is not the individualism of other countries." The principle of equality of opportunity demanded the abandonment of an individualism based upon " 'every man for himself and the devil take the hindmost.' " Hoover admits that this form of individualism may have made an appearance in the nineteenth century but argued that a purer principle had evolved than in the days of laissez-faire. Lincoln is assigned the Hegelian role of reinterpreting a new form later confirmed by legislation. Hoover even argues that Lincoln's concept of fair chance has evolved into a notion of "fair division" and that even this formulation is now in the process of merging into an even higher formulation, one described by Hoover himself as "progressive individualism." There is no place in the American system, says Hoover, for one who "throws bricks at the social edifice." The "strong and dominant" have learned that our individualism imposes "certain restrictions."[27]

But if the American Idea was "special" even as it had evolved into higher and higher forms, it was in Hoover's mind the Idea of America as well. "No European state will lay claim" to this idea, but on the other hand to attack the concept of individualism was to attack the very essence of American identity. "Salvation will not come to us out of the wreckage of individualism." There is for Hoover a papal edict of a sort for Americans: There is no salvation outside the American system. In return for participation in a system that "shall safeguard to every individual an equality of opportunity" to take his "position in the community to which his intelligence, character, ability, and ambition entitle him" he "in turn must stand up to the emery wheel of competition." Anyone who sought to alter this contract was part of "malign social forces" that "would destroy our progress."[28]

New powers of production might set up "temporary roadblocks" upon equality of opportunity. Hoover himself is quite willing to cite "things [that] have happened that never ought to happen." He offers a long list, one that shows progressive sensibilities. These include the uncertainty of employment in some callings; the deadening effect of certain repetitive processes of manufacture; the twelve-hour day; arrogant domination by some employers; child labor; some fortunes "excessive far beyond the needs of stimulation to initiative"; survivals of religious intolerance; "poltical debauchery of some cities." But there is a "deadline" between our system and socialism. Hoover, with all the certainty that Hegelian logic and language provide, declares that "regulation to prevent domination and unfair practices . . . are in keeping with our social foundations. Nationalization of industry or business is their negation."[29]

Supporters as well as critics have assumed that the essence of America lies in its nature as a commercial society. To be an American is to be one who sells and buys. The measure of the health of our society, perhaps our only measure, is general prosperity. The measure of individual success, the mark of the good citizen, is his own material success. In its essence a kind of Hegelian logic results: If the publicly shared ideal is private acquisition, then there is no public.

Hoover is very much aware of this paradox and seems to attempt to return to the original Jeffersonian formulation as a solution. Acquisitive instincts in themselves ought not to be celebrated. It is wrong to say that individualism has "as its only end the acquisition and preservation of private property—the selfish snatching and hoarding of the common product." The defense of private property in republican thought centered around the assertion that ownership sprang from "natural wants" and thus in principle all had a right to property and all property owners had a common interest. Hoover put his position this way: "Our development of individualism shows an increasing tendency to regard right of property not as an object in itself, but in light of a useful and necessary instrument in stimulation of initiative to the individual; not only stimulation to him that he may gain personal comfort . . . but also because . . . ownership is a basis of selection to leadership. . . ." Hoover's conception of property then had a definite Jeffersonian cast. Property was not just a thing to be exploited, it was a means of "self expression" for Hoover not just economic but spiritual. Property was very much like Locke had described it, "Life, Liberty and Estate."[30]

Ironically, Hoover was committed to what Leon Samson has called a socialist's conception of private property.[31] Here was an institution to which all had a right and from which all benefited. Thus Hoover could contend that corporate capitalism actually represented a higher level of property ownership than the collection of Jefferson's yeomen:

The overwhelmingly largest portion of our mobile capital is that of our banks, insurance companies, building and loan associations and the vast majority of this is the aggregated savings of our people. Thus large capital is steadily becoming more and more a mobilization of the savings of the small holder—the actual people themselves and its administration becomes at once more sensitive to the moral opinions of the people in order to attract their support.[32]

American Individualism did not offer any kind of ascetic ideal. For Hoover, however, prosperity was a reward, even simply a by-product, that the American system provided. His therefore was a measured and tempered materialism. The 1924 Democratic Party platform complained that "the Republican party is chiefly concerned with material things." Hoover did not deny that high and increasing standards of living and comfort should be the "first of considerations in [the] public mind." Government needs to make "no apology" in its promotion of economic development. The American system in the last four decades had "added electric lights, plumbing, telephones, gramophones, automobiles" to our standard of living. Moreover these new "comforts," begun as luxuries, were now in wide diffusion. "Seventy or eighty per cent of our people participate in them." But all this has been given us by the American system: "it [the system] plowed two score of great states; it built roads, bridges, railways, cities. . . ." If we remain faithful, the system will provide: "so long as we maintain our individualism we will have increasing quantities to share and we shall have time and leisure and taxes with which to fight out proper sharing of the 'surplus.'" But so Hoover also reminded "the slightest reduction of the impulse to produce will at once create misery and want."[33]

The third premise of his philosophy was a conception of individualism that Hoover believed he had discovered in the process of the evolution of the American system he had thus described. "Every man for himself" was only a lower manifestation of the "divine spark in each person." "Self-expression" does not exist in the creation of private property as a "fetich" but is manifested most clearly in service to the community. Hoover contends that "when we rehearse our own individual memories of success, we find that none gives us as much comfort as memory of service given." He asks, "Do we not refer to our veterans as service men? Do not our merchants and businessmen pride themselves in something of service given beyond the price of their goods?" There were "great mystical forces" of the past seven years, "glorious spiritual forces," that suggested the existence of "a rising vision of service."[34]

Hoover saw the expansion of interest groups as evidence of the existence of this service individualism. Chambers of commerce, trade associations, labor unions, bankers, farmers, propaganda associations were all, of course, institutions that represented mixtures of altruism and self-interest. But Hoover insisted that these groups, in providing individuals an opportunity for self-expression, were a "field for training" in service to the whole. Each group itself represented "a realization of greater mutuality of interest," each contains "some element of public service."[35]

Hoover's philosophical vision was a paradoxical one. The concept of individualism suggests that a person's rights and needs come before the demands of any collectivity. It also suggests that individuals have at least the capacity to discern these rights/needs. The principles of individual rights and individual autonomy are in important ways denied by Hoover. Not only does he seem to offer positions that the critics of the New Era had made (entrepreneurs were often a threat to prosperity and the American standard of living was more often than not the result of factors other than their initiative, prosperity needed to be diffused across the population, every man for himself was not the operative ethic of a good society) but he offered philosophical positions that represented the antithesis of the liberal tradition. He argued that individualism was a social construct that could function only under certain conditions of cooperation. In this sense, despite the open polemics of his entire career after 1932, Hoover was a collectivist. In an important sense, he was on the other side of that great divide that separates individualists from collectivists.

In a way, in fact, Hoover was far more of a collectivist than was FDR. This point needs to be examined more fully in a moment, but let me take this opportunity to explain Hoover's collectivism. Political theorists tend to assign positions on the dichotomy under discussion on the basis of a writer's commitment to mediating institutions. From one vantage point Hoover was clearly a defender of social and economic and political groups. Nationalization of industry, he had intoned, was the "negation" of our social foundations. His opposition to the use of direct federal authority during the depression was unwavering. In *American Individualism* Hoover had warned that socialism entails "the bureaucratization of the entire population." On the other hand groups for Hoover were morally epiphenomenal. They were to be supported only to the extent that they exhibited a mutuality of interests, and Hoover had openly worried that a government dominated by groups would produce a "syndicalist nation on a gigantic scale." FDR's concert of interests approach, which I shall discuss shortly, paralleled Hoover's position. The difference, I think— and it is a difference that neither Hoover's nor Roosevelt's supporters saw—was that the concert implied that there were a set of common interests that conflicting groups might discover, while Hoover's mutuality implied that groups were deserving of moral recognition only to the extent to which they served the interests of the whole. At bottom Hoover's American system was so tethered to his Hegelian interpretation of American exceptionalism that it accepted the legitimacy of no group or set of groups but only the American Idea of individualism. Accept service, Hoover told the business elite, accept the social contract that demands submission to the emery wheel of competition, he told those in distress.

Was Hoover a "corporativist?" No more than he was a progressive. His system was a unique distillation of both the remnants of the progressive tradition as well as an emerging corporate ideology. Certainly his suspicion of interest groups, except as training grounds for leadership; his disdain for legislatures and politicians generally; his love for rational organization—all were elements congenial to the development of an American counterpart to European corporatism. But what made his position so successful in 1928 and so vulnerable in 1932 was his commitment to the simple substantive content of his collectivist vision.

Hoover in his commitment to Jeffersonian principles had grasped the power of individualism as a Volkgeist in America. When he said he was an "unabashed individualist" Hoover was expressing his commitment to a collectivity, to, in his words, the American system. George Santayana captured the essence of Hooverism when he explained that "to exploit business opportunities and organize public service useful to all" constitute the "tasks of a good citizen." "In America there is only one way of salvation; to work and to rise by that work, adhering to a regimen not less strict than that of the monasteries for the sake of an ill-defined but somehow better future."[36] Here was the American's collective duty. It was the duty to be an "unabashed individualist," to be sure, to work and rise by that work, and it was a duty that was absolute.

The threat to liberty from corporate power was always acknowledged but Hoover's preference for corporate organization, particularly in the new mass-production industries, revealed a real lack of concern for their centralizing power that was decidedly un-Jeffersonian. What Hoover admired in businesses like International Harvester and Goodyear were, in fact, their rationalizing stabilities, their capacity for innovation and efficiency as well as their potential for public spiritedness.[37] In short, what Hoover found attractive in these new forms of capital were those features that were destroying local markets and the viability of state rather than federal supervision. While it is true that Hoover supported decentralization within the corporation particularly in regard to labor issues, he believed that efficiency, diffuse stock ownership, and labor peace made the corporation, if not an ideal, certainly an acceptable vessel for individualism under modern conditions.

There can be no doubt that Hoover took the concept of service individualism seriously. When he urged Americans to contribute $10 million to the drought relief fund of the Red Cross the message had something of the language of an executive order about it: "It is imperative in the view of the experienced directors of the Red Cross that a minimum of ten million dollars be contributed to carry this relief project to completion." When Congress pushed for direct appropriations, he insisted that any other method of relief would "break down this sense of responsibility and mutual help" and "not only impaired something infinitely valuable in the life of the American people but have struck the roots of self-government." This was not simply a question of the most efficient method of relief nor "the cost of a few score millions" but the creation of an "abyss of reliance in future upon Government charity in some form or another." Hoover concluded that the demand for appropriations was, of course, a "natural anxiety for the people of their states." Privately he believed that Southern congressmen were using the demand for funds to avoid any direct help to sharecroppers.[38]

Hoover had developed a political philosophy that took as its central premise the uniqueness of America and with Jefferson, a belief in the indispensability of local community. Hoover's own geisteswissenschaften permitted no deviation from the American idea of individualism. Within these restraints, however, Hoover was more than willing to pursue reforms that would rationalize the American system. Hence Hoover's reputation as a progressive in 1928 and the first eight months of his presidency.

The 1928 campaign perfectly illustrated the complex character of Hoover's system. Hoover himself notes in his memoirs that prosperity was his "great ally" in 1928 and the depression his "major enemy" in 1932. The remark in the context of Hoover's political philosophy means a good deal more than simple partisan strategy. Prosperity allowed the American public to hear the positive side (the "charm," to use Hartz's phrase) of Hoover's version of American exceptionalism. His acceptance speech at Stanford University emphasized the recent achievements of the American system (3.5 million new homes, 9 million more electrified dwellings, 6 million more telephones, 7 million new radios, 14 million new cars) as well as its possibilities. He presented a vision of truly utopian potential for America. Not only did Hoover promise "larger comfort" and "equality of opportunity for all irrespective of faith and color," he claimed that "we in America today are nearer to the final triumph over poverty than ever before in the history of any land." Hoover, admittedly without specific programmatic recommendations, placed not only the alleviation of want on the political agenda but the abolition of poverty itself: "we shall soon with the help of God be in sight of the day when poverty will be banished from this nation."[39]

While Hoover himself would have been the first to admit that these were the promises inherent in the American system, the press portrayed Hoover as "the hero of a new organized and efficient industrialized America." The "Great Engineer" whose office looked more like a machine shop than a room, whose mind commanded all experience, and "whose wave of the hand organized fleets of rescue vessels and millions of contributions" was a figure enormously appealing to the suburban middle-class businessmen, managers, professional men, and white-collar workers who "benefited most fully from the prosperity of the 1920's in terms of self-esteem as well as personal income."[40]

Page Smith has argued that the small town rarely produced robber barons.[41] The psychology of the small town inculcated a kind of diluted Puritan calling for service that made the scientific, legal, and managerial professions the career choices of young men. This special elite may have attempted to apply the ideals of the small town to reform as Hoover himself would claim to do, but in the process they contributed to the nationalization of American society and the demise of a nation of villagers. But in 1928 Hoover seemed to represent a synthesis of a Jeffersonian, rural America and the new Enlightenment of applied science. Hoover's August visit to his home town in West Branch, Iowa, was a spectacular illustration of this theme and certainly the most successful media event of the campaign.

The Jeffersonian ideal envisions America as a series of gardens. "I have often thought," wrote Jefferson in 1811, that "if heaven had given me a choice of my position and calling, it should have been a rich spot of earth, well watered, and near a good market for the productions of the garden."[42] And here was Iowa in August with, in Hoover's words, "the wonder at the growing crops, the joining of neighbors to harvest, the gathering of apples, the pilgrimage to the river woods for the annual fuel and nuts, the going to school, fishing in creeks, the hunting for prairie chickens and rabbits in the hedges and woods." Childhood memories magnify sensual pleasures, and Hoover visited and spoke about the swimming hole of his youth and in a Tom Sawyer-ish evocation mentioned the "inherent joys of getting muddy." Hoover even had his own Aunt Polly who disapproved not only of the mud carried home but also of the "godlessness of sliding down hill."[43]

The newspapers loved the entire event. The *New York Herald Tribune* saw this significance in the "home-coming": "one cannot help feeling that it was from his precious heritage of small town frontier life, rich in affection, that Mr. Hoover took the major inspiration of his life."[44] Overlooked in accounts of the speech were Hoover's assessment of the small town. He described the "milestones of changes" in the microcosm of West Branch. There were the early days when the town was settled by "the courageous and the adventurous," the creation of the "richest stretch of agricultural land that ever blessed any one sovereign government." A mile from where he stood was the farm of his Uncle Allen, where he had spent his boyhood "just at the passing stage of the great pioneer movement." Hoover remembers a Jefferson utopia: "We ground our wheat and corn on toll at the mill; we slaughtered our hogs for meat; we wove at least part of our own clothing; we repaired our own machinery; we got our fuel from the woods; we erected our own buildings; we made our own soap; we preserved our own fruit and grew our own vegetables." About 20 percent of the farm products were sold in a market to purchase "the small margin of necessities" not produced and to pay on the mortgage. But that self-sufficiency is gone and it has been gone for some time. Hoover now describes farm life thus: "We have improved seed and live-stock; we have added a long list of mechanical inventions for saving labor; we have increased the productivity of the land." Farming now was a "high specialized business," actually a dozen different industries with 80 percent of production for market use.[45]

Hoover admitted that he had "sometimes been as homesick for the ways of those self-contained farm homes of forty years ago" as he had been "for the kindly folk who lived in them." But those early days did have "lower standards of living, greater toil, less opportunity for leisure and recreation, less of the comforts of home, less of the joy of living." And in any case the choice was not available. It was no more possible "to revive those old conditions than it is to summon back the relatives and friends in the cemetery yonder."[46]

One could not utter a more direct pronouncement on a basic institution in American society. Hoover had said that the desire to restore the family farm and by implication the autonomy of the small town was equivalent to raising dead relatives from their graves. The metaphor is culturally an accurate one because indeed, despite criticism, the small town and the self-sufficient farm were the institutional inventions of centuries of republicanism. In place of peasants in America there would be free farmers. Jefferson had hoped that "all our citizens would be husbandmen." The convented town was the political adjunct to this economic structure assuring a literate citizenry who managed its own affairs. Both structures held such emotional appeal in part *because* they were autonomous and self-sufficient institutions. And Hoover had said that they were dead, dead now for forty or fifty years.

Why had not headlines read, "Hoover Announces Death of the Family Farm" or "Hoover Declares Age of Rural America at an End" or "Hoover Proclaims Home Town a Ghost Town?" The media, however, reported the event in celebratory terms, and while we do not know directly what the fifteen thousand farmers who listened to the speech thought, the *New York Times* reported that Hoover had received the "hearty approval of the plain folk who listened to him."

Hoover had assured his audience at West Branch that what was lost was not essential: "While we recognize and hold fast to what is permanent in the old-time conditions, we must accept what is inevitable in the changes that have taken place. It is fortunate indeed that the principles upon which our government was founded require no alteration to meet these changes." This recognition, and even embrace, of modern life was coupled with an assurance that nothing of value was under challenge. Hoover closed his speech with an account of the "enduring nature of American integrity." The "self-reliant," "rugged," "God-fearing" fathers had given "a genius to American institutions that distinguished our people from any other in the world." The legacy of the Jeffersonian yeoman was not the family farm but a collective American character. Here lay "the real basis of American democracy." Hoover repeated verbatim his analysis in *American Individualism:* "When we rehearse our own memories we find that none give us such comfort and satisfaction as the record of service we have been able to render." As our fathers had "combined to build the roads, bridges and towns," as they "cooperated together to erect their schools, their churches, and to raise their barns and harvest their fields" they would in the future find new outlets for "neighborly cooperation and mutual service."[47]

Hoover in essence had said at West Branch, "Jefferson Is Dead, Long Live Jefferson." Whether the public simply heard in the evocations of rural America a restatement of American principle rather than a eulogy, or whether they heard only the promise of the abolition of the poorhouse and of "larger comfort," Hoover did elucidate in his five remaining campaign speeches his new synthesis.

Each of his addresses recapitulated the relationship between American prosperity and American exceptionalism. In Newark he reminded his audience that nearly 6 million people had been unemployed in 1921. That figure had now been reduced to under 2 million. Hoover created an international wage index that compared U.S. and foreign wages if applied to the purchase of "composite pounds of bread and butter." The American worker might not be swimming amidst reefs of roast beef and apple pie as Sombart had alleged, but at least according to Hoover he could buy on his wages about twice as much bread and butter as his British counterpart and almost twice as much as the German worker. All this had been done in America without the dole, Hoover reminded his audience. Nor had prosperity been built "upon the bowed and sweaty backs of oppressed and embittered people."[48]

Each speech repeated the assertion that prosperity, while it rested upon the genius of the American system, also was based upon a new structure: "This higher standard of living, this new prosperity, is dependent upon an economic system vastly more intricate and delicately adjusted than ever before." In Boston he told his audience that the subjects of international trade, the tariff and other economic issues, are "no longer remote from any one of you." A shortage of shipping to New Orleans and at once the Kansasan farmer suffers; "touch the tariff on textiles" and North Carolina feels the influence as well as Massachusetts. The "old local decisive issues are largely gone."[49]

Intricate, delicate, big and growing bigger were Hoover's repeated descriptions of the American economic system. But if Hoover implicitly told Americans they must cease to think like villagers in regard to economics, he celebrated the Jeffersonian ideal in other areas. In Elizabethtown, Tennessee, he praised the aid given to victims of the Mississippi flood and outlined his conception of local community as the institutional unit for mutual aid. Noting his own resentment of "sneers at Main Street," Hoover spoke of "the cottages that lay behind the street." Service and mutual aid need not, indeed could not, be nationalized. Hundreds of villages and towns had undertaken "the instant work of rescue, the building of gigantic camps, the care of children, the provision of food, the protection of health of three-quarters of a million people." No modernization, no "fine tuning" was needed here. The Jeffersonian model could proceed without revision: "in no other country does there exist the intelligence, the devotion, the probity, the ability . . . that exists in the Main Street of the American town and village. . . . I do not wish to disparage the usefulness of Broadway, Pennsylvania Avenue, or State Street, but it is from Main Street and its countryside that the creative energies of this nation must be replenished and restored."[50] In this context, he echoed the Jeffersonian critique of urban life: "History shows that crowded cities too often breed injustices and crimes, misery and suffering."[51]

In the penultimate speech of his campaign Hoover raised the specter of un-Americanism. The charm of American exceptionalism involved evoking America's past, recounting current American prosperity, and projecting future achievements. The terror of American exceptionalism involved determining how others may be straying from an acceptance of America's uniqueness and predicting the horrific consequences that will surely follow from this alleged infidelity. In his memoirs Hoover reported that his advisers recommended against a speech of this sort, arguing that "the subject was not of public interest or importance, and harping on it carried liabilities." Hoover, however, was "determined that the Republican party draw the issue of the American system as opposed to all forms of collectivism."[52]

The Commerce secretary had been scrupulous in his treatment of Governor Smith's religion with all the connotations of immigrant and foreign influences the issue raised in the minds of Protestant drys. In fact, Hoover had appealed to Americanism in his defense of toleration. He certainly did not need to utilize this side of American exceptionalism for the sake of electoral victory. Yet the speech was extremely aggressive, "nearly demagogic" is Martin Fausold's characterization,[53] and quite similar to the Madison Square Garden address Hoover would deliver four years later almost to the day, when he certainly was desperate and when, at least from his point of view, the American people were also desperate enough to stray from the principles of the American system.

Part of the reason for his decision to attack Democratic proposals as an "abandonment of our American system" and a turn to "state socialism" was his distaste for the Democratic Party coalition. For Hoover here was a collection of groups decidedly un-Hegelian in terms of their relationship to the American system. Composed of the "extreme conservatism" in the South, "radical labor and agrarian groups" in the North, "corrupt city machines," and a growing left-wing intelligentsia, Smith's electoral base was not "philosophically very discriminating" despite the fact that Smith himself "conscientiously believed in the American system." Hoover saw in the relatively moderate proposals that Smith had espoused the genesis of a majority coalition that threatened his conception of the American system. The 1928 Democratic Party platform included general comments on unemployment and water development but it clearly was a Jeffersonian document. "We demand," the platform read, "that the constitutional rights of the states shall be preserved in their full vigor and virtue." Local self-government was a "bulwark against centralization and the destructive tendencies of the Republican Party." But Hoover was convinced that "some assurances" had been given to Senator Norris and John Dewey's "socialist group" that the government would go into the power business and that the governor had submitted to pressures from the "radical agricultural group" that price fixing schemes be adopted.[54]

The New York speech then is a prophetic one. Hoover had looked into the future and seen the New Deal coalition. Even in the Democratic Party's position on prohibition Hoover saw state socialism. State purchase and sale of liquor, as well as agricultural relief and public utilities, raised the question: "Shall we depart from the principles of our American political and economic system, upon which we have advanced beyond all the rest of the world, in order to adopt methods based on principles destructive of its very foundations?" Four years later Hoover would predict that grass would grow in the streets of New York if Roosevelt were elected. Here his admonitions are more general but no less apocalyptic. Free speech, he warned, "does not live many hours after free industry and free commerce die." Bureaucracy will not tolerate the "spirit of independence"; it will "spread the spirit of submission into our daily life." Roosevelt had attempted to recall the spirit of cooperation in wartime as a basis for national reform. Hoover saw in the war effort America's first experience with socialism: "For the preservation of the state the Federal Government became a centralized despotism which undertook unprecedented responsibilities, assumed autocratic powers, and took over the business of citizens. To a large degree we regimented our whole people temporarily into a socialistic state." In Hoover's language, within the American system are health, vigor, independence, youth. Beyond it is "infection," submission, "depressed spirits," enfeeblement.[55]

In 1928 Hoover had already betrayed Jefferson—or at least half of him—in the name of an American system that was defended at least in part on Jeffersonian principles. Of course, he was not the first president, or the last, to do so. The battle for the heart and soul of Jefferson would be waged again on different terms four years later. But in New York Hoover had described what was to be the New Deal's central dilemma in victory. Business, Hoover had admitted, requires a concentration of responsibility. Self-government, on the other hand, requires "decentralization and many checks and balances to safeguard liberty." Boards and commissions must be employed by government to avoid too great a concentration of authority. Each member in order to be responsible to the public must have equal authority. The result is a conflict of ideas and lack of decision that would ruin any business. Moreover, these commissions must be representative of different sections of the community. In addition legislative bodies cannot completely delegate authority to administrators. "Thus every time the Federal government goes into commercial business, 531 Senators and Congressmen become the actual board of directors of that business."[56]

One can see from his telling critique of the near future how Hoover himself had abandoned a Jeffersonian economic structure. His analysis is based upon the acceptance of an oligarchical economic system that he willingly accepts but warns cannot be extended further. "Our government to succeed in business would need become in effect a despotism" was the Hooverian warning. Was it already despotic in its economic structures? Not as long as it was "private ownership under public control," was Hoover's answer. But could a Jeffersonian-inspired political structure control the corporation? Hoover had held enough progressive sensibilities to answer that it could.

3

Is There a Jefferson on the Horizon?

The Great Depression tore apart Hoover's American system. The president initially publicly minimized the severity of the economic situation. "Over-optimism as to profits" had led to an "inevitable crash." As a result "a reduction in the consumption of luxuries and semi-necessities" was a logical result. There had "necessarily" been some unemployment but Hoover warned business leaders about "undue pessimism, fear, uncertainty, and hesitation." "These emotions, being emotions, if they had been allowed to run their course would, by feeding on themselves, create difficulties."

But Hoover appeared to have seen the consequences of the crash almost immediately. Privately he determined that the depression would be a long one and that its depths were not known. In the early months he struggled to minimize its consequences. Speaking among industrialists he refused to support Mellon's view that the crash opened Darwinist opportunities. There must be no liquidation of labor, he insisted, for labor was not a commodity. Industrialists must accept the burden of the depression. Wages must remain stable and the unemployed cared for. [1]

But if Hoover did act with dispatch he rarely employed the language of crisis. Lincoln, the Republican symbol of national unity, is largely ignored. In fact, Hoover used his 1931 radio address on Lincoln's birthday to remind the American public of the dangers of "centralized government." Lincoln's role as the Great Emancipator is reviewed but Hoover does not see in this exercise of state power precedent for a major expansion of responsibility in fighting the depression. On the contrary, the Lincolnian example is one that provides for equality of opportunity. "If Lincoln were living, he would find that this race of liberated slaves, starting a new life without a shred but the clothes in which they stood, without education, without organization, has today by its own endeavors progressed to an amazingly high level of self-reliance and well-being." Federal control would destroy the "opportunity of every individual to rise to that highest achievement of which he is capable," and ultimately lead to a "superstate where every man becomes the servant of the State and real liberty is lost." This was not the government "Lincoln sought to build." Hoover insisted that the union that Lincoln had preserved was a nation of villagers and it was at the local level that the Depression would be beaten: "Victory over this depression and over other difficulties will be won by the resolution of our people to fight their own battles in their own communities, by stimulating their ingenuity to solve their own problems, by taking new courage to be masters of their own destiny in the struggle of life."[2]

Hoover's eschewal of a crisis vocabulary was coupled with an analysis of the depression as an event that was almost exclusively external in origin and effect. The depression was repeatedly described as a "storm" that had broke upon American shores from Europe. Hoover would admit that "reckless speculation" had played a part in creating the current economic situation but always insisted that Americans had already paid the "moral penalty" for "speculative mania." The countries of Europe, however, had "proved unable to withstand the stress of the depression." "Disease and starvation" brought on by the war, "poisoned springs of political instability" as a result of the armistice treaties, "fear and hate" doubling armament expenditures, "enlarged government" borrowing had sent "violent shocks" with every month that reached the United States with "hurricane force."[3]

The belief that "the major forces of the depression now lie outside of the United States" led Hoover to assume that recovery was being stalled from a lack of confidence on the part of both consumers and industrialists. The Reconstruction Corporation was thus described in terms of the "temporary mobilization of timid capital." To an increasingly restive and angry Congress, Hoover replied that a "return of confidence" would only be "clogged by fears" if larger amounts of money were to be spent on public works.[4]

Hoover had arrived at an assessment of the depression that was derived from his earlier commitment to American exceptionalism. The American system, while obviously not depression proof, nevertheless was radically different from European politics. Those who would attempt to copy the measures used to fight the depression abroad were only advancing the sickness. And if the depression was primarily brought on by the war it followed that even attempts to apply programs used in the World

War were mistaken. Hoover admitted that "from the apparent success of governments in war in dealing with great emergencies there has grown up among our people the idea that Government is a separate entity, endowed with all power, all money, and all resources; that it can be called upon at any hour to settle any difficulty." But while Hoover would on occasion employ the war emergency analogy himself (he once compared his efforts to Washington at Valley Forge)[5] he contended that it was our duty to "free ourselves from these influences." More specifically, Hoover seemed to be saying that battles there can be but they must be fought primarily on Jeffersonian terms. In a "land of homes, churches, schoolhouses" it is "not the function of government to relieve individuals of their responsibilities to their neighbors, or to relieve private institutions of their responsibilities to the public. . . ."[6]

In terms of the requirements of American political culture Hoover's outline of the depression was impervious to challenges. Americans could withstand the depression's admittedly tremendous force by adhering to their unique system. But by 1932 the numbers seemed to suggest "our institutions" were not "sustained intact." The gross national product had declined 40 percent since 1929, industrial production, 50 percent, residential construction, 75 percent. Unemployment had reached over 13 million. Passivity was giving way to protest and sporadic violence, resentment and bitterness were rising against the rich, and most of all the fear was spreading and deepening.

"He was no local American! He was no little American"

Roosevelt's response to the American system that Hoover had constructed was much less a frontal attack than a set of substitute arguments. He too accepted American exceptionalism (the concept of the "middle way" as a later justification of the New Deal captured American uniqueness as well as "ordered liberty"). He too was a Jeffersonian. In fact FDR was to argue that it was Hoover who was the real Hamilton and he the real Jefferson. The central point in which Roosevelt differed from Hoover was on the question of the origins of the depression. FDR not only blamed Hoover personally for encouraging speculation, minimizing the gravity of the crash and delaying relief; more important, he blamed the entire American business elite.

The full theoretical implications of FDR's new political theory are present in his prenomination "Forgotten Man" speech. Emendations would, of course, follow. But this very short address, drafted by Raymond

Moley, reveals the outlines of a theory for reform that FDR had struggled to produce in earlier campaigns. The thesis is simple: combine the analogy of war mobilization with the Jeffersonian idea of decentralization. During the last great national emergency, the world war, the United States had a "great plan" because it was built "from bottom to top and not from top to bottom." What is wrong with the Hoover administration is that "it has either forgotten or does not want to remember the infantry of our economic army."[7] As I have noted, Hoover had in fact argued that the depression could be beaten only by the actions of thousands of local communities. Roosevelt's shift here is subtle but significant. These villagers need to be mobilized for the emergency at hand.

The symbols derived from Lincoln and Jefferson are juxtaposed throughout the brief speech. There are the Lincolnian military metaphors: the "emergency," the "battle," the "generalship," the "infantry," "mobilization." FDR also draws upon the fractional terminology of the Civil War president: "No nation can long endure half bankrupt." But Roosevelt's analysis of the depression is based upon a conception of America as a nation of villagers. "How much do the shallow thinkers realize," he asks, "that approximately one-half of our population, fifty or sixty million people, earn a living by farming or in small towns whose existence immediately depends on farms?" Men and women of "Main Street," "home-owners," "farm-owners," "little local banks," "local loan companies" are the focus for FDR's intimations of a "planned program."[8]

Public works projects are rejected as "the habit of the unthinking." Instead Roosevelt presents a cure for the depression based upon the restoration of the purchasing power of the yeoman and his village counterpart. The "little fellow," not the "big banks, the railroads, and the corporations" needs "permanent relief." It is in the context of FDR's appeal to the great American petit bourgeoisie that the call for the recognition of the forgotten man is made. Moley had borrowed the phrase from William Graham Sumner. While the decision to use a concept from a Darwinist of the Gilded Age is usually seen as part of the speech writer's license in eclecticism, the choice was not totally inappropriate from a theoretical viewpoint. Sumner might have intoned that "God alone could give distributive justice" but "in this world in which we are" He had not "seen fit to provide for it at all." But his heart also went out to the forgotten man, the "simple, honest laborer," the "clean, quiet virtuous citizen," the "industrious self-supporting men and women who have not inherited much to make life luxurious for them."[9] It was to this class that Roosevelt appealed in this speech. Jeffersonian in political outlook, the "little fellow" could and had in the past swung into concerted political action. Pushed rightward, he would attack urban cultural elites as well as newly emerging groups. Pushed leftward he would attack big business. Jeffersonianism's tendency to drift toward this unstable Jacksonian alternative is recognized in the "forgotten man" speech and Roosevelt lets its explosive possibilities stand between both alternatives. The offending (or encouraging) remarks, depending upon one's own political position, were exquisitely poised in April.

"These unhappy times call for the building of plans that rest upon the forgotten, unorganized but indispensable units of economic power. . . ." Put our "faith once more in the forgotten man at the bottom of the economic pyramid," Roosevelt had urged. Was the remark part of an effort "to get back to fundamentals" by using Lincolnian precedent for Jeffersonian means? Toward what cause was the "little fellow" being urged? Was he being reminded that relief to the cities was the result of the "illusions of economic magic"? Was he being encouraged to take on a Jacksonian attack on big banks? The speech clearly states that the "forgotten" are those only recently dispossessed, the "home-owner and the farm-owner," but had a rhetorical and theoretical wedge been suggested by the word "unorganized"? Certainly, the "industrious" and the "self-supporting" saw themselves as forgotten, but there were others who were at the very "bottom of the economic pyramid."

The so-called Jeffersonian democrats saw the last interpretation as a dangerous possibility. Al Smith warned: "We should stop talking about the Forgotten Man and about class distinctions."[10] For the most part Roosevelt did. His next major preconvention address continued his effort to nationalize Jefferson without the hint of a Jacksonian revival.

Two broad models of policy-making are drawn in the Jefferson Day speech in St. Paul, Minnesota. FDR returns to the old Hamilton-Jefferson debate on the role of the federal government in the promotion of economic policy. But here both Jefferson and Hamilton are portrayed as nationalists, Hamilton as nationalist-elitist and Jefferson as nationalist-democrat. Both were planners although "the great financial genius" of Hamilton rested upon the belief that "certain sections of the Nation and certain individuals within those sections were more fitted than others to conduct government."[11]

The case for a new Jefferson is based upon three aspects of the original Jefferson's career. Jefferson "devoted years to the building of a political party" as a "definite and practical act aimed at the unification of the country in support of common principles." Roosevelt emphasizes

Jefferson's cosmopolitanism. Along with Franklin and Theodore Roosevelt, Jefferson "knew at first hand every cross-current of national and international life." As an international figure he understood "the yearnings and the lack of opportunity, the hopes and fears of millions." Finally Jefferson's boldness as an executive is recounted. He had been "willing to stake his fortunes on the stroke of a pen" when he purchased "an imperial domain which trebled the size of the nation over night." FDR concludes: "He was no local American! He was no little American!"[12]

By contrast Hamilton and the "early Federalists" are drawn as men who attempt to lead from the perspective of local vision. And, of course, the Hoover administration's policies were in the "true Hamiltonian tradition."

The entire course of American history is described in terms of this conflict between nationalisms, and Roosevelt reviews the "great leaders of every generation" who successfully transcended the Hamiltonian viewpoint. Lincoln as well as Jackson, Theodore Roosevelt, and Wilson are all extensively quoted. But even more telling in terms of FDR's general attempt to provide a theory of reform is the analysis of the nature of public life and action in America as a liberal society. Roosevelt begins by using a joke by Chesterton, who had said that the members of the British Empire are like the passengers in an omnibus. They get to know one another only in case of an accident. So too is American society. "In normal times" we live in the "isolation of sectionalism." America is "a loose association of communities, with little common thought and little realization of mutual interdependence." Only in crises have Americans looked to wider concerns. Then presumably the traditional Hamiltonian-Jeffersonian battles are refought.

In his speech Roosevelt attempted to break this pattern through his reinterpretation of Jefferson. A "concert of interests" is possible to construct that would create a permanent "shared public life." Jefferson showed how it might be constructed. A national political party based upon common participation and led by men and women who understand the "hopes and fears of millions of their fellow human beings" is the institutional structure that Roosevelt recommends. Upon what principles would this common life be based? Here FDR is much less clear. He speaks of "imaginative and purposeful planning" but reminds his listeners that he speaks not of an "economic life completely planned and regimented."[13] He does cite a single "practical example." Here he resorts to the "public utilities socialism" of the 1928 campaign. Asserting the principle of the "historic and fundamental control over certain industries which, by their very nature, are monopolistic," Roosevelt argues that common-law practice extending back to before independence had produced a consensus on the need for government regulation of toll roads and ferries later to be extended to canals, railroads, gas, electricity, and telephones. FDR quotes himself as governor and reviews his policies on public power on the St. Lawrence River.

The Jefferson Day speech had offered a far more sophisticated analysis of the problem of permanently expanding the public realm in American society than Roosevelt had ever presented. His reading of Jefferson, while no doubt a tortured one, was designed to shift the debate over the use of public power from the question of national vs. local scope to an examination of whether its base were to be democratic or elitist. Roosevelt had hinted that even the terminology of crisis might not be a strong enough metaphor since American society may be moving toward a level of interdependence that required permanent planning. Was a remodeled Jefferson a stable enough base for such a departure? Roosevelt had admitted in St. Paul that he was stating his case "conservatively." Was FDR, to put the problem in another way, ready to publicly abandon the doctrine of American exceptionalism, not only in its Hooverite form but in any other formulation? In late May, goaded by a friendly reporter who had complained that his speeches had lacked the boldness necessary for the times, Roosevelt delivered an address at Oglethorpe University that intimated answers to these questions.

The speech began with a description of the world in 1928. Roosevelt spoke of it in parody of New Era politicians. In the "rose-colored days," Americans were told they "could sit back and read in comfort the hieroglyphics called stock quotations which proclaimed that their wealth was mounting miraculously without any work or effort on their part." But this "eternal future" of "easy-chair" living was a "dazzling chimera," a "mirage" fostered by financial leaders and men in high public office, for beneath this "happy optimism" was "lack of plan and great waste."[14]

Roosevelt reviews Hoover's analysis of the origins of the depression and passes over the question of whether problems brought on by the world war and the international monetary system were an "original cause, an accentuating cause, or an effect." There had been in America "haphazardness," "gigantic waste," "superfluous duplication," "continual scrapping of still useful equipment," "profligate waste of natural resources." Above all, wages had not risen in proportion to the reward to capital. "We accumulated such a superabundance of capital that our great bankers were vying with each other, some of them employing questionable methods, in their efforts to lend this capital at home and abroad."[15]

There are hints in the Oglethorpe address that America had reached an economic stationary state. "We can now make more shoes, more textiles, more steel, more radios, more automobiles, more of almost everything that we can use." But the thrust of Roosevelt's remarks were focused upon the depression as a failure of American political elites. Industrialists had shortsightedly refused to pass on profits to workers, they had been lured to "thousands of dead-end trails," they had wasted precious resources. In short, industrialists, who had held the economic structure in a kind of trust, had failed to plan. Finance capital is judged even more harshly. Here was a "small group of men" whose outlook "deserves the adjectives selfish and opportunist!" And public officials who might be expected to guide the economy promoted this inequitable and wasteful expansion through "the very instruments of Government which they controlled."

FDR's theory of the depression as a massive failure of elites inverted Hoover's exceptionalist theory. Hoover's contention that the "storm" was worldwide but could be resisted by adherence to the American system was replaced by the argument that the real causes of the depression were internal. The depression for Roosevelt, despite the situation in Europe, was an American phenomenon and as such could be fought by locating and attacking its internal sources. Pushed to extremes this approach could lead to an abandonment of American exceptionalism as Roosevelt seemed to suggest in his October Commonwealth Club speech.

If American elites had so failed to guarantee the continued functioning of the "economic machine" that that machine had collapsed, the natural question to be raised was who were to take their place. Again Roosevelt did not explicitly answer this question, but the speech does suggest the need to create a liberal apparatchik. We must bring about a "more equitable distribution of national income," FDR told his audience. How was one to build an "economic machine capable of satisfying the wants of all"? Roosevelt said that when the nation becomes "substantially united in favor of planning," then "true leadership must unite thought behind definite methods."[16]

Inserted at the close of the speech were the lines that made the address famous: "The country needs and, less I mistake its temper, the country demands bold, persistent experimentation. It is common sense to take a method and try it; if it fails, admit it frankly and try another, but above all, try something. The millions who are in want will not stand by silently forever while the things to satisfy their needs are within easy reach."[17]

What had Roosevelt meant? Although he suspected that the startling passages may have simply been the result of FDR's resentment at Hoover for making him wait at the recent Governor's Conference, Rexford Tugwell was thrilled by the speech. "Planning and experimentation were words I had been conditioned to suppose no candidate would mention in public." But the *New York Times* saw the address differently and had described FDR as "indefinite, abstract, irresolute. . . ." Tugwell was ultimately disappointed: "The speech had been pulled apart and attacked. . . . Altogether, the bold new doctrine was a political failure."[18]

In point of fact the address, which has come to be regarded as one that captured the later spirit of New Deal reform, was neither startling nor indefinite. Here is what Roosevelt had done. While he blamed the depression on economic and political elites, he had not criticized the economic or political system as such. While he suggested that major economic growth had been completed, he assumed that "needs were in easy reach," and that the "economic machine" was "capable of satisfying the wants of all." In a broader sense, he had accepted the Jeffersonian commitment that the goal of government was to ensure the pursuit of happiness. He had even conceded that waste is the "inevitable by-product of progress in a society which values individual endeavor. . . ." What he envisaged was a system in which the reward for a day's work would be greater and the return on capital less. The "average citizen" would expect a smaller return on his savings in return for a greater return upon his principal. Like the Marxists, FDR had identified a ruling capitalist class with interests separate from the rest of society. Unlike the Marxists, FDR had identified, not a proletariat, but a mass of tiny capitalists whose dreams of "living in their own homes" each "with a two car garage" were shattered by an irresponsible ruling class. To say that Roosevelt had redefined the Jeffersonian yeoman as the central figure in the American order may be stretching the point, but he had identified a different kind of capitalist order, one that placed much more emphasis on stability. In his acceptance speech Roosevelt asked what do Americans want, and answered, "work and security."

But FDR had implicitly admitted that the Jeffersonian notion of a natural virtue was no longer automatic. A new elite was now necessary to ensure the millions of fellow citizens that "sense of security to which they have rightly felt entitled in a land abundantly endowed with natural resources." This new leadership may have to use "drastic means" to correct the faults in the system. To the youth at Oglethorpe who listened he met Stuart Chase's challenge. Chase had asked, "Why should Russians have all the fun of remaking a world?" FDR closed his speech thus: "Yours is not the task of making your way in the world, but the task of remaking the world which you will find before you."[19] The consequences of FDR's formulation were not apparent until years later, but with hindsight one can see the paradox that he had created. For Roosevelt had called forth groups of public-spirited citizens whose goal was to construct and preside over a system whose major objective was the fulfillment of private satisfactions.

"The dream was the dream of an economic machine"

The story of Roosevelt's nomination in Chicago is well known. It is frequently argued that with the nomination the influence of the Brains Trust waned as FDR sought to broaden his political base. With the exception of the famous San Francisco address, Roosevelt's speeches do fit into a pattern of more conventional campaign rhetoric. At Columbus, Pittsburgh, and Madison Square Garden, Roosevelt delivered the traditional attacks against the party in power. There was also the series of policy speeches to major constituencies. In Topeka he offered his promises to farmers. In Salt Lake City he discussed railroads, in Portland, public utilities.

But throughout the postnomination stage of the campaign, the themes outlined in the controversial Oglethorpe speech are still present. There is always some evidence of the martial rhetoric of Lincoln (usually with Wilson as proxy) with its menacing implications. In Chicago FDR called up the "great, indomitable, unquenchable progressive soul of our Commander-in-Chief, Woodrow Wilson" to make his point about the need for united action. Yet always the crisis is to be resolved through some sort of Jeffersonian risorgimento. The planning which has thus far been implemented to meet the depression was Hamiltonian. "There are two ways of viewing the Government's duty in matters affecting economic and social life," Roosevelt told the convention. The one "sees to it that a favored few are helped." And that theory belongs to "the party of Toryism." Nearly every American had been "forgotten": "The consumer was forgotten . . . the worker was forgotten . . . the stockholder was forgotten. . . ."[20] The "new deal" FDR promised was then offered in a sense in the language of remembrance as much as new-world building. Roosevelt promised a return to some essence of Americanism.

In this context the traditional attacks on incumbents carried broad implications. Hoover had not only failed as a leader: Roosevelt used Hoover's analogy of the depression as a "storm" to suggest "incompetence": "there are glimpses through the clouds, of troubled officers pacing the deck wondering what to do. . . ." Hoover had presided over a profligate capitalism. "It was a heyday of promoters, sloganeers, mushroom millionaires, opportunists, adventurers of all kinds." FDR's message is clear. The predepression economic and political elites could not continue as guardians of the republic. These were not men of virtue. They had themselves created a period of "loose thinking, descending morals, an era of selfishness." "Let us be frank to admit," Roosevelt reminded his listeners, that many of us too "have made obeisance to Mammon."[21] The people themselves had been corrupted (although not hopelessly so) by these leaders.

Roosevelt was much less clear about the new guardians. In part this vagueness was the result of the adoption of the Jeffersonian paradigm. Planning was to come from the bottom up through a concert of interest in which "the top of the pyramid and the bottom of the pyramid, must be considered together." But FDR was also clear that no Gosplan was being considered. His Jefferson Day speech had assured his audience that he had not envisioned an "economic life completely planned and regimented." In Columbus he reiterated his belief in the "sacredness of private property." This inability to explore fully the basis of a new elite left Roosevelt and the New Deal apparatchik open to the charge that they were in fact the new Hamiltonians, that they too had betrayed Jefferson. Curiously this was a criticism of both the American left and the right. Hoover spoke of New Deal planning as a "deliberated plan for centralizing authority to a point where we the people can be made to do what starry-eyed young men in Washington think is good for us—whether it is good for us or not." A "multitude of code administrators, agents, or committees has spread into every hamlet," and he darkly intimated that once the letter names for agencies had run out there were still more letters in the new Russian alphabet.[22] Norman Thomas saw in the National Industrial Recovery Act (NIRA) a Hamiltonianism with fascist coloring. In truth, the New Deal had betrayed Jefferson, but not completely and almost never without theoretical battles. I shall discuss this point more fully in a moment but first I turn to the most comprehensive attempt to consider the full philosophical implications of the New Deal.

The Commonwealth Club address, delivered in late September, was not only very positively received but reaches a level of political discourse well beyond the immediate goals of the campaign. Yet commentators have been reluctant to give it much weight as an example of FDR's thought. Schlesinger notes that it is a "powerful" and "serenely philosophical" speech but contends that it represents more of Berle's thinking than that of Roosevelt's. Tugwell too questions the degree of FDR's participation and assent to its broad assertions. But while there does appear to be a good deal of last-minute preparation the general idea of an address of this sort had been under consideration for some time. The candidate's advisers, with FDR's encouragement, had planned a speech that would directly refute Hoover's concept of individualism. The original title of the address was to be "Individualism, Romantic and Realistic."[23]

The speech is structured around sets of pairs. Roosevelt compares the growth of central governments to that of centralized industry. He compares the rise of European monarchs to the new "princes of property." He compares Jefferson to Hamilton. He compares the needs of a country with a frontier to one whose "plant is built." The theme of the essay deals with one of the central preoccupations of political philosophy: how are rights preserved and exploitation avoided across time?

Often overlooked in analyses of the address is Roosevelt's presentation of great leaders, portrayed here in ambivalent terms, not unlike in Lincoln's Lyceum address. Lincoln had spoken of the need for men of great ambition at the time of the founding and the threat they posed in an established republic. Roosevelt recounts the contributions of the "creators of national government" in Europe. "The people preferred the master far away to the exploitation and cruelty of the smaller master near at hand." The people, by and large, had wanted "a strong stable state to keep the peace, to put the unruly nobleman in his place, and to permit the bulk of individuals to live safely." These were, however, "ruthless" men and when there came a growing feeling that "ambition and ruthlessness" had "served their term," the people sought a "balancing—a limiting force." Roosevelt describes the new institutional forms created for this purpose—town councils, trade guilds, national parliaments, constitutions, and elections—as well as the formulation of the tenet that a ruler bore a responsibility to his subjects.[24]

America had come into existence as part of this struggle. Our own institutions reflected this concern with the oppressive consequences of centralized political power. But new kinds of creators came to fulfill a similar role in this country. Roosevelt traces their emergence to the industrial revolution and the "new dream" it created. "The dream was the dream of an economic machine, able to raise the standard of living for everyone; to bring luxury within the reach of the humblest; to annihilate distance by steam power and later by electricity, and to release everyone from the drudgery of the heaviest manual toil." But there was a "shadow over the dream." "To be made real, it required use of the talents of men of tremendous will and tremendous ambition. . . ." The American people accepted these men "fearlessly" and "cheerfully." "It was thought that no price was too high to pay for the advantages which we could draw from a finished industrial system." The methods of these men were "not scrutinized with too much care." The "financial Titans" were "always ruthless, often wasteful, and frequently corrupt." FDR estimates that investors paid for railroads three times over. But the railroads were built and "we still have them today." With this task now completed, however, these American creators threatened the people like the old feudal barons; "great uncontrolled and irresponsible units of power within the State" were a danger to everyone's ability to earn a living.[25]

As with all of Roosevelt's speeches, Jefferson is turned to for a solution. Roosevelt had beaten back the Hamiltonian challenge that only "great and strong group of central institutions," led by "a small group of able and public spirited citizens" could best govern. In its place he had devised two sets of rights. Those of "personal competency" such as freedom of speech required limitations on governmental power. Property rights, so argues Roosevelt, are historically variable in their implementation.

"But even Jefferson realized that the exercise of the property rights might so interfere with the rights of the individual that the Government, without whose assistance the property rights could not exist, must intervene, not to destroy individualism, but to protect it."[26] But even Jefferson! FDR too had said in effect, "Jefferson is dead! Long live Jefferson!" He tacitly admits that the original Jeffersonian solution, a nation of villagers, is now irrelevant. "The happiest of economic conditions made that day long and splendid" but now a "re-appraisal of values" was necessary. Admittedly, FDR's solution is presented in Jeffersonian terms. A new "social contract" is required. "Every man has a right to life; and this means that he has also a right to make a comfortable living." "Every man has a right to his own property; which means a right to be assured, to the fullest extent available, in the safety of his savings." If the economic elite cannot meet these requirements, the "Government must be swift to enter and protect the public interest."[27] The "apparent Utopia which Jefferson imagined for us in 1776" was still obtainable. Perhaps Roosevelt had held true to the essence of Jeffersonianism, perhaps all he was doing was applying Jeffersonian principles to "new conditions." Or had he used Jefferson to reach a Hamiltonian solution in which "a great and strong group of central institutions" led by "a small group of able and public spirited citizens" would be the guardians of happiness?

But whatever kind of Jeffersonian reconstruction was offered, it was dependent upon Roosevelt's assessment in San Francisco of the nature of American economic development. For FDR's "new conditions" assumed that the American economy had reached a permanent stationary state. "Our last frontier has long since been reached . . . there is no safety valve in the form of the prairie to which those thrown by the Eastern economic machines can get a new start." American exceptionalism is not simply an economic theory, but here FDR had argued that the unique features of American society of the past had largely been erased. Roosevelt had himself quoted Jefferson's famous observation that in America there were no paupers. In America the laboring classes possess property and are able to "feed abundantly, clothe above mere decency, to labor moderately and raise their families." Even the rich "cannot live without labor" and they were "few and of moderate wealth." But he had responded that more than half the population no longer live on farms and "cannot derive a living by cultivating their own property." We are now providing "a drab living for our own people." And rich there were. Six hundred corporations controlled two-thirds of American industry. "Put plainly, we are steering a steady course toward economic oligarchy if we are not there already."[28]

Here is a Roosevelt so pessimistic that commentators question whether his commitment to the principles in the speech are "more notational than real."[29] It is certainly correct that the Commonwealth Club address presented an account of the depression far broader than FDR's repeated view that the crisis was the result of elite failure. But to appreciate the autumnal tone one must focus upon the general goal of the speech. The analysis throughout is contractarian. If the implicit contract between the American people and the promoter was no longer to be judged beneficial, then FDR was forced to draw up a set of conditions that showed unequivocally that the "organizer of more corporations is as likely to be a danger as a help." As long as major economic growth was judged to be a possibility, the "contract" between the entrepreneur and the people could be reactivated, so to speak. Certainly FDR portrayed entrepreneurs in the most unflattering terms, but he had admitted that they had fulfilled their contractual obligation. Railroads and factories had been built. "The ambitious man" had been given "free play and unlimited reward" provided only that "he produced the economic plant so much desired." The depression had shown that not only could the entrepreneur no longer deliver but that his services were no longer needed. "Our industrial plant is built; the problem just now is whether under existing conditions it is not overbuilt." Added to this analysis was the observation, Jeffersonian and liberal in spirit, that these were after all dangerous men, Ishmaels "whose hand is against every man's," who would become the despots of the twentieth century.[30]

As important as the changed terms of the contract is the fact that the government is to replace business as one of the parties. "Our task," said Roosevelt, "is not discovery or exploitation of natural resources, or necessarily producing more goods. It is the soberer, less dramatic business of administering resources and plants already in hand. . . ."[31] Business had in America served as the guarantor of happiness, and now FDR said that the State would become the new party. It should be noted that Roosevelt did not call for the complete dismantling of the economic elite, which would still function but in a more limited sense. The two new economic rights, a "comfortable living" and the safety of savings, were to be "satisfied, in the main, by the individuals who claim and hold control of the great industrial and financial combinations which dominate so large a part of our industrial life." Only when the economic elite used its collective power contrary to the "public welfare" should the government intervene. Indeed it must be "swift to enter" to protect the public interest but should engage in economic regulation only as a "last resort."

Did Roosevelt believe that America had reached a permanent plateau of economic development? The skepticism that he did may result as much from our unwillingness to imagine an America in terms any other than unlimited growth. The Commonwealth Club address did consider this more as a consequence of the failure of current economic elites than as an independently established assessment. But the genius of the speech originates from a slightly different focus. Roosevelt had identified one of the central aspects of American exceptionalism not just in his analysis of the premise of the "dream of an economic machine" able to "bring luxury within the reach of the humblest" but in his portrayal of how Americans historically saw the fulfilment of this dream. Economic elites were in a contractual sense, if one can call a cultural consensus contractual, "fearlessly" given authority to make this dream real. Roosevelt was hardly the only public figure to state that they had failed. What is so remarkable about the analysis is how that failure is recast into other aspects of the American exceptionalist theory. The new social contract included all the basic elements of America's unique political heritage. No elite could be fully trusted. This much FDR cheerfully applied to the business community. The goal of government must be to secure the pursuit of happiness. This FDR carefully reiterated and even expanded. In faith in America lies our salvation. To this FDR openly appealed.

It is easy to see the election of 1932 in narrow terms, primarily as a conventional partisan contest with only the most basic and timidly conceived symbolic and rhetorical overtones. But both Hoover and Roosevelt had explored the viability of the central political tenets of the American republic. It is certainly true that the political careers of both men as well as the campaign itself required this focus. Both men were actors in the same regime. They had built their careers upon participation in the American system as they understood it. In the context of their quests for electoral office each had managed to confront the crisis of the depression through an examination of the phenomenology of the American regime. Both saw very clearly—although they reached different conclusions—how the American political system functioned as a system of beliefs, and both men fought to confront the current crisis through the philosophies of past regime figures. Hoover's understanding prevented the use of either Lincoln or Jackson, but his exploration of Jefferson as an exemplar that could not be abandoned was the most thorough of any president. Roosevelt was more willing to consider the models of past regime actors but he too quite early fixed upon Jefferson as the key to both the election and the crisis. Depending upon one's own political perspective, Roosevelt's use of Jefferson was more opportunistic or more flexible than Hoover's. Still it must be remembered that no matter how imaginative these men were in their understanding of the limited number of models available, the depression stood before both as a brute fact. The crisis shattered a seemingly impregnable adaptation of Jefferson for Hoover and would pose severe contradictions upon the implementation of the New Deal itself.

4

The Parade

Edmund Wilson described the inauguration of Roosevelt in comic-tragic terms. "Everything is gray today," Wilson observed.[1] The weather seemed to describe the state of the nation. Things were vaguely ominous, "clouds in colorless light threaten rain or snow," "the people seem dreary," there was "general blankness and dismay." The address itself also fit the mood of both the weather and the nation. The phrases of the speech (which Wilson did not like much) were "shadowy"—"plain-speaking followed by the old abstractions," the "old unctuousness, the old pulpit vagueness." And there is at the close "a warning, itself rather vague, of a possible dictatorship."

But it was the inaugural parade that most caught Wilson's attention. First passed the branches of the service. There was General MacArthur, "who drove the veterans out of Washington last summer," followed by a flare of flags from the First Division and the Knickerbocker cadets, "tall and rigid, in gray." Next came the Marines dressed in white caps and gaiters and with a red and yellow rattlesnake flag. Behind them were "Negroes in khaki, always with a white officer at their head" and followed by the Richmond Blues and Grays "all with white plumes and pre-Civil War uniforms." The martial portion of the parade was fun—"It was fun to hear 'The West Point Cadets March' and 'The Stars and Stripes Forever'— they bring back the America of boyhood: the imperial Roosevelt, The Spanish War." But at this point the procession "crazily degenerates." The inaugural reminded Wilson of some college reunion where the classes dress up in crazy costumes. The event took on "qualities of grotesque idiocy which make the Carnival at Nice look decorous." High school bands exude a "musical-comedy air." Then come the governors followed by more bands. There is a "fairy drum-major" whose "specialty is hip-wiggling and mincing." And as the weather grows "darker and more ominous," the parade becomes "more fantastic." Wilson is momentarily startled by the appearance of American Legion Posts, whose home-made uniforms and volkishness seem to remind him of Brownshirts. But the legions are followed by a "cute-kid cowboy" on a donkey and a man dressed up like Abraham Lincoln who is so unintentionally comic that one expected to see him do a clowning act, "perhaps puff smoke out of his stovepipe hat."

The spectacle becomes even "more phantasmagoric." Lodges and marching clubs pass by with men in "curled up shoes and fezzes, dressed in hideous greens, purples and reds." There are Indians, "terribly fat, with terribly made-up squaws." The airplanes of the first portion of the march have been replaced by an auto-gyro that proclaims on its banner: "Re-Tire with Lee's Tires." Tom Mix with his white suit and white sombrero gets the biggest ovation of all. Hollywood takes over the close of the procession with waving beauties poised on wicker chairs against a background of giant tulips and with costumed figures, some with great feather headdresses and others with flowing robes "tinted with celestial pinks and blues."

The parade ended. It could not have lasted any longer anyway. It was now too dark and too cold. Wilson was glad it was over: "The America it represented had burst, and as you watched the marchers, you realized that it was getting sillier and sillier all the time. The America of the boom definitely died today, and this is the ghost it gave up."

Press reactions were much more positive than Wilson's. But the crankiness that was part of Wilson's genius as an interpreter of American culture acted as a kind of crowbar that opened up for view the kind of dilemma that faced FDR and in more general terms, any American president. Wilson was wrong in concluding that the parade eerily symbolized the death of America as we knew it. But he was right to juxtapose the gray doom that hovered over the republic, one that made everyone look and act alike, and the crazy cacophony of colors and shapes of a heterogeneous and commercial society. The one seemed to call for immediate, drastic, even dictatorial action, the kind of action that was without precedent in America. But the parade itself—exciting, vulgar, and occasionally menacing (much like a carnival)—illustrated the real essence of a liberal society, one that blithely mixed commercial goals with the great and solemn events of the republic. Tom Mix vaguely represents both the frontier experience and the movie industry, the costumed Lincoln becomes a circus figure, the war technology of the martial phase of the march is used to advertise tires, the Knickerbocker cadets become the

Loew's Theatres Cadet Band. Here symbolized was a society in which thousands of local communities produce many thousands of associations all alike but also all a little bit different and all profoundly nurturing in their provincial settings but not a little comical or even ludicrous at this "day of consecration." Here symbolized was a society in which pockets of more disciplined communities are imbedded in Babylon (Marines in white caps, "legionnaires in orange, as hussars," even Tammany Hall marching in "solid ranks" in silk hats and carnations "on and on like an army"). Here symbolized was a society in which oppressed and forgotten people manage to live in some dignity ("Negro lady hussars" in "gorgeous bright purple stockings," "real Cherokees in white fringed suits and headdresses of pink-tipped feathers").

"An emergency no less serious than war"

This day, March 4, 1933, Franklin Roosevelt spoke a language, "solemn and a little terrifying," that reflected the threat of the weather over a "stricken Nation." In the ensuing months for the most part, however, FDR was to employ a language more congenial to the parade.

There is some controversy surrounding the drafting of the inaugural address. Rosenman reports that the speech "was one of the very few of which the President wrote the first draft in his own hand" and dates its composition on the night of February 27.[2] James MacGregor Burns describes the drafting in historically picturesque terms:

The evening of February 27, 1933, at Hyde Park was cloudy and cold. A stiff north west wind swept across the dark waters of the Hudson and tossed the branches of the gaunt old trees around the Roosevelt home. Inside the warm living room a big, thick-shouldered man sat writing by the fire. From the ends of the room two of his ancestors looked down from their portraits: Isaac who had revolted with his people against foreign rule during an earlier time of troubles, and James, merchant, squire, and gentleman of the old school.

Franklin D. Roosevelt's pencil glided across the pages of yellow legal cap paper. "I am certain that my fellow Americans expect that on my induction to the Presidency I will address them with a candor and a decision which the present situation of our nation impels." The fire hissed and crackled; the large hand with its thick fingers moved rapidly across the paper. "The people of the United States want direct, vigorous action. They have made me the instrument, the temporary humble instrument"—he scratched out "humble"; it was no time for humility—"of their wishes."

Phrase after phrase followed in the President-elect's bold, pointed slanting hand. Slowly the yellow sheets piled up. By 1:30 in the morning the inauguration speech was done.[3]

This is wonderful stuff, the top side of Wilson's jaundiced observations. And it fits neatly the historical impact that the inaugural was intended to achieve and did in fact succeed in achieving. The Burns account also uses the weather as symbolic of the crisis facing the nation. FDR represents the incarnation of an earlier America, one that faced different kinds of threats but faced them with courage and resoluteness. The address seems to materialize automatically; we know now that Roosevelt kept the fire of liberty burning.

Actually, according to Raymond Moley, the themes of the address were conceived as early as September. FDR seemed more impressed with the parallels to Lincoln than to Wilson. Moley himself was afraid to take notes. If the opposition learned of the tenor of the speech, "there would be dangerous cries of dictatorship." The address was discussed again at Warm Springs in early February and Moley left for New York, again taking precautions in the interest of secrecy. On February 27, before that symbolic fireplace, FDR copied and dated Moley's draft, making some minor changes in the process. When Louis Howe saw the draft the next morning he inserted the now famous phrase "the only thing we have to fear is fear itself." Moley disputes Rosenman's suggestion that the line was taken from Thoreau, and that Roosevelt had a copy of the philosopher's book in his Mayflower suite. Howe probably got the phrase from a sign he had seen in a department store window. Some final changes were made on the day of delivery, including the addition of the sentence, "This is a day of national consecration."[4]

The address, then, was one written like most major modern presidential speeches. It was a collaborative effort carefully conceived but not without serendipitous elements. But Moley's account notwithstanding, FDR had conceived of the inaugural address as an occasion to outline the depression in terms of a national crisis. There was already too much "optimistic preachment," he had told Moley. In the face of a "confused population" there must be an announcement of an "emergency no less serious than war."[5] Once this decision was made it was not just fitting but unavoidable that Roosevelt use Lincoln as his exemplar. No other presidential discourse existed except Lincoln's to describe a national crisis of such apocalyptic proportions.

Roosevelt had selectively used Lincolnian metaphors during the campaign. In the "Forgotten Man" speech he had asserted that "No nation can long endure half bankrupt." At Chicago he had raised the question of whether the depression has an act of retribution for America's "obeisance to Mammon." But always the Lincolnian conception of crisis had been modified by the Jeffersonian ideal that any unity must come from the "bottom up." Now the inaugural relied exclusively upon Lincoln. In fact, in a certain sense its essence was more Lincolnian than the "Great Emancipator's" first inaugural. That speech too was delivered in an atmosphere of national crisis. Guards had ringed the inaugural stand. But Lincoln's speech, despite the closing evocation of the "mystic chords of memory," had the ring of the lawyer's brief. Part of this difference is due to the fact that Lincoln faced imminent action on the part of "dissatisfied fellow country-men." The speech was laced with threats ("no state, upon its own mere motion, can lawfully get out of the Union . . . acts of violence, within any state or states, against the authority of the United States, are insurrectionary or revolutionary"), entreaties ("Nothing valuable can be lost by taking time"), and assurances ("The government will not assail you").[6]

FDR, on the other hand, had simply announced that "the money changers have fled from their high seats in the temple of our civilization." The campaign charge that the depression had been caused by economic elites was now treated as a foregone conclusion. The economic collapse that had occurred in the interregnum had made Roosevelt's theory axiomatic. Lincoln had linked civil conflict to Providence. The first inaugural had repeated that interpretation. "*You* have no oath registered in Heaven," Lincoln reminded the Southerners, "while I shall have the most solemn one. . . ." Roosevelt too now connected the depression to a crisis of the spirit that affected all America. The fear was of fear itself, and FDR paused as he described a collective feeling. It was a "nameless, unreasoning, unjustified terror."

What Roosevelt had said was something that politicians, including Hoover, had been saying since 1929. The depression was continuing because there was an absence of economic confidence. If only business would believe that markets could be resuscitated, if only consumers would buy, the depression would be over. But FDR's use of the idea was different. First he had described something broader and deeper than lack of business confidence. He had described individual panic that was so widespread that it had become a collective fear for survival. What he described was not the traditional economic problems of a liberal society. This was no longer a case of sets of individual problems, an uncle who could not find work, a family who lost its breadwinner, a factory that had closed, a missed mortgage payment. It was of course, all these things, but grossly magnified. And now in the winter of 1933–34, the very infrastructure of society was collapsing. The depression had created a sense of unity unknown in American society, and that cement was fear.

As Lincoln had insisted that the Civil War involved more than tariffs, or states' rights, or even slavery, FDR had asserted that the depression was more than an economic slump. As Lincoln had argued that secession violated universal law, FDR charged the old economic elites with a defilement of the American dream. The New Testament analogy placed this elite in the same position as that of the money-changers who had brought on Jesus' wrath. They had seduced a whole population into believing that happiness lie in "mere possession of money"; they had no vision; they knew only self-seeking in the "mad chase of evanescent profits." But the question that FDR logically faced was: What were the "ancient truths" to be restored? What vision did a commercial people have? Here, although Roosevelt speaks in the language of restoration, he offers a basic alteration for an American political culture. We must apply "social values more noble than profit," our "true destiny" is to "minister to ourselves and to our fellow men." Without "unselfish performance" it is "small wonder that confidence languishes." Without changes in ethics we "cannot live."[7]

Roosevelt received one of the loudest expressions of approval from the audience when he then announced that restoration called not only for changes in ethics but "for action, and action now." Military metaphors now cascaded. Putting people back to work must be accomplished as we "would treat the emergency of war." Americans must move forward "as a trained and loyal army," willing to submit their "lives and property to such a discipline," pledging a "sacred obligation with a unity hitherto envoked only in time of armed strife." And then there was the warning. A "temporary departure from the normal balance may be called for." If Congress should fail to act and act without delay, Roosevelt would ask for "broad executive power to wage a war against the emergency, as great as the power that would be given to me if we were in fact invaded by a foreign foe." If the Constitution, "simple and practical" as it was, could not be bent to permit the formation of a nation into a "trained and loyal army," Roosevelt suggested that it must be broken.[8] Of course FDR's warning was not acted upon nor was it repeated (even during the Jacksonian turn in 1935–36). Scholars do not speculate upon what Roosevelt meant or under what conditions he might have tried to implement it. But there is no evidence to suggest that it was an idle threat, and one wonders whether it rests as a half-hidden exemplar for some future president.

Students of the New Deal have placed a great emphasis on the first hundred days, so much so that subsequent presidents are evaluated in terms of that same time frame. Here was a period of almost no opposition. Fifteen messages were sent by FDR to Congress; fifteen laws were enacted. The president's banking bill message was read as freshmen representatives were still trying to find their seats. No copies of the bill were available when the House passed the measure unanimously after less than forty minutes of debate. The Senate was ever so slightly recalcitrant (the vote was 73–7) as it approved the measure at 7:30 that evening. An hour later the legislation had the president's signature.

But his unprecedented political success also gives rise to the charge that FDR acted timorously and/or unimaginatively. A "confused population" was at his feet. He could have nationalized the banks (William Lemke charged that the president "drove the money changers out of the Capitol on March 4th—and they were all let back in on the 9th");[9] he could have nationalized the railroads (instead we got the Railroad Coordination Act); he could have nationalized big business (we got the ill-fated National Recovery Administration [NRA]); he could have proposed scores of TVAs (later he did attempt unsuccessfully to introduce seven); he could have confiscated the plunder of the wealthy (he proposed his "soak the rich" tax plan in 1935); he could have unleashed the Brains Trust (instead he stuck them throughout New Deal agencies). The list of course can go on and on. But, at least in the "first" New Deal, Roosevelt did not follow the route that he had opened up in the inaugural address. To pursue any one of the possibilities above would have required pushing at and expanding the edges of the Lincoln exemplar. An enormous cultural opening, almost revolutionary in its suddenness, stood before Roosevelt in 1933. It closed somewhat in 1935 and 1936 and then snapped shut in 1938. When it was open FDR chose to pursue Jefferson rather than Lincoln. It was not, I think, that Roosevelt was incapable, either in an intellectual or moral sense, of constructing a new order. He had declared that he would not "evade the clear course of duty" should the crisis demand it. The inaugural itself and the reaction it produced showed that Roosevelt had the theoretical tools to transform American political thought. The intellectual climate was more than willing to accept the war analogy.[10] Many of his advisers awaited his word to begin the transformation of the

American system. Instead FDR chose Jefferson. It is on these terms that FDR and the New Deal must be judged.

"We are reviewing all kinds of human relationships"

In a sense Roosevelt's decision was the more difficult route in 1933. Edmund Wilson was right to view the America of the parade as the ghost that was given up. The martial alternative must have seemed more real, more accessible in 1933. The fireside chats and the innumerable speeches to those sorts of groups that paraded in March could have been part of a scenario that would be written for an American Kerensky. In the months following the first hundred days FDR offered a thematic structure to the New Deal that would characterize his entire administration. Jefferson had declared that the purpose of government was life, liberty, and the pursuit of happiness. This was to be the opening from which Roosevelt justified the New Deal. But happiness in the Jeffersonian model had dimensions that were systematically ambiguous. Was happiness the pursuit and satisfaction of private desire or the creation and maintenance of a just political order?

In the difference between these two understandings lies the distinction between and the arguments over liberal and republican thought. Gary Wills in his reinterpretation of Jefferson argues that the Declaration meant to express the latter definition. If Jefferson intended the second definition, the American people then never quite understood him.[11] Hannah Arendt probably better captures the American understanding of the concepts contained in the concept when she concludes that the distinction is blurred in the Declaration, that "the historical fact is that the Declaration of Independence speaks of the 'pursuit of happiness,' not public happiness" and that the "chances are that Jefferson himself was not very sure in his own mind what happiness meant."[12] Whatever Jefferson meant, these terms themselves break down and create more interpretations. Is happiness-private the private life itself, which suggests a whole structure of affection? This was Jefferson's view when he wrote of his yearnings for an existence "in the lap and love of my family, in the society of neighbors and my books, in the wholesome occupations of my farms and my affairs." Or is happiness-private material and social success? Here there will not be much time to enjoy Jefferson's affective realm for, as as George Santayana said, there is "only one way" in America to happiness, and that is "to work and to rise by that work, adhering to a regimen not less strict than that of the monasteries for the sake of an ill-defined but somehow better future."[13] Then there is the happiness-private of the reflective American, like Ralph Waldo Emerson, who reminded Americans: "It takes a good deal of time to eat or to sleep, or to earn a hundred dollars and a very little time to entertain a hope and an insight which becomes the light of our life."[14] There are, of course, more—many more—interpretations and variations of happiness-private, and the number indicates how much effort Americans historically have spent on the Jeffersonian axiom that governments exist to promote happiness.

Happiness-public, by contrast, has a less rich American history. It is instructive to note that despite the efforts of both Arendt and Wills to remind us of this aspect of the concept, the phrase public happiness is an archaic one. Any American can tell you what he or she thinks happiness-private means, few can speak so readily about the other concept in the concept. But even if happiness-public is often articulated as a "second language" in American political culture,[15] it does have its interpretations. The primary distinction—and the one which FDR's conception of the New Deal never quite confronted—involves the question of whether the quest for happiness-public is in some way autonomous of, or morally prior to, happiness-private. Winthrop's insistence that it was the duty of all to create the best city possible as well as the constant reflections of the revolutionary republicans offer a tradition that expresses one view. But, despite all the effort of recent scholarship it is historically the minority view. Happiness-public, defined as a set of institutions and practices that permits the pursuit of happiness-private (however defined), is the culturally dominant interpretation. To quote Santayana again, the American social contract is an agreement to "exploit business opportunities and organize public service useful to all." This is, then, the consensus that Americans have arrived at with regard to Jefferson, whatever the Sage of Monticello might have meant to say.

Even when it emerges periodically in American history the spirit of reform seems to be devoted to restoring some version of the happiness-private relationship. Few writers or politicians have been willing to challenge this point. Perhaps the bravest of all who wrote in the American idiom was Herbert Croly, who insisted that Jefferson (as he was interpreted) was wrong. The test of happiness was not "the comfort and prosperity of the individual," the promise of American life was not "a system of unrestricted individual aggrandizement and collective irresponsibility." But Croly could turn only to Hamilton for a solution: "the nationalism of Hamilton, with all its aristocratic leaning, was more democratic than the indiscriminate individualism of Jefferson."[16] But if Americans were wrong in their devotion to their interpretation of Jefferson, Croly was wrong about Hamilton. It was not that Hamilton could not be democratized or even, as FDR managed to do, not that Hamilton could not be democratized in the name of Jefferson. What Croly was mistaken about was his assumption that a stronger national government—even a stronger national government devoted to reform—implied an alteration in the formula that read happiness-public guarantees happiness-private.

FDR nearly established a theoretical model that not only nationalized Jefferson and democratized Hamilton but also altered the relationship between happiness-public and happiness-private, but he did not quite succeed. This failure, unnoticed for at least a generation, provided for the deconstruction of the New Deal by other presidents and even through the very exemplars that Roosevelt had used.[17]

In the months following the first hundred days, FDR addressed some of those cacophonous groups of which Wilson had spoken and explored the relationship between happiness-public and happiness-private. At the Naval Academy he reminded graduates that while "esprit de corps, pride of profession is a delightful element in the making of a good officer" it does not in a democratic society make one a "valid member of the aristocracy of life." "Avoid an exclusive relationship to your own clan" was Roosevelt's advice. "Remember to cultivate the friendship of people, not alone your own class or profession, but the average run of folks, the same folks you would have known and liked and affiliated with had you not chosen to enter and to graduate from a highly specialized institution of higher education." Neither an officer nor a civilian ought to be "set apart as a clique with different interests and different ideas from those of the rest of the country." Think of the people you serve, FDR continued, "not as an abstract, theoretical mass, but as one hundred and twenty millions of men and women and children in forty-eight states—on sea coast, on plain and among the mountains; in city, in village, and on the farm; rich people, people of moderate means, poor people; people employed and people out of jobs."[18]

This graduation address is hardly a philosophically inclined speech even by standards of presidential ceremonial politics. But it does illustrate the general theoretical perspective of the first New Deal. Virtually absent are any appeals to the icy clarity of martial virtues (and this is a military organization that FDR is addressing, one that on Roosevelt's own terms has learned "discipline, responsibility, industry and loyalty").

While there is a populist tinge to FDR's advice, it is constrained and largely implied, much like the "forgotten man" campaign address. The advice, clearly and simply stated but moderate in intensity, is offered largely in negative terms and in precepts that can be easily, almost naturally met. Don't forget the "average run of folks" is all that FDR is asking. There is certainly a sense in which the ethics of the address reach for the lowest common denominator of national unity. FDR is offering a breezy democratic ethos, not without its own kind of esprit de corps, as we shall see in a moment, but one in which the spirit of America as revealed in that parade is preserved. Remember the average folks not as an "abstract, theoretical mass" but in the contexts of their own lives and communities.

There is a real delicacy to FDR's formulation, one that one would not expect to find in the midst of a crisis so harrowing as the depression. Hamiltonianism must be democratized but not through populist outrage. Jeffersonianism must be nationalized but not through the abolition of local sentiment. The symbol that FDR selected to pursue these aims is the American pioneer. At an extemporaneous speech before students at Washington College, Roosevelt criticized the previous speaker's reference to the pioneer as an individualist: "It is true that the pioneer was an individualist; but, at the same time, there was a pioneer spirit of cooperation and understanding of the need of building up, not a class, but a whole community."[19] At Vassar College a month earlier FDR spoke of "extending to our national life the old principle of local community, the principle that no individual man, woman or child, has a right to do things that hurt his neighbors." "What is good for my neighbors is good for me, too" was announced as an old precept to be applied to the New Deal.[20] Before the National Conference of Catholic Charities, Roosevelt announced that "we have recaptured and rekindled our pioneering spirit. . . . A democracy, the right kind of democracy, is bound together by the ties of neighborliness."[21] The New Dealer as pioneer implementing the values of neighborliness at the national level was an image that transformed the old Hamiltonian-Jeffersonian debate that FDR had said during the campaign repeated itself throughout American history. The New Dealers were not, as Jeffersonians might charge, a new technocratic elite. They were pioneers, men and women with an esprit de corps without cliquishness. They remember the forgotten. In fact they saw them as neighbors. To the Hamiltonians, defeated but not broken by the depression, there was the threat, not stated often, that "modern Tories" would not be tolerated, that a new leadership was now in place. "We are guilty of great experimentation," FDR boldly told a Georgia audience as he quoted J. S. Mill, "one of the fathers of all economists":

History shows that great economic and social forces flow like a tide over communities only half conscious of that which is befalling them. Wise statesmen foresee what time is thus bringing and try to shape institutions and mold men's thoughts and purposes in accordance with the change that is silently coming on. The unwise are those who bring nothing constructive to the process, and who greatly imperil the future of mankind, by leaving great questions to be fought out between ignorant change on the one hand, and ignorant opposition on the other.[22]

But the easy naturalness of a new pioneer ethic should not blind one to the total character of the appeal. Roosevelt may have left basic American politicoeconomic structure intact, but he had grasped the enormous power of American democratic reform. "We are asking a new question in an old form. We are saying, 'Is this practice, is this custom, something which is being done at the expense of the many?' " Along with neighborliness came a new vigilance. "The many," FDR explained are "the neighbors."[23] No one was special because we are all special was the New Deal precept, and in it is contained the spirit that conservatives feared would unleash leveling. And Roosevelt had said that he did not need any four- or five- or ten-year plan of the sort dictatorships imposed. With "support" from "average citizens," the country could move further in a "shorter space of time without giving it a definite number of years." In truth, the New Deal apparatchik as neighbors were not nearly as thorough or nosey as the speeches implied. But FDR was committed to a few general rules. He told the audience at Washington College that the wider a distribution of wealth we can have, in the "proper sense of that term," the more likely the goals of democracy could be reached. Every man and woman had two duties to perform: (1) to "apply that education intelligently to the problems of the moment"; (2) to "obtain and maintain contact with and understanding of the average citizens of their own country." His statement on the NIRA in June, while noting business cooperation in World War I, included the warning that "no business which depends for existence on paying less than living wages to its workers has any right to continue in this country."[24]

It is difficult to overestimate the manner in which the simple precepts of social democracy (for that is what FDR had articulated) encapsuled in the American homey concepts of neighborliness and pioneering overtook the entire agenda of American politics if only for a short period of time. T. V. Smith has remarked how successful was Roosevelt in "politicizing the whole of American life."[25] This in his Vassar address seemed to be precisely FDR's goal: "more and more men and women are taking an individual, a personal interest in all the problems—the social and economic and political problems—than ever before in the history of the Nation. . . ." The search for happiness was now to be a public activity, "what is good for my neighbors is good for me, too."[26]

FDR had led, and helped create, a cultural revolution in America, one that grasped for a brief moment the Jeffersonian idea of happiness-public as praxis. Critics (FDR called them "modern tories" and "doubting Thomases") have historically reminded us about the totalitarian possibilities of democratic reform, and the New Deal was a perfect illustration of the cause of this skittishness. FDR had avoided for the most part the Lincolnian martial alternative but the Jeffersonian principle hit nerves ("roots" in the New Deal vocabulary) that brought forth a kind of Jacksonian nationalism that preceded by years the famous "left" turn of FDR. Walter Lippmann's complaint in 1934 that the New Deal had many plans but no Plan is not exactly correct.[27] For while the bureaucratic and policy relationships between the NRA and the AAA may have been tenuous or even inconsistent, these and all the proliferating alphabet agencies reflected a common spirit of neighborliness and pioneering that sought to transform American culture. And how can one say conclusively that a Hegelian-like consistency is not more real than a seemingly chaotic administrative structure? This is not to say that New Deal programs were not in some Hegelian sense Hamiltonian in themselves (a point to which we shall return) but that FDR's report that "we are reviewing all kinds of relationships" so captured the principle of happiness-public that his question, "Is this practice, is this custom, something which is being done at the expense of the many?" was asked again and again nationwide.

The sense in which New Deal programs were to become profoundly undemocratic and paternalistic was rarely perceived in FDR's first term. For above all else the New Deal had established the happiness-public principle in a culturally hegemonic way. It pulled in nearly every conceivable group idea. Back-to-the-land proponents, technocrats, Southern agrarians, "independent" liberals, decentralists, Popular Front communists, socialists—the entire community of ideas in America found that it could not fully resist the appeal of neighborliness and pioneering. Even those leaders and groups who were said to offer alternatives, the Townsend and Share the Wealth and EPIC clubs, the Coughlinites, those very groupings that are alleged to have turned FDR leftward in 1936 were only intuiting, sometimes in grotesque ways, the precepts of the New Deal. To attack the New Deal in its particulars was possible (this was in large part Landon's strategy as well as that of the press in general), to be a sympathetic critic was possible, but to take a position that stood outside the New Deal placed one outside society and meant the loss of one's identity as an American.

5

Oh, Shade of Jefferson

If we assume then that the New Deal in eschewing the Lincolnian alternative pushed the Jeffersonian exemplar hard—as hard as it could possibly be pushed—toward social democratic directions, how successful was its cultural revolution? What structures of public happiness were built? The record, needless to say, is mixed. But the standard assessments seem to almost uniformly miss the point. The liberal argument of James MacGregor Burns, for instance, that FDR's policies were insufficiently Keynesian and that Roosevelt failed to create a permanent liberal party coalition by forgetting "the great lesson of the inaugural speech of 1933," or the socialist argument of Howard Zinn that New Deal policies were too piecemeal and only narrowly experimental fail to treat the New Deal's exploration of Jefferson on its own terms. [1]

"If Jefferson were alive . . ."

More to the point is a 1935 essay by Robert K. Gooch, who focused his attention on what seemed to almost form a genre in contemporary assessments of the New Deal. [2] "If Jefferson were alive, what would be his position on the New Deal?" was a question that commentators found immensely important, one noticeably lacking in subsequent analyses. Gooch's answer in itself is not profound. If Jefferson were alive today, as a man of "encyclopedic interests" he "would undoubtedly concern himself with the workings of the multi-form agencies associated with the New Deal; and with respect to them he would probably form definite opinions as to whether they are working, will work, or can work." Gooch could not be sure what Jefferson's specific ideas would have been. But of this much he was certain: "he would . . . be unequivocally on the side of a deal that assumes the priority of the welfare of all the people over the privilege of the few and that proceeds on the belief in the superiority, which no repetition or sneers can render banal, of human rights over all others. It is inconceivable that he should stand on any other side."[3] Hoover himself found that he was forced to respond similarly although of course with opposite conclusions. He would not quarrel with "the avalanche of oratory" on behalf of the "common people," the "average man," the "economic middle class," and the "rank and file." (Who could, in 1936?) But he would respond to FDR's references to past presidents that he used to "enliven the effervescence of righteousness." Jefferson had said, "Were we directed from Washington when to sow and when to reap we should soon want bread." "Apparently," said Hoover, "this was forgotten when they created the AAA [Agricultural Adjustment Administration]." Jefferson had also said, "the principle of spending money to be paid by posterity, under the name of funding, is but swindling futurity on a large scale." That would "seem even truer to the children of this generation."[4]

In the spirit of these depression commentators, can we ask how had the New Dealers succeeded in building an edifice of happiness-public? I would like to suggest that the great achievement of FDR and his administrators lay with their efforts as community builders, that in various ways that I shall discuss the New Deal built or fostered a myriad of communities devoted to the Jeffersonian principle of public happiness. But without exception these structures disintegrated, and when the Jeffersonian-inspired superstructures disappeared what remained was a Hamiltonian bureaucracy; the major reason for this development lay with alteration of New Deal theory in the left turn of 1936. This conclusion is admittedly a paradoxical one for it suggests that Raymond Moley was right for the wrong reasons and that it was the class appeals of 1936 that brought the New Deal back once again to the conventional nature of a liberal society and its preoccupation with happiness-private. But before fully stating the argument let us take a closer look at the Jeffersonian happiness principle and the attempts of the New Dealers to create arenas of public happiness.

As Hannah Arendt has shown, the idea of public happiness is intimately related to the idea of revolution. The revolutionary spirit occurs in part out of a mass desire to obtain public happiness, an arena of human freedom. No contemporary is more aware than Arendt of the recurring tragedy of modern revolution, of how this desire for freedom leads again and again to the creation not of a constitutio libertatus but of new structures of oppression. Often the cause for these failures was the role that poverty played in revolution. How, Arendt asks, can men and women build structures of freedom when a whole population so suffers from the weight of necessity? Despite the profound problem posed by this "social question" (one that the American revolutionaries did not have to answer but one that also first appeared in the depression) every modern revolution produced spontaneously new and unplanned forms of direct representation. These conciliar forms (soviets, communes, ratts, councils) were invariably crushed and replaced by institutions of dictatorship. While the American revolution did not follow this pattern precisely, an analogous pattern emerged. The social question may not have weighed on the minds of the founders but the general problem of establishing order did. And herein lies a more general but deeper contradiction between revolution and the quest for freedom. For if the aim of a revolutionary spirit "was not merely the spirit of beginning something new but of starting something permanent and unending; a lasting institution, embodying this spirit of encouraging it to new achievements, would be self-defeating."[5]

There is then a conceptual contradiction between the Declaration of Independence and the Constitution that reaches even deeper than the current controversy over the extent to which republican political theory was abandoned at the founding. The American Revolution had no Reign of Terror, it produced no dictatorship; but it did in Arendt's analysis fail to incorporate the conciliar system into its Constitution. In their desire to solve the problem of republican government the founders chose to substitute representation for direct political action. While this alteration bears none of the cynicism and ruthlessness of Lenin's slogan "All Power to the Soviets," it represented the great tragedy of the American Revolution. This in his later life Jefferson saw. Jefferson "knew, however dimly, that the Revolution, while it had given freedom to the people, had failed to provide a space where this freedom could be exercised."[6] The failure of the founders to incorporate the township and the town meeting into the Constitution was to be remedied by Jefferson by a subdivision of the country into wards. Here a citizen would be a "participator in the government of affairs, not merely at an election one day in the year, but every day." When there is not a man in the State "who will not be a member of some one of its councils . . . he will let his heart be torn out of his body sooner than his power wrested from him by a Caesar or a Bonaparte." For Arendt the genius of Jefferson's proposal lay in the fact that this proposal advocated a new form of government rather than a mere reform of it or a mere supplement to existing institutions. For "the basic assumption of the ward system, whether Jefferson knew it or not, was that no one could be happy without his share in public happiness, that no one could be called either happy or free without participating, and having a share, in public power."[7]

"Everybody here was equal"

In 1932, when the "social question" hung over America as it had never done before and when many saw America in the same situation as pre-revolutionary France, or more properly prerevolutionary Russia, FDR had indeed moved in Jeffersonian directions. He had rejected the Lincolnian exemplar; he had introduced the concept of public happiness through the concepts of neighborliness and pioneering. New Deal programs were not a conscious introduction of a counciliar system to America. In many areas FDR moved very reluctantly in accepting new political forms, in others he actively opposed them, almost always he saw them as temporary. But consistent with Arendt's analysis, new arenas of freedom emerged spontaneously, unplanned in the era of planning.

Let us review some of them. The various New Deal relief projects—the CWA (Civil Works Administration), the WPA (Works Progress Administration), the CCC (Civilian Conservation Corps), the NYA (National Youth Administration)—were all regarded as emergency programs. FDR canceled the CWA after three and a half months, partly on the grounds that the program was designed to get people through the winter and that "nobody is going to starve during warm weather."[8] In 1937 he drastically reduced WPA appropriations. There were also a number of important restrictions. Government work projects could not compete with private business (although here Harry Hopkins could be very creative) or engage in ongoing government projects. There was the problem of competition with union wage scales and, in the South, rates for black workers. The relief projects were, of course, in an important sense in direct contradiction to the concept of the free citizen. Workers were dependent upon the political structure for employment. From their inception both the New Dealers and their critics expressed concern that a permanent dependent class could be created. But this fact, as important as it is, notwithstanding the relief projects, contributed to the ideas of happiness-public and the Jeffersonian ideal in other ways. In its short existence the CWA built or improved 400,000 schools, laid 12 million feet of sewer pipe, built 469 airports, employed 50,000 teachers in rural schools, built 3,700 playgrounds. The PWA (Public Works Administration) and the WPA "changed the face of the land."[9] Here is William Leuchtenburg's summary of its activities:

> The PWA built thoroughfares like the Skyline Drive in Virginia and the Overseas Highway from Miami to Key West, constructed the Medical Center in Jersey City, burrowed Chicago's new subway, and gave Natchez, Mississippi, a new bridge, and Denver a modern water-supply system. Few New Yorkers today realize the long reach of the New Deal. If they cross the Triborough Bridge, they are driving on a bridge the PWA built. If they fly into La Guardia Airport, they are landing at an airfield laid out by the WPA. If they get caught in a traffic jam on the FDR Drive, they are using yet another artery built by the WPA. Even the animal cages in the Central Park Zoo were reconstructed by WPA workers. In New York City, the WPA built or renovated hundreds of school buildings; gave Orchard Beach a bathhouse, a mall, and a lagoon; landscaped Bryant Park and the campus of Hunter College in the Bronx; conducted examinations for venereal disease, filled teeth, operated pollen count stations, and performed puppet shows for disturbed children; it built dioramas for the Brooklyn Museum; ran street dances in Harlem and an open-air night club in Central Park; and, by combing neglected archives, turned up forgotten documents like the court proceeding in the Aaron Burr libel case and the marriage license issued to Captain Kidd. In New York City alone the WPA employed more people than the entire War Department.[10]

The NYA built tuberculosis isolation huts in Arizona, raised a milking barn at Texas A&M, landscaped a park in Cheboygan, Michigan, renovated a school house in North Dakota. The CCC, the longest-lived New Deal relief agency, enrolled over 2.5 million youths in its existence working in reforestation, soil conservation, and parks projects. The Federal Arts Project of the WPA included in its final report that it had created 15,666 murals, 17,744 pieces of sculpture, 108,099 paintings, 240,000 copies of original designs. Photographers for the FSA (Farm Security Administration) shot over 100,000 photographs. Over 2 million students were taught art in over 160 community centers. The Federal Theatre Project staged over 1,000 plays, musicians performed the compositions of 14,000 American composers. The Federal Writers Project published about a thousand works, including fifty-one state and territorial guides (the first since the Baedaker series of the 1890s), some thirty city guides and regional studies, a 150-volume "Life in America" series, a group of ethnic studies, as well as supported novelists such as Richard Wright,

Saul Bellow, John Steinbeck, Ralph Ellison, Eudora Welty, John Cheever, and Nelson Algren. [11]

There is a severe contradiction between FDR himself and Congress and the middle-level administrators and participants themselves regarding the theoretical justification of these programs. The relief projects were regarded as a necessary expedient by New Deal supporters. Hopkins himself complained about criticism that the New Deal had created a nation of "leaf-rakers" by arguing that many seemed to prefer direct relief. "Let these fellows . . . sit home and get a basket of groceries, that is what a lot of people want."[12] Roosevelt too defended the projects as the only way to avoid the "narcotic" of receiving relief. "Usefulness" was usually the strongest defense of the projects. But participants tended to see these efforts in broader terms. A CCC member pointed out the "big trees you see along the highways" and recalls planting them in an atmosphere that taught people that "everybody here was equal." Another looks at the Children's Zoo in Central Park: "This was built during the Depression by WPA workers. It's an absolutely lovely place. I go to the Park often. And I cannot help remembering—look, this came out of the Depression. Because men were out of work, because they were given a way to earn money, good things were created."[13] The unemployed were engaged in public projects in a deeper sense than the New Dealers chose to speak. They were creating projects designed to promote happiness-public and in an inchoate way were participants in a new arena of public freedom.

As I noted, WPA and other public project workers were in an important sense still dependent citizens. Not only were they employed as a last resort but their status as "workers," receiving a wage for a task assigned independent of their participation, was not substantially different from those who were employed in the private sector. But there were signs of transition in this regard. The WPA itself brought into being the Workers Alliance, which made demands for more and new kinds of projects.

It is in the areas of the arts that one sees the clearest articulation of the idea of happiness-public both because of the nature of the activity and the creativity of its several directors. Here again Hopkins tended to be aggressively utilitarian. Responding to criticism of the Federal Arts Project, he replied, "Hell! They [artists] have to eat just like other people."[14] But directors such as Hallie Flanagan (theater), Holger Cahill (art), Nikolai Sokoloff (music) advanced the concept of "cultural democracy" as a theme for work relief projects. The directors worked under many of the same restrictions as the WPA in general. Ninety percent of the participants were required to be registered on relief rolls, the quality of talent was variable, and there were those who, like Alfred Stieglitz, argued that unemployed artists should be given a weekly allowance and kept away from paint. In addition there were the legitimate fears that this kind of federal support for the arts would turn the American intellectual community into an agitprop structure for the New Deal (which in a sense it did, though not in the way congressional critics imagined it would and later charged that it did).

The directors and their participants pursued Jeffersonian ideas in several ways. First, they argued that in democratic societies support for the arts tended to be limited to "legacies from rich men's houses" and that the bulk of the population was alienated from its own heritage. Thus, under Flanagan the Federal Theatre Project was conceived in terms of "people's theatre" in which the stage as a place "where sophisticated secrets are whispered to the blasé initiate" would be abandoned and replaced by a theater that was accessible and devoted to American themes and history. In Flanagan's mind people's theater required new experimental techniques in order to break away from the elitist tradition. Arthur Arendt's documentary theater, the "Living Newspaper," was one example of this attempt. Flanagan herself had proposed dramatizing the WPA guides. The New Deal cooperative ethic of "neighborliness" was pursued in a number of original plays much to the concern of HUAC in its 1937 investigation. One play, *The Revolt of the Beavers*, was designed to teach children "never to be selfish"; another, *Power*, explored the case for public ownership of utilities. Staff members attempted to attract as wide an audience as possible by encouraging block ticket purchases for union locals and WPA workers. Cahill helped create community art centers for the employment of artists in small cities and for training for amateur artists. In an effort to provide "a work of art for every American home," the Federal Arts Project sold graphics for as little as $2.50.[15]

Second, the directors took very seriously the belief that a national art is foremost a regional one. Perhaps in no other set of New Deal programs was the effort to invigorate Jeffersonian principles of localism through federal support more successful. Everything American was the goal of all the project directors, and American meant the rediscovery of regional and vernacular art forms. The music project, perhaps the most traditional of the programs, transcribed traditional folk music. The artists who worked on the Index of American Design copied quilts, stoneware jugs, dolls, carvings, weathervanes, ironwork, all the reminders of America's "true artistic past."[16]

Perhaps the most enduring legacy in the arts are the mural commissions, especially the post office murals created under the direction of Edward Bruce in the Treasury Department. Walter Quirt, a WPA/FAP artist from 1935 to 1943, complained that the American muralist was denied the "common ideology in the form of religion" that the Renaissance artist enjoyed. Nor did he have the common ideology of revolution to convey "simply and clearly in murals for an illiterate population" as had the Mexican artist. This was an important restriction in a medium whose "first task" was "ideological."[17] Yet the WPA muralists, led by a committed "Section" board, did develop its own ideology. Every region of the country had its own history portrayed. New England muralists attempted to capture the revolutionary experience, Mid-Atlantic artists, the rise of industry. Southern muralists, who were especially handicapped by the special history of the region, focused upon the relationship between work and a bucolic culture while the Midwestern and Western artist sought to portray the interaction between human beings and the vastness of the prairie. In all these works, the famous are conspicuously absent. The theme of the muralist was a people's history. Folk heroes made their appearances. Arthur Covey painted three panels on the life of John Brown; a mural depicting Molly Pitcher was commissioned for Freehold, New Jersey. Foremost, however, are murals illustrating collective activity of anonymous Americans: Saul Levine's "Ipswich Tax Resistance," Gerald Foster's pictorial account of the battle of Milburn Bridge, Mary Earley's "Down-Rent War," Anton Reffreiger's "Sand Lot Riots." Every region of the country celebrated its pioneers, from Leopold Scholz's pioneer woman defending her family against bears in Angola, New York, to Edward Chavez's "Building a Sod House" in Geneva, Nebraska, to Anton Reffreiger's "The Donner Party" in San Francisco.[18]

The New Deal symbols of neighborliness and pioneering were thus given an artistic rendering for America's ubiquitous post offices and courthouses. When muralists were not depicting the people's struggle against authority and the elements, they interpreted the collective and social nature of American life. FDR had insisted that pioneering involved a "spirit of cooperation and understanding,"[19] and these murals prominently display an American geist that celebrates work as a collective activity. Every conceivable form of work is promoted on these terms. There may be bosses in the foreground or background, but it is the communal and creative nature of the enterprises of lettuce-picking, peach-growing, cypress-logging, mining, cotton-picking, paper-making, threshing, and building that the artists attempt to capture. Leisure too is given a collective interpretation. Simple socializing is a very common theme. Street themes in cities and small towns show groups of people conversing. Peppino Mangravit's "Family Recreations" in Atlantic City is a panel that celebrates the most basic forms of leisure (biking and horseback riding, swimming, dancing, sun-bathing, chatting on park benches). Lee Allen's mural depicting fishing and hunting even manages to achieve a collective aspect.

FDR's reliance upon Jeffersonianism was based on the assumption that Jefferson could be "nationalized," that a reinterpretation of localism and self-government would reveal an inner unity (public happiness) among Americans that would make the Lincoln alternative unnecessary and that would explode the elitist cast of the Hamiltonians. At a cultural level the arts projects achieved just that. There is an Arcadic element in the most industrial of the murals, a sense of industrial discipline in all the depictions of farm activity. Doris Lee's "General Store and Post Office" portrays all the myths of rural sociality, the chatty store owner, the community of women engaged in shopping, the men around the cracker barrel. Kinred McLeary's "The Lower East Side" panel shows tenements in the background and conspicuously depicts different ethnic and racial groups, but its essence is the same as Lee's. Children peer appreciatively into a baby carriage, men talk over their newspapers, street vendors are tiny points of momentary conversation. Work itself is transformed. As we noted, the most regional and specialized economic activities are the subjects, but in all the murals, work is stripped of its alienating character. As communal effort it becomes as Thoreau once remarked on seeing the boatmen, stone masons, and lumberers along the Merrimack River: then activities were "less like toil and more like a game of chess."

The mural projects, and in a more blatant ideological way, the Federal Theatre, articulated the utopian aspects of the New Deal. Here were images of public happiness, drawn from but scaling far beyond reality, that were not portrayed as temporary measures. They were, as critics charged, agitprop for the New Deal but at the same time they stood as utopian criticisms of an administration that was committed to the principles of neighborliness and pioneering for more limited purposes or—to put the point more kindly—for more immediate objectives. In what directions would the New Deal have had to proceed in order to politically and bureaucratically capture the visions of the federal artists?

This is a question that does not appear to have been asked beyond the confines of the section apparatchik, and it may be that no political-administrative structure could capture the idealized nationalized Jeffersonianism of the various projects. But the point I am trying to make here is that these temporary and utilitarian efforts brought forth efforts to conceive new kinds of public space intuited from American experience.

It is difficult to assess the impact of the art projects on the population at large. In typical New Deal fashion, formal procedures for democratic decision making were ad hoc. The section staffs, who had a clear preference for realism and an open bias against allegorical paintings, demanded in general an American art accessible to the public. Local tastes were to be accommodated through the artist's visit to the proposed site; the postmaster had a formal veto on the content of any project. Mass reaction to the murals tended to be favorable overall, as was the case with the art projects in general. But "art for the millions" never achieved the proportions conceived in the dreams of the directors. By 1943 the last of the FAP and writers' programs were eliminated or funneled into the war propaganda effort.

As to the participants themselves, Stuart Davis's account of the period to 1939 is an illustration of the way the New Deal inadvertently created new forums of happiness-public.[20] Davis chronicles the position of the American artist in the 1930s in terms of a series of stages. The first phase is characterized by the collapse of the artist's world. Unemployed, possessing skills that are unrelated to even the limited employment opportunities available, and without patrons, the artist, like the rest of the population, sinks into despair. He or she may attempt to re-create the world through outdoor exhibitions and sales, but like the street-corner apple vendors, he or she is overwhelmed by the new economic conditions. The early New Deal work relief programs give that artist a sense of hope "based on the new sense of social responsibility." In other words, the projects themselves create an evaluation of a new concept of art.

Elizabeth Olds's attack on the concept of the print is a good illustration of Davis's point. Olds contended that the notion of the limited edition print was equivalent to the medieval practice of chaining Bibles to the pews of churches. She argued that lithographs and woodcuts could be printed on power presses by "the thousands instead of tens" comparable to "the nineteenth century democratic popular prices of Currier and Ives prints." Then ways must be found to bring the mass-produced print to the public. Eschewing market mechanisms, she proposed that "picture textbooks" be created by artists for schools and public libraries, and that original prints be distributed to people directly along with agricultural manuals and reports. Along these same lines, Cahill attacked the concept of the "masterpiece" as a "collector's idea."[21]

The third phase involved the creation of various artist's organizations that attempted to challenge the work-relief character of the federal projects, to demand participation in the decisions regarding the nature of activities, and to attempt to negotiate wage levels. These organizations were hardly welcomed by New Deal administrators or for that matter much of the public at large. There was concern about communist domination, charges that the unions were the self-interested attempts of incompetent or mediocre artists. But in a sense these efforts followed along lines set by FDR's general ideology and the reevaluations of art unleashed by it. Where there was no independent collective action, there was now a myriad of artist's congresses and associations, all emerging from a structure created to relieve individual dependency.

"A rich spot of earth . . . well watered . . . near a good market"

But if the New Deal gave inadvertent and reluctant birth to new communities it also consciously attempted to create its own community. The New Deal community program, initially under the direction of Harold Ickes as part of the NIRA and subsequently managed by M. L. Wilson and finally by Rexford Tugwell, was an openly experimental attempt to create examples of a "new organic society." Although only a small part of New Deal expenditures, approximately 100 communities were built. The most famous were the "greenbelt towns," which absorbed one-third of the total cost of the experiments.[22]

But the money devoted to community building does not capture the vision held by the New Deal administrators. FDR himself had long advocated resettlement as a solution to the plight of the urban poor. A farmer even in the worst of times had shelter and food supply while the urban worker had neither. The depression, however, had altered this perspective. Both farmer and laborer were without the means of subsistence and early Roosevelt presidential addresses contained the poignant expression, "stranded populations."[23] Privately Roosevelt still held to a utopian belief in the Jeffersonian ideal of rural life. Tugwell has complained that FDR "always did, and always would, think people better off in the country." In 1931 he mused to his Brains Trust adviser: "Suppose one were to offer these [unemployed] men opportunity to go on the land, to provide a house and a few acres in the country and a little money and tools to put in small crops?"[24] Congressmen too invoked the Jeffersonian ideal of the American farmer as one of God's chosen. Robert Green of Florida described an America without "congested industrial centers" and "once again self-sustaining . . . vast and fertile farms, pasture, and prairie lands. Herein lies the real hope for the bright destiny of America." William Stafford of Wisconsin supported legislation to remake the urban laborer into a farmer. On a farm the poor could have a pig and a cow and "make a step toward relieving themselves and those dearest to them by cultivating God's native soil."[25] The back-to-the-land movement saw in the New Deal new hope for its ideal of a rural decentralized America.[26]

But it was under M. L. Wilson and Tugwell as well as the intense interest of Eleanor Roosevelt that this aspect of the Jeffersonian ideal was transformed. Wilson, while quite willing to administer subsistence homesteads designed to simply return stranded populations to the land, reserved funding for a number of homesteads that would be devoted to experimental purposes. These homesteads represented what Wilson called the "community idea." They were to represent a praxis for the creation for a new cooperative America. The communities themselves were to be "a cradle" for a new society. "Somehow . . . attitudes and lives of the families who occupy these communities must be integrated so as to provide a new and different view of life and a new and different set of family values."[27] Tugwell, who assumed head of the new Resettlement Administration in 1935, provided another redefinition. Tugwell was certainly the most un-Jeffersonian of New Deal administrators. In 1930 he had declared the farm to be an area of "vicious, ill-tempered soil with a not very good house, inadequate barns, makeshift machinery, happenstance stock, tired, overworked men and women—and all the pests and bucolic plagues that nature has evolved. . . ." It was a place where "ugly, brooding monotony, that haunts by day and night, unseats the mind."[28] Convinced then of the Marxist principle of the idiocy of rural life, Tugwell focused his utopian vision on the greenbelt towns. These were to be entirely new cities with populations of up to 10,000, encircled by farms. Tugwell hoped that there would eventually be 3,000 of them.

Wilson's "community idea" had taken the Jeffersonian concept of the yeoman farmer to new and experimental forms. The family farm was to be transformed into collective agriculture. Subsistence, if seen as a self-contained, noncash economy, did not presuppose poverty but modest material comfort and community, an abandonment of what Wilson called "the psychology of 'whitelighters,' never satisfied, but excited."[29] Tugwell's vision of a nation of greenbelt towns represented an attempt to move even further from the Jeffersonian ideal. Tugwell had described the Bankhead bill as a plan for little more than a "contented and scattered peasantry." But still the meaning of greenbelt, as Tugwell had conceived it, was derived from the theories of Ebenezer Howard and the English garden greenbelt movement.[30] The connecting link to Jefferson was submerged but nevertheless partially visible. An environment that was gardenlike, "a rich spot of earth," "well-watered," and "near a good market" was the aim of both Howard and the greenbelt planners. Tugwell had simply insisted that the garden take on new forms other than the family farm. The small city was Tugwell's new organizational structure for the farm. Workshops need not be limited to Europe, as Jefferson had once insisted, but industry incorporated in a new organizational structure. Unlike John Crowe Ransom and Ralph Borsodi, and even FDR in his utopian moments, Tugwell did not want the government to empty the cities and rebuild a yeoman class but, to empty both city and country into a new structure.

Tugwell has concluded in retrospect that the New Deal community programs were bound to fail.[31] There were enormous technical problems involved in dealing with the problem on a large scale. Land had to be found and acquired, facilities built, and demoralized families immediately provided for. The decision to proceed with pilot projects created a special set of problems. Political opponents of the New Deal unmercifully focused upon every detail of the settlements from the cost of grease traps at Arthurdale to concrete slabs at the New Jersey homesteads. Paul Conkin describes the unenvious role of the settlement participant: "When a simple farmer, wide-eyed with wonder and expectancy, or a hardened, cynical coal miner, so inured to hardship and struggle as to expect only more of the same, moved to a glittering new subsistence homestead or resettlement community, he was entering a social show window. Willingly or unwillingly, knowingly or unknowingly, he was a human mannequin in a great exhibit. . . ."[32] These communities were after all conceived and built by a modernist elite. It is not surprising then that there would be disputes over the progressive educational philosophy taught at many of the settlement schools, complaints about entertainment (the residents at Penderlea returned government recordings and requested country music instead), opposition to new agricultural methods.

There were serious theoretical criticisms as well. The assessment of the *New York American* that Greendale was the "first Communist town in America" may have been hyperbolic but it did raise the question of how elastic was the Jeffersonian ideal. Spokesmen for labor wondered if the subsistence homesteads represented an organized abandonment of the American dream by means of "planning for permanent poverty." Louis Hacker expressed the fear that the government was consciously seeking to build a "sheltered peasant group as a rural reactionary bloc to withstand the revolutionary demands of the organized industrial workers."[33] None of these concerns, of course, was well founded.

Bit by bit the government sold off the property to individual homesteaders. As with all New Deal programs there was a tension between focus on the temporary measures designed to meet the pressing needs caused by the depression and the long-range planning necessary to produce a transformation of the whole society. The greenbelt towns and the subsistence homesteads may illustrate the limitations of utilizing pilot programs as a way to bridge between the two objectives. In defense of the New Dealers, the resettlement of entire populations is the most daring project that any regime can undertake. A certain amount of caution may say more about the humanity of the administration than a lack of imagination. But what may have been as determining a cause in the demise of the effort was the inability or the refusal of elites and the public at large to accept a major reinterpretation of the Jeffersonian yeoman ideal. Back-to-the-land intellectuals gave up on the RA and focused their attention on the Bankhead bill. Eleanor Roosevelt was unable to persuade Dubinsky to support the Heightstown project. Perhaps most telling of all is the story told by C. B. Baldwin about his experiences with a homestead in Arkansas:

We built these houses, put in a school, nursery . . . they had individual garden plots. It was diversified land-livestock, cotton, fruits, vegetables. They were paid so much a month, and at the end of the year, when the crops were in, they'd divide the profits. It had been operating about two years. They were doin' pretty well. . . .

Will Alexander spent several days on the project visiting with these families. He'd talk to them in the evening, when they were relaxed. They'd say, "Dr. Alexander, this is wonderful. You know, if we're able to stay here four, five years, we'll be able to go out on our own farm."

It came to us as sort of a shock. See, this hunger for land ownership. . . . Although they were happy and more secure than they'd ever been in their lives, they were lookin' forward to gettin' out and ownin' their own land. You have to reckon with this kind of thing.[34]

What would America have looked like had there been 1,000 greenbelt towns built? What would America have looked like had there been at least one subsistence homestead in every rural county in the farm belt? Many questions would need to be answered before an evaluation can be offered. But in terms of the point of our discussion the conclusions are more clear. The New Deal community programs had imaginatively attempted to provide a new set of structures for the Jeffersonian ideal. If there were to be new institutions for pioneering and neighborliness the New Dealers had offered a vision of how they might look. But Americans seemed intent on exploring other versions of happiness.

"If we are successful here, we can march on step by step"

One of the few institutions devoted to the New Deal interpretation of pioneering that was not dismantled by Congress was the Tennessee Valley Authority. William Leuchtenburg has observed that in general the New Dealers consciously avoided the moralistic approach to public policy that they associated with progressivism. But along with the greenbelt towns, the TVA qualified as a Heavenly City for the New Dealers.[35] The antiutopian, scientific orientation of the reform apparatchik fell away when the TVA was under discussion. Here engineering, both of the physical and social kinds, was mixed with rapture. For David Lilienthal the TVA was the story of the taming of a "wandering and inconstant river," an "idle" and "destructive giant," into a "chain of broad and lovely lakes which people enjoy, and on which they can depend, in all seasons, for the movement of the barges of commerce that now nourish their business enterprises." For Tugwell the TVA stood for tall transmission towers, white dams, glistening wire strands, a place where "a vision of villages and clean small factories has been growing in the minds of thoughtful men." Even Norman Thomas paid a back-handed compliment: the TVA was a "beautiful flower in a garden of weeds." FDR himself preferred to see the TVA in terms of his reinterpretation of the frontier experience: "This in a true sense is a return to the spirit and vision of the pioneer. If we are successful here we can march on, step by step, in a like development of other natural territorial units within our borders."[36]

In truth, a case can be made that the ideological foundation for the creation of the TVA was more limited and eclectic than these commentators suggest. The TVA was, after all, the fulfillment of a progressive, not New Deal, dream. FDR's own interest in the project derived in large part from his earlier battles over the St. Lawrence Seaway as governor of New York.[37] The "TVA idea" was in an important sense a leftover from the politics of the 1920s. But this qualification cannot be permitted to miss the basic theoretical role that the TVA played in the New Deal. For many the TVA, not the relief projects or the NRA (which seemed to please no one), represented the essence of the left possibilities of the New Deal praxis. For here was government planning—permanent planning under the principle of government ownership. Here was the so-called middle way in action. For instance, Lewis Mumford, upon his return from a tour of the valley, described the facilities as "as close to perfection as our age has come" and was all the more impressed because it was the first such project of this magnitude (the twenty-one dams were in their combined mass more than a dozen times that of the Great Pyramids) to be undertaken with free labor.[38] Max Lerner proposed that the concept of the TVA yardstick be applied to the "opinion industries." We must avoid a government monopolized press as in Germany, Italy, and Russia, argued Lerner. But what about creating a Federal Radio chain "run noncompetitively and without advertising" to serve as a standard for other chains to live up to and to "serve to broadcast the merciless truth about our social conditions when the other chains fear to?" Lerner also proposed the funneling of "socially conscious money" to compete with Hollywood in the movie industry and the private press "leviathans" in the newspaper industry.[39] Whatever the origins of the TVA, its supporters always saw in it more than the development of fertilizer and electricity, or more accurately, they saw in these technical goals the achievement of broader aims.

If the TVA was, however, the Heavenly City of the New Dealers it was a city that rested uneasily, if imaginatively, upon Jeffersonian ideals. One can identify no less than four Jeffersonian-inspired visions for the valley: that of its first chairman, Arthur E. Morgan; the Harcourt Morgan–Lilienthal approaches; and the critique offered by Donald Davidson. The "grassroots" visions of Harcourt Morgan and Lilienthal, of course, become the authoritative one only to be replaced by a more narrow technocratic model. New Deal hagiology tends to portray Lilienthal as the giant killer of the private utilities, with Arthur Morgan as the unwitting ally of the forces of greed and Davidson as a quixotic gadfly, but the battle over the TVA as a prototype for a new community was much more complex than this.[40]

Arthur Morgan was soft on the private utility companies. He believed, as an aide to Lilienthal concludes, that the TVA could be made so perfect and idealized that the utilities would copy it: "one demonstration farm and one demonstration cooperative and one TVA municipal power company would be enough."[41] But Arthur Morgan was fired not only because of his fellow traveling with the Commonwealth and Southern but because in other ways he supported a handicraft conception of Jeffersonian community. One critic had complained "that the one planning body so far established by the government should meantime be representing planning as a Davy Crockett-coonskin-cap retreat from life seems a great shame."[42] The first director also inclined toward an authoritarian edge in implementation. He spoke of replacing money with script in the valley, of reducing the number of counties in Tennessee, of ridding the valley of real estate developers, of confiscating the land of farmers who refused to prevent soil erosion. In short, Arthur Morgan had a vision of a Jeffersonian risorgimento. A focus on public power would only delay or even prevent the conduct of a "great experiment." He always insisted that his vision had the support of the president and he quoted FDR's remarks, that "power is really a secondary matter. What we are doing there is taking a watershed with about three and a half million people in it, almost all of them rural, and we are trying to make a different type of citizen out of them."[43]

Arthur Morgan's replacement, Harcourt Morgan, made his own concessions to the powers that be. In his oral memoirs Harcourt Morgan defended his cooperation with agricultural interests: "If it weren't for the power of agriculture, the leadership of these land grant institutions, the Department of Agriculture and the leadership of the farm organizations, you would have a peasantry."[44] The second TVA chairperson preferred to call his vision of the valley the development of "common moorings," an ecological concept that Lilienthal further transformed into the highly successful ideological battle cry, "grass roots democracy." Harcourt Morgan's realism in regard to the administration of TVA agricultural programs (he essentially wrote off the small farmer) was combined with a mystical interpretation of resource development in general:

It has not been an easy task . . . for nature throughout the millions of centuries to keep the elements and compounds within the evolutionary program so that when man should appear he would find a universe of complex interacting interdependent elements and compounds at his service. These have been so governed by laws that man's environment has permitted not only his existence, but that of all plants and other animals. This complex has definitely challenged man to discover his relation to his Creator and the creative process through his relation to his environment and to the mineral, plant, and animal kingdoms in which he found himself. This challenge has not stopped here. Over the centuries there has developed within man a sense of responsibility and moral obligation to assist nature in augmenting, through intellectual concepts not available to any other beings, the program that brought him into being.[45]

At the end of his career he had complained that Lilienthal had never really understood his concept of common mooring. He had only focused on administrative structure. Lilienthal "didn't get what I was after at all."[46]

Lilienthal may not have understood Harcourt Morgan, but he did understand American political culture. Aside from Tugwell, who so often unwittingly served as the New Deal ideological point man, Lilienthal was the most intellectually astute administrator in America during the 1930s. A man of considerable personal ambition as well as political vision, Lilienthal was able to capture the essence of Roosevelt's ideological revolution more sharply than any other New Dealer.[47]

Writing in his diary in 1939, Lilienthal reveals the Machiavellian aspect of his policies. Electricity was the key to the success of the TVA: "all the eloquence about land and water omits two factors almost essential to wide public interest of a lively kind, to wit, emphasis upon human beings and a fight. In my activities 'crusading' on the power issue, . . . I sensed the crucial importance of stressing the human factors, the concrete picture of men and women benefitting from low electric rates, etc. It was something that came into everybody's life and affected it. The farm electricity matter was especially good in that connection. And, of course, the utility companies furnished the 'fight' element."[48]

Indeed that emphasis on "human beings and a fight" was placed in the context of a nationalized Jefferson or a democratized Hamilton. Lilienthal's belief in the liberating force of technology was unqualified. "There is almost nothing, however fantastic, that (given competent organization) a team of engineers, scientists, and administrators cannot do today" is the assertion made in the first chapter, appropriately entitled "One Valley—and a Thousand," of *TVA: Democracy on the March.*[49] But while Lilienthal may have had the faith of a technocrat, he always conveyed his beliefs in the language of the poet. The Jeffersonian image of the garden is never left unstated. Describing the results of land policies Lilienthal speaks of "the cover of dark green" left to form after the "large scale modern machinery" has done its work. Jefferson himself would have been pleased. "The farmers have built 128,000 miles of terraces on a million acres and more; their graceful design, following the contour, makes a new kind of landscape, one that led Jefferson, observing the effect upon the face of his own Monticello acres, to exclaim that in 'point of beauty nothing can exceed' contour plowing with its 'waving lines and rows winding along the face of hills and valleys.' "[50]

The two pillars of Jeffersonian thought, decentralization and experimentation with new political forms, that have historically made the model a refuge for both local elites and reformers are merged in Lilienthal's ideological justification of the TVA. Jefferson had warned—and Jeffersonians like Hoover had repeated the warning—that should Washington direct when to sow and when to reap the country "would soon want for bread." Lilienthal never challenged this position. In fact he managed to turn the TVA into part of an axiom. "A national capital almost anywhere is bound to suffer from lack of knowledge of local conditions, of local customs," wrote Lilienthal in support of Jefferson.[51] The director did remind his readers that centralization had already done its work in the economic sphere, and he captured the contradictions of American culture when he remarked that "a wondrous state of confusion arose in the minds of men": "they ate food bought at a store that had its replica in almost every town from coast to coast; they took their ease in standard chairs; they wore suits of identical weave and pattern and shoes identical with those worn all over the country. In the midst of this uniformity they all listened on the radio to the same program at the same time, a program that bewailed the evils of 'regimentation,' . . . urging them to vote for a candidate who said he would bring an end to centralization in government."[52] But Lilienthal respected the authority of American political culture and like the dutiful member of an organization that has officially spoken, he accepted the verdict, at least in major outlines. If decentralization there was to be, it would be made to fit the goals of a new age.

"Decentralized administration of centralized authority" was the ideological axiom that transcended the limitations of at least one aspect of Jeffersonianism. For authority, Lilienthal reached for Tocqueville and even Hamilton as well as Jefferson. Tocqueville had claimed that centralization might be able to create a "drowsy precision in the conduct of affairs" but the citizen as "passive spectator" would never produce the "conditions on which the alliance of the human will is to be obtained." For this, freedom and responsibility were required and unless these were granted it was better that the citizen remain a passive spectator than "a dependent actor in schemes with which he is unacquainted." Even Hamilton, "himself a constant advocate of strong central authority," said Lilienthal, had said as much—"The more the operations of the national authority are intermingled in the ordinary exercise of government," the more the national government will "touch the most sensible chords and put into motion the most active springs of the human heart."[53]

How to avoid the dangers of centralization? For Lilienthal, Jefferson had always held the key with which to solve the dilemmas: in "citizen participation lies the vitality of a democracy." The government in Washington would not tell the farmer when to sow and when to reap but it would show him how to do both. It was Jefferson who voiced his hope that "this would be an age of experiments in government," and Lilienthal described the whole of the TVA as one vast educational experiment. Farms were themselves "schoolrooms of the valley." Farmers would be called in by their agricultural agent and would select some to their number to have their farms serve as "demonstration projects" for new techniques including the use of phosphate fertilizer. Since single, scattered farms were not as effective in demonstrating the utility of new methods, "area demonstrations" were encouraged. These "little valleys" became sites for visits by other farmers. Jefferson too was a farmer and he had seen that "education is the foundation of a democratic nation." These "students" would compare one man's methods to their own; "the 'lessons' learned are taken back to be tested at home."[54]

Here was for Lilienthal "grass roots democracy" and as always he gave the program a human face: "I recall when two busloads of farmers from the great dairy state of Wisconsin came to the valley 'to see for themselves.' They spent days walking over Tennessee and Alabama demonstration farms. . . . For me one of the pleasantest experiences of my years with TVA was the sight of a Wisconsin farmer sitting on an automobile running board with an Alabama farmer, both completely absorbed, talking over together their experiences with their land. Their grandfathers may have fought at Shiloh. These citizens, however, would never think of Alabama and Wisconsin in the same way again."[55]

Like his predecessors, Arthur E. and Harcourt Morgan, Lilienthal openly admitted that the TVA was more than just phosphates and electricity. These were important but as "technical levers" or "fulcrums" for the creation of new communities. As fertilizers were the tool to be used to create a "common purpose so deep and broad" as to raise "the spirit of men," electricity was a fulcrum to get farmers to work together "organizing their own electric cooperatives, sometimes against the opposition of private agencies." There were other benefits as well: "When an electric range or refrigerator comes into a farm kitchen the effect is always the same: the kitchen gets a coat of paint, is furbished up; not long after, the rest of the house spruces up; a new room is built on, pride begins to remake the place—pride supported by added income that comes from 'smart' use of electricity for farm purposes. You can follow the trail of new electric lines in many sections by observing the houses that have been thus tidied up."[56]

In truth it is contestable as to how much democracy there was in "grass roots democracy." Lilienthal had not created the American equivalent of Stalin's machine tractor stations but Lilienthal never seemed to regard the farmers under the authority of the TVA as other than peasants who would never alter their practices except on the terms he had outlined. *TVA: Democracy on the March* is filled with stories of farmers who, while never openly described as ignorant, generally behave as if they were. They puzzle over "contraptions" like electric hay driers; they are a suspicious and rumor-prone people. One story involves a farmer who believed that once he put his TVA phosphate in his soil, the land would henceforth belong to the "gov'ment." (Given the subsequent history of the American farmer, this skeptical Tennesseean may have been correct.) On Lilienthal's terms it is not unfair to say that the beneficiaries of the TVA were not Jeffersonian yeoman ready for aid but peasants who had to be made into yeomen. The school analogy itself, while it no doubt is employed to convey the restraint of the federal government (after all, the engineers and agricultural experts knew from the beginning the liberating potential of fertilizer and electricity), also suggest the Tocquevillian role of dependent actor for the farmer.

No writer perceived this aspect of grass roots democracy and the possible violation of Jeffersonian ideals in the name of Jefferson more clearly than Donald Davidson, whose two-volume masterpiece, *The Tennessee*, represents yet another interpretation of Jefferson. Arthur Morgan had contended in a 1934 speech that one of the reasons FDR had chosen the Tennessee Valley as an area for economic development was that the people of the valley "never really had an economy." The slave economy prevented the formation of a free labor force; the market for King Cotton was located in the North. As a consequence the white man was forced to flee to the hills, where he and his family "lived hand to mouth, sometimes almost like the Indians in the woods." After the Civil War, the lack of railroads and roads left the area economically underdeveloped. The hill people were again forced to immigrate, this time to the cities of the North. When jobs there were unavailable, they returned again to the hills, and the region became "a relief station for the great industrial centers." Whenever economic opportunities did arise, as in the cases of hardwood and oil booms, the area was ruthlessly exploited. "Trachoma, tuber-culosis, and pellegra exist everywhere. Schools and local government are breaking down financially. A man seldom sees conditions as bad in city slums as those that exist in that county."[57]

One can see from this speech why Arthur E. Morgan flirted with revolutionary methods in his plans for the TVA: "Rugged individualism had abandoned these areas." Davidson was more than willing to accede to portions of Morgan's assessment. The Indian wars had "diverted popula-tion movements and stamped the pioneer pattern deep upon the valley culture." There was the "terrible destruction of the Civil War" and the "cruel bleeding of its aftermath" as well as the industrial preeminence of the North.[58] But Davidson found in the economy (or lack of it, from Morgan's perspective) of the valley and hill people a set of functioning values that, while deeply structured by the historic exploitation of the region, constituted an autonomous culture.

Everywhere he looked, Davidson found attempts to destroy and completely remake this culture. Over 14,000 families were forced to move from the reservoir areas, more than three or four times the number of persons evacuated during the Cherokee Removal. Generally federal au-thorities were reasonable about compensation. Officials even undertook the removal of cemeteries (5,000 remains were disinterred at Norris). No federal troops supervised the removals, only occasionally was a marshall necessary. But Davidson reminds the reader that "one may take arms against a sea of troubles . . . but one cannot take down a rifle to fight an actual, practical flood. When TVA surveyors came through the valley and put bold marks on trees and barns to show where the water would come, the argument was really over. Tears might be shed, and angry words might be passed, but the only questions worth discussion were: How much will you pay? Where do I go next?"[59] Nearly 500,000 acres were flooded, of which 298,000 were farm land. Gone forever were huge sections of garden that had been Tennessee for eons.

As for the agricultural programs, Davidson contends that the histor-ical reliance on cash-crop, row farming was discouraged in favor of dairying, cattle and sheep raising, poultry, and small grains because the agricultural experts wanted to create a market economy in the region (live "on," not "off" the farm was the advice) and the engineering experts feared plowing would fill the reservoirs with silt. Where Lilienthal saw Jeffersonian gardens, Davidson saw the destruction of an existing econ-omy, "by no means as backward as the nation had been taught to think."

In its place were artificial lakes and land designed to go to pasture. The effect on the landscape, he contended, of the valley would be much like the effect of the enclosures of Henry VIII's time.[60]

Lilienthal had described the renovation of farms and the return of pride. Here is Davidson's assessment:

But if, in the long run, the TVA program succeeded, the transformation of the land would certainly take place. The effect on the landscape of the Tennessee Valley, combined with other tendencies of similar kind, would be much like the effect of the enclosures of Henry VIII's time, and later, upon the England of Elizabeth and succeeding monarchs; and it might have some of the social effects which later made acid for the pen of Karl Marx. Green fields would be many, and tillage would be small. The Tennessee farmer would become a cattle raiser, a dairyman enslaved to the aching, compulsive teats of a herd of cows and to the trucks and price scale of Borden, Pet, Carnation. And then he might also become—though in 1946 he still detested the idea—a forester, a mountain guide, an operator of tourist homes and hot-dog stands, a tipped purveyor and professional friend to tippling fishermen, hunters of ducks unlimited, abstracting artists, tired neurotics, and vacation seekers of all sorts. Under the TVA agricultural plan it might even turn out, eventually, that the various rural dialects of the valley would acquire a marketable value and could be entered among farm assets, along with the blooded bulls, hogs, alfalfa, and refrigerators.[61]

The sharpest criticism of Lilienthal and the TVA, however, involved Davidson's analysis of grass roots democracy. The directors had powers that rivaled kings and despots. More so, argued Davidson, for Northern technology gave the administrators godlike powers. "They could change the natural environment to such an extent that the natural order might be deeply and even permanently affected; and in changing the natural order they might change the course of human life in seven states." When there were complaints about the proposed construction of the Douglas Dam, the TVA was "unruffled by this spate of guerrilla bullets. . . . Like the Yankee gunboats of other days," the TVA, "happily armor-plated . . . chugged stolidly on." The TVA was impregnable to local criticism, "what the nation might think about TVA or the TVA idea was for the nation to decide."[62] In the end the position of the citizen under its authority was fundamentally the same as that of a medieval peasant (the passive spectator in Lilienthal's gloss of Tocqueville).

The visions of community presented to the citizens of the valley and to the nation at large were extremely complex. Each saw his model in

Jeffersonian terms. Each saw his model as fulfillment of FDR's concepts of neighborliness and pioneering. Arthur Morgan hoped to create a local community that had never had a chance to develop, one in which real estate developers and unecological farmers were not welcome but responsible power companies were. Harcourt Morgan saw a reactionary edge to the commitment to the subsistence farmer and envisioned agricultural elites as the basis for a "common mooring." Lilienthal saw the TVA as a great experiment in a new kind of democracy, one which those committed either to a "basket-weaving" economy or to private electric power opposed. Davidson, as critic, attempted to expose what he saw as the Hamiltonian grounding to the whole venture. Phosphates to renew tired soil and the elimination of malaria were fine endeavors, but Davidson was asking in essence where was the commitment to the principles of the inaugural parade that Roosevelt had promised? It is unlikely that FDR himself appreciated the significance of all these formulations especially in all their complexities. He seemed satisfied enough that Lilienthal's model was "a return to the spirit and vision of the pioneer."

"A seed bed out of which many other activities and experiments grew"

If it gave accidental as well as planned birth to new communities the New Deal also, as in the first instance reluctantly and without full forethought, permitted through other policies the conception of still more communities. The NIRA was designed to create a whole new economic infrastructure. While they were not unsympathetic to labor's cause, Gen. Hugh S. Johnson and NRA bureaucrats did not envision free and independent trade unions as an essential part of the new order. Johnson would contend that "we did more for labor through NRA, in a few months, than all the strikes and all the unions in this country from the beginnings."[63] When decisions were being made about the bureaucratic location of the new NLRB (National Labor Relations Board) he had told Frances Perkins (who wanted the new board in the Labor Department) that "when this crisis is over and we have the recovery program started, there won't be any need for a Department of Labor or a Department of Commerce, and perhaps some other departments as well."[64] Much to the concern of labor leaders, Johnson and his counsel, Donald R. Richberg, had declared that the executive order creating the NLB still permitted business to negotiate separately with groups representing a minority of workers in a plant.

Although Johnson had accepted the principle of labor representation in the NRA (National Recovery Administration) and while there is no doubt that he believed that wages were far too low, his model for the future was heavily influenced by European corporatism. While Perkins herself knew that he "had the interests of labor at heart," she worried when Johnson gave her a copy of Raffaello Viglione's *The Corporate State* with its glowing tribute to the Italian system.[65] The emblem of the blue eagle, probably the most successful public relations campaign of the New Deal, was a symbol of national participation. While America was never to be subject to *gleichschaltung*, the NRA was hardly Jeffersonian in inspiration. In fact, the agency was clearly the most Lincolnian structure of the New Deal. Johnson's tastes in books aside, the model for the NIRA (National Industrial Recovery Act) was drawn from the board structure of World War I. Herein lies the institutionalization of a crisis mentality for the purposes of national unity outlined in the inaugural. FDR had compared the blue eagle to a "bright badge" worn by soldiers in night attacks to help separate friend from foe.[66] The NRA slogan read "We Do Our Part," and Johnson, who spoke of the "great army of the New Deal" and referred to criticism as "enemy propaganda," publicly described the NRA in terms of the new concept of total war:

Our men had the leading part in the Revolution which *made* the nation— and in the Civil War which *united* it, and in the World War which *glorified* it. But, this time, it is the women who must carry the whole fight of President Roosevelt's war against depression, perhaps the most dangerous war of all. It is women in homes—and not soldiers in uniform—who will this time save our country from misery and discord and unhappiness. They will go over the top to as great a victory as the Argonne. It is zero hour for housewives. Their battle cry is "Buy now under the Blue Eagle!" and the bird is blazoned on the banners in their van.

Those who are not with us are against us, and the way to show that you are part of this great army of the New Deal is to insist on this symbol of solidarity exactly as Peter of the Keys drew a fish on the sand as a countersign and Peter the Hermit exacted the cross on the baldric of every good man and true. This campaign is a frank dependence on the power and the willingness of the American people to act together as one person in an hour of great danger. And that brings us to the critical point of the program which I must make with all the emphasis at my command.[67]

But Frances Perkins had said, "The NRA was a seed bed out of which many other activities and experiments grew."[68] Out of this legislation inspired by a flirtation with corporativism and justified by Lincolnian metaphor emerged unexpectedly new Jeffersonian structures. The specific seed bed here was section 7a of the NIRA, which declared that every code must permit employees to "organize and bargain collectively through representations of their own choosing . . . free from the interference, restraint, or coercion of employers. . . ." The labor movement itself was in a state of near collapse or severe retrenchment. In 1930, only 9.3 percent of the labor force was unionized, and even this figure does not convey the fragile hold that unions had on employees. Sidney Hillman's Amalgamated Clothing Workers (ACW) had 180,000 members in 1920 and 60,000 in 1933, of whom only 7,000 were paying dues. David Dubinsky's International League of Garment Workers (ILGW) had lost nearly two-thirds of its predepression membership. But section 7a gave public legitimization to the union. The organizer's speech repeated throughout the country began with "The President wants you to join the union." The AFL was overwhelmed by requests for organizers. By August 1933 one union simply ran out of dues books and payment stamps. The AFL gained about 500,000 members in 1933 and 400,000 in 1934. The deskilling of workers that had progressed steadily throughout the 1920s had produced thousands of semiskilled and unskilled workers who could not be easily fit into the traditional structure of the AFL forcing the federation to charter new groups and then place them temporarily in "federal" unions. John L. Lewis, president of the United Mine Workers and later a major nemesis of FDR, undertook two bold risks. First he committed his union's modest finances to a major recruitment drive, and then in 1935 he broke with the AFL leadership to organize industrial unions through the CIO, which in the words of Robert Zieger "truly transformed the labor movement."[69]

The opening for the creation of these new and expanded organizations was small and tenuous. The Supreme Court decision to declare the NIRA unconstitutional, as well as FDR's dilatory behavior in regard to the Wagner Act, threatened to close the opening completely. The Labor Advisory Board, which was created to deal with employer violations of section 7a, was seriously understaffed to deal with the volume of complaints it was receiving. Moreover, the corporate ideology of the NRA in general tended to be reflected in a bureaucratic structure that regarded strikes as counterproductive to the goals of national economic recovery.[70] Unions with strong leadership and resources would receive a hearing while newer and weaker organizations were left to fend for themselves.

The NRA was soon called the "National Run Around" by labor leaders. The old miners' ballad did seem to accurately reflect labors' task: "You've got to go down and join the union / Join it for yourself / Ain't nobody there to join it for you / You've got to join the union for yourself." Moreover, the opposition of employers was organized, sustained, and often vicious.[71] After passage of the Wagner Act, American Liberty League lawyers urged employers to disregard the new labor law on constitutional grounds. The La Follette Civil Liberties Committee obtained an inventory of weapons in two steel plants and concluded that there was an arsenal adequate for a "small war."[72]

Roosevelt's position through all this turmoil was mildly sympathetic to unions but almost invariably remote. FDR could be rapturously attentive to the details of farm prices but he never exhibited the same interest in labor disputes. In 1937, in exasperation over labor unrest, FDR told reporters that unless unions and employers soon found a way to settle their differences both he and the American public would be entitled to say, "A plague on both your houses."[73] This ambivalence is captured by Perkins's recollections of Roosevelt's comments on the sit-down strikes in Flint, Michigan. The tactic of the sit-down was probably one of the most inventive in American labor history. Designed in part to deal with the problem of scabs, the sit-down in strategical terms veered close to syndicalist radicalism. The workers, after all, took the strike literally into the factory. The threat of expropriation was always carefully avoided, but the fact that workers did have physical control of the plants raised the stakes on both sides. An early attempt by local police to storm the factory was met with violent resistance. The sit-down itself illustrated the extent to which labor had organized itself at both the local and the national level. The "takeover" itself was the result of delicately timed organization. The six-week sit-in revealed the existence of a myriad of workers' networks, including the Women's Emergency Brigade. New labor elites negotiated with police and state and national politicians. Most of all the strike visibly showed a newly won sense of mastery on the part of labor. It was "the most significant labor conflict in the twentieth century."[74]

In a broad sense, the workers were the new pioneers of whom Roosevelt had spoken. They were, as FDR had said at Vassar, "reviewing all kinds of relationships." Yet according to Perkins, Roosevelt was puzzled by these strikes. He seemed to work at fitting the incidents, rather than within a Jeffersonian model of community, within a Lockean framework, albeit a sympathetic one. The sit-downs were wrong, both strategically and morally; there was no need to do something like this in the United States. Workers now had rights under the law and eventually the government would get around to seeing that those rights were recognized. On the other hand, employers had been "difficult" and FDR could not understand their intransigence. On one occasion Roosevelt mused over the sit-down itself:

Well, it is illegal, but what law are they breaking? The law of trespass, and that is about the only law that could be invoked. And what do you do when a man trespasses on your property? Sure you order him off. You get the sheriff to order him off if he tries to pitch a tent in your field without your permission. If he comes on your place to steal, why, you have him for theft, of course. But shooting it out and killing a lot of people because they have violated the law of trespass somehow offends me. I just don't see that as an answer. The punishment doesn't fit the crime. There must be another way. Why can't these fellows in General Motors meet with a committee of workers? Talk it all out. They would get a settlement. It wouldn't be so terrible. [75]

Locke had spoken about "measures of punishment" in the state of nature, and while FDR's thoughts on the sit-down are not so reflective there is a hint in his remarks, slight as they are, that worker-employee relations were in a kind of state of nature. The government was only on the verge of recognizing legal rights for labor. In that context both parties were essentially on their own in regard to protection of their rights, and employers were under a moral obligation—in Locke's words—"only to retribute to him, so far as calm reason and conscience dictates, what is proportionate to his transgression."[76] This is probably the most sympathetic reading of the sit-down that one could derive from a Lockean model, but as Perkins notes, "there were many things about trade unions that Roosevelt never fully understood." Most significant of all was FDR's inability to apply imaginatively his revised Jeffersonianism to the rise of labor in the 1930s. He never understood "what solidarity means in the trade union movement. He tended to think of trade unions as voluntary associations of citizens to promote their own interests in the field of wages, hours, and working conditions. He did not altogether grasp that sense of their being a solid block of people united to one another by unbreakable bonds which gave them power and status to deal with their employers on equal terms."[77] But while FDR did not see the Jeffersonian potential in the labor unions his kindly Lockeanism prevented him from seeing its syndicalist threat as well. It seems that within that theoretical space the modern labor movement was born.

"Jeffersonianism . . . brought to higher levels in Marxism-Leninism"

Another community, less benevolent in its goals and certainly less democratic, emerged from the policies of the New Deal. The American Communist Party began the decade of the 1930s in strident opposition to the New Deal. In 1936 it seemed to have concluded that FDR was not a Louis Bonaparte but a Louis Blanc. With the exception of the brief period between the Soviet-Nazi Nonaggression Pact and the invasion by Hitler of the USSR, the Party constituted a small but important part of the New Deal apparatchik. The New Dealers prided themselves as planners but the Party had its own Plan within this plan. For the Communist Party too presented its own reinterpretation of Jefferson during its Popular Front period.

If the New Deal Jefferson was strained, the CP version was grotesque. It was one thing to appeal to the sense of tolerance in the liberal consensus by asserting that communists like baseball and dating and are no different from other people except that "we believe in dialectical materialism as a solution to all problems." But it was quite another to declare that with only minor revision there could be a "complete amalgamation of Jefferson's teachings with those of Marx, Engels, Lenin and Stalin."[78] It is difficult to say how many of the 80,000 party members and thousands of fellow travelers actually believed this. It is hard to believe that the core of the Party did, especially given the number of Party professionals who came of political age during the Third Period. It is certainly possible, as Irving Howe contends, that the popular front communists, left on their own, might have developed a party into the American equivalent of Eurocommunism.[79] Yet how Jefferson might have been read under these circumstances is impossible to guess, although it is difficult to imagine a significantly more honest reading.

It is probably more profitable to push these kinds of speculation aside and look briefly at the kinds of communities the Party did create within the New Deal. The chaos occasioned by the immediate need for a bureaucratic caste provided opportunities for communists that had never existed before in American life. Earl Latham describes the confusion in Washington in 1933 and the need for rapid recruitment as something of a "frontier town" in which any candidate with bureaucratic skills was welcomed. Networks of Party members were created in the Department of Agriculture (the Ware group that was to be so infamous in the 1950s) the NLRB, the WPA and the writers' and theatre projects, the Department of

State, government unions, even in the FBI. Here were the submerged members of the Party.[80]

Nathaniel Weyl described a new kind of communist, "no different from other people," but one committed to a plan of colonization:

Under Stalinist leadership the lineaments of the archetypical underground Communist had entirely changed. The resolute and romantic organizer of street war had been put away in a museum. Into his place had stepped the iron bureaucrat—the well-dressed, soft-spoken, capable executive who sat in the board room or on the Government committee. The man with a briefcase led a secret life of his own. If Communist rule should be proclaimed in this country, he would move to the head of the table.[81]

These "members at large" communists often were quite different from this description (although Hiss did fit the model nicely), nor was the Plan as well formulated as Weyl suggests. Even Chambers was vague about the actual functions of the Ware group. He admitted that this group had not engaged in espionage per se but insisted that it was considerably more than the Marxist study group that Lee Pressman described before the House UnAmerican Activities Committee. If Herbert Fuchs's testimony is to be believed, the NLRB cell could not consistently maintain officers or meet with regularity. On general issues of patronage, however, these networks were much more successful. Fellow members routinely scuffled individuals without assignments to congressional committees and recruited from committee staffs. La Follette complained about a grapevine that extended into executive sessions. Earl Latham, however, cautions that the CP was only one of many functioning networks in the government, a number of which appear to have been overlapping. It is sometimes difficult to separate old school ties and professional connections from Communist Party membership in tracing an individual's bureaucratic advancement.[82] Most impressive about this system, however, is the psychological tenacity that these groups had over their members. Part of the explanation for this phenomenon lies with the secrecy of the networks. The Ware group was not discovered by Congress until fourteen years after its formation. Fuchs spoke of a psychological "trap" created by the conspiratorial nature of the groups. Some members, like Elizabeth Bentley and William Remmington, seemed addicted to the underground nature of their activities.[83]

The government cells were tiny communities, though no doubt deformed by their conspiratorial nature and commitment to democratic centralism. But the CP's special cooperation with the New Deal also produced a flowering of organizations more public in character. The Party created scores of what it called "mass organizations," commonly known as front groups.[84] The most well known included The Unemployed Council, TUUL (Trade Union Unity League), the John Reed Clubs, and the American League against War and Fascism. Many of these efforts were begun in the Third Period but these fronts grew to very large proportions during the Popular Front. One New York Party member claimed over 100 different mass organizations in his district. In fact the numbers became so large that their management strained the resources of the CP membership. As one functionary complained, "we send out an organizer into a new territory. He becomes the Party organizer, he becomes the TUUL organizer, the ILD organizer, the WIR organizer, etc. The result is that he is so confused he actually [doesn't] know where he stands."[85]

The above comment reveals even more than simple organizational problems. It may have looked like the CP's commitment to Americanism led to a frenzied Tocquevillianism, but in fact the Party seemed obsessed with assuring control over its fronts, a point that the Socialists grimly discovered. The Congress against War, for instance, was composed of over fifty organizations of which only two were openly communist (the Party itself and the YCL [Young Communist League]). But thirty-four others were Party auxiliaries.[86] In this sense the CPUSA perversion of Jefferson in rhetorical terms was mirrored in practice. For the fronts looked like citizens' groups exercising their right to petition their government when in fact they often prevented participation. Herbert Benjamin, himself a Party member, wrote, "Where non-Party workers are attracted to our movement, they find themselves excluded from all participation in the *actual* work of *planning* and *leading* actions." Max Bedacht was even more explicit: noncommunists were not members of a real organization, but at best "a tolerated wall decoration in sham organizations."[87] Yet without conceding the point that the fronts were ruthlessly managed by the Party, there was still a sense in which these organizations provided an arena of happiness-public for their participants. As Harvey Klehr has remarked, few members of fronts were genuine innocents. Most were fellow travelers, unwilling to join the Party but willing to accept Party direction.[88] For them the fronts were the way they chose to participate in the issues of the day.

As for the rank and file communist, there is no question that the

Party provided bonds of comradeship. Sara Gordon's memory is illustrative:

My God! How I hated selling the *Worker!* I used to stand in front of the neighborhood movie on a Saturday night with sickness and terror in my heart, thrusting the paper at people who'd turn away from me or push me or even spit in my face. I dreaded it. Every week of my life for years I dreaded Saturday night. And then canvassing! Another horror. A lady would shut the door in my face before I'd gotten three words out—and if she was a socialist she'd *slam* the door—and I'd stand there sick. I'd tell myself a thousand times: It's not *your* face she's shutting out. . . . God, I felt annihilated. But I did it, I did it. I did it because if I didn't do it, I couldn't face my comrades the next day. And we all did it for the same reason: we were accountable to each other. It was each other we'd be betraying if we didn't push down the gagging and go do it. You know, people never understand that. They say to us, "The Communist Party held a whip over you." They don't understand. The whip was inside each of us, we held it over ourselves, not over each other.[89]

Recent scholarship suggests branch organizations, held together by the bonds Vivian Gornick recounts in her oral history, expressed concerns and held perspectives independent of Party leadership.[90] Still it seems that when voices could have been raised, these communities of radicals, sustained as they were by rich and flourishing subcultures, were largely silent.

John L. Lewis had calculatedly used CP organizers in the formulation of the CIO. When asked if he was concerned that the Party might take over the new organization, he replied, "Who gets the bird, the hunter or the dog?"[91] New Dealers never seemed to take anything resembling as focused an assessment of the role of the Party. In 1933 Lorena Hickok reported to Hopkins that communists were "working like beavers," something that both she and Hopkins took for granted. Rexford Tugwell, so frequently described by the media as a red, was fervently anticommunist. When William Wirt testified before a congressional committee in 1934 that several governmental officials related to him their plans for takeover, FDR had joked to reporters, "In Washington, apparently you people have been going from Wirt to Wirt."[92] Privately, Roosevelt did undertake investigations of selected individuals and smarted from Hearst's allegations in the 1936 elections. On the whole, he and the New Dealers did not appear particularly interested in the CP one way or another. The Party (and the Comintern) spent a great deal of effort in its attempt to assess the New Deal. Roosevelt expended almost no energy on it. When the country did come to reflect on the Party, the CP's secret communities and "mass organizations" completely collapsed.

There were even more communities brought into existence by the New Deal. Governmental networks of women, vague and fragile but observable, emerged.[93] FDR's racial policies were especially timorous but even here he created small openings. His denunciation of lynching as a "vile form of collective murder" even gave hope to W. E. B. DuBois. His promise that as there would be no forgotten men there would be "no forgotten races" was largely unfulfilled, but it did in altering party alignment break the "pervasive despondency on the immutability of the racial status quo."[94] Outside the New Deal, thousands of Townsend clubs (5,000 by 1935) and Share the Wealth clubs as well as the National Union for Social Justice threatened for a brief moment to overwhelm the New Deal itself.[95] These groups may not have been neighborly but they were composed of groups of neighbors. Most important, they too saw themselves as engaging in their own form of "pioneering."

6

The Jacksonian Turn

The second New Deal has become a standard interpretive concept in historical scholarship and in American political thought. Curiously, however, there is a considerable amount of disagreement as to exactly what its significance was. Nearly all commentators recognize a certain continuity between the two New Deals but insist that some sort of major departure occurred in 1935. Basil Rauch, the first scholar to make the distinction a central concept in the history of the New Deal, places the shift with Roosevelt's January 4 annual Message to Congress and argues that economic security, rather than recovery, became the "central objective" of reform. Arthur Schlesinger largely accepts this characterization, emphasizing that throughout 1934 FDR had been in a "stew of indecision" before his inauguration of the modern welfare state. Raymond Moley in his memoirs emphasizes the "left" turn of FDR and sadly reports the use of demogogic rhetoric and the abandonment of the "concert of interests" for class politics. Rexford Tugwell sees the shift as moving not to the left but to the right. The Brandeisians, the "old justice's" disciples, had "infiltrated" the New Deal apparatchik to "an almost incredible extent" and moved the president back to the progressive orthodoxy that he had always naturally gravitated toward. James Mac-Gregor Burns, always emphasizing the "gadget" character of FDR as a thinker, attributes the change to goals almost exclusively opportunistic and political. Control of Congress now required a shift leftward, the invalidation of the NRA serendipitously moved FDR closer to labor through the salvaging of section 7a through the Wagner Act, and, most important of all for Burns, the open desertion of business personally angered the president and eliminated a right-of-center coalition as a strategy in 1936.[1]

"Evils overlap and reform becomes confused and frustrated"

If we look at the New Deal as a reading of presidential exemplars that represent the theoretical directions of American political culture, the picture becomes clearer. FDR never gave up the reform of American society along the lines of the image provided in the inaugural parade. Jefferson was never discarded. Many of the communities fostered by the New Deal continued or were initiated or sprung up on their own well after 1935. The Farm Tenancy Act, perhaps the most Jefferson-inspired legislation of the New Deal, was passed in 1937. But a new interpretative layer was added in 1935–36, not entirely un-Jeffersonian but one that emphasized other aspects of American political culture. In this sense it may be helpful to characterize the second New Deal as the Jacksonian, rather than the left, turn. The Jacksonians did not challenge basic features of the Jeffersonian vision. The belief in the inventive capacities of the people is affirmed as well as the doctrine of American exceptionalism and the limited state. But Jacksonianism is foremost a political philosophy of risorgimento and it is this perspective that gives the exemplar its uniqueness. The Jeffersonian enemies are more powerful and the list itself is expanded. Moreover, if the republic is under imminent threat, new measures must be considered.

We saw how the Jeffersonian exemplar had to be inventively modified during the 1932 campaign and the early days of the New Deal. Somehow the Jeffersonian vision had to be subjected to centralization, else Hoover's interpretation and that of the "Jeffersonian Democrats" would remain dominant. This meant an accommodation with the ideological enemy of Jeffersonianism, the Hamiltonians, that was never fully recognized by the New Dealers. "Democratic Hamiltonians" actually is not an inaccurate description of both Moley and Tugwell. But the Hamiltonian structures of the New Deal, especially the AAA and the NIRA, seemed to continually give birth to Jeffersonian communities. The commitment to Jefferson was strong enough to permit these communities to flourish, sometimes by sufferance, sometimes on the edges of the practical thrust of the New Deal.

It seemed to Tugwell that the rise of the Brandeisians represented a fatal retreat by embracing the old Jeffersonian shibboleth of small is better. Thus he writes that the policies of the second New Deal were the "kind of thing the old gentleman on the Supreme Court approved." "Relief could be given, welfare measures could be enlarged, public works could be undertaken; but he must abandon his leaning toward collectivism." He could, Tugwell continues, have "refused to conform." He did not; "he gave in."[2] But Tugwell's analysis depends upon a dismissal of the operational ideology of the welfare state. While there is a certain amount of insight in ignoring the capacity of the service state to truly alter the "obsolete social philosophy" of individualism, Tugwell did not see the new welfare measures for what they were. There was Hamiltonianism in the first New Deal in the president's reading of Jefferson, and there was Hamiltonianism in the second New Deal in the president's reading of Jackson. The welfare state, no matter how forcefully it justifies its existence as a battle against elites, is a state that administers to its people.

But this new Hamiltonianism was not so apparent to New Deal factions in 1935. Moley, Tugwell, and the Brandeisians saw the turn more in terms of past American reform and did not fully appreciate the imagination with which FDR was confronting the American political tradition. This Jacksonian turn is all the more significant given Roosevelt's own personal predilections. Arthur Schlesinger's emphasis on the indecisiveness in the months preceding the annual message illustrates the difficulty of FDR's position, as does Burns's assessment of what he calls FDR's own natural conservatism. Had Roosevelt been a British politician he might have been a Disraeli rather than a Gladstone, but an aristocratic critique of the threat of capital that might have come from a Dutchess County patrician had already been transformed by the power of the American setting. FDR had already and irrevocably invoked Jefferson or democratized Hamilton. The annoyance (which was real and increasingly embittered) which Roosevelt frequently expressed toward ungrateful capital (had he not saved the entire class?) does suggest an assessment made by an outsider. But it was one thing to talk of the forgotten man, complain about the failure of elites, even call for a concert of interests and speak of the values of neighborliness and pioneering, and quite another to talk of "our resplendent economic autocracy" who would "gang up against the people's liberties." It was one thing to refer to the "debauch" of business elites as he had done in 1930, another to refer to them as "privileged princes" and the "resolute enemy." But this FDR did.

There is another sense in which the Jacksonian turn was a theoretical risk. The Jacksonian exemplar is foremost an attack on elites. It is true that in the logic of risorgimento this populism requires a centralization of authority. Jackson, after all, is universally listed as a "strong" president. He destroyed the Bank, but his administration stood for a populist nationalism and he did also threaten to send in troops to South Carolina.

But—especially in America—the baiting of one elite runs the risk of destroying others. As such, the turn represented a difficult step for the construction of a welfare state. Yet in 1935 FDR seemed to have no choice. The extra-New Deal movements of Huey Long, Father Charles Coughlin, and Francis Townsend had already made the transition from Jefferson to Jackson. Here were men that had also intuited their own version of Jefferson. They had promised to remember Jeffersonian forgotten men, the farmers, and added the entire petit bourgeoisie, shopkeepers, small-town newspaper editors, even local bankers, which in America amounts to a majority coalition. A reader of the Long paper, *American Progress,* wrote:

The forgotten merchant is one who has the forgotten man on his books and has not asked the government for an appropriation to take care of the millions of dollars in lost credits. The forgotten merchant is responsible for keeping the forgotten man with food, drugs and clothing, etc. thereby keeping many people well and happy through this past period of chiseling and starvation wages. The powerful groups responsible for chiseling and starvation wages have contributed nothing towards the upkeep of the forgotten man. By slicker methods they are already crowding the forgotten merchant. . . .[3]

These dissidents had attacked the New Deal as unalloyed Hamiltonism. Long had insisted that "we can allow our people to accumulate and grow prosperous" but "beyond that point where accumulation . . . becomes a menace to our society and the well-being of others no one should be permitted to go." He compared the NRA to programs in Italy and Germany and complained that "the Farleys and Johnsons combed the land with agents, inspectors, supervisors, detectives, secretaries, assistants, etc., all armed with the power to arrest and send to jail whomever they found out not living up to some rule in one of those 900 catalogues." Townsend's pension, Long's Share the Wealth, Coughlin's monetary plans—all of them would restore America without a New Deal apparatchik. Wall Street had always had a plan to divest the citizenry of its rights, now the New Deal had a "blueprint" for a "new form of government abolishing States Rights." Long and others had added governmental elites to financial ones as the threat to Americans' status as "free men."[4]

Louis Hartz's thesis that FDR never had to answer critics of property and that this was responsible for the intellectual flabbiness of the New Deal[5] misses the problem that the president faced by 1935. FDR was confronted with fully developed movements that had constructed clear ideological alternatives. To these he responded with precision and imagination. The force of the challenge from these new dissident Jeffersonians was so strong that it took FDR some time to create an effective response.

The Annual Message to Congress offered hints of a Jacksonian answer. Roosevelt reviewed the achievements of the New Deal, emphasizing the constitutionality of its measures in times of crisis. The New Deal had operated through processes that retain all "the deep essentials of the republican form of representative government first given to a troubled world by the United States." But FDR raised the question of whether recovery itself was enough. A convalescing man needs not only treatment of symptoms but removal of the cause of the illness. Changes in the economic and technological spheres have been so rapid that "succeeding generations have attempted to keep pace by reforming in piecemeal fashion this or that attendant abuse." As a result, "evils overlap and reform becomes confused and frustrated." We must, Roosevelt continued, strip away the confusion to agree upon "our ultimate human objectives." In early 1935 the problem as FDR saw it was a "population suffering from the old inequalities, little changed by past sporadic remedies." FDR admitted that "in spite of our effort and in spite of our talk, we have not weeded out the overprivileged and we have not effectively lifted up the underprivileged."[6] Both conditions, no doubt related, had "retarded happiness." Here succinctly stated was the Jacksonian premise that FDR was to carry through 1936. It was not the first time that Roosevelt had employed this model. He had, after all, blamed the depression itself on the failure of elites in the 1932 campaign. He had already raised the specter of the "forgotten man" and he had in his Inaugural noted that the captains of industry had fled from the American temple. Here then the Jacksonian premise was simply being repeated. Yet there was now a difference. Before, economic elites had led a population astray; they had failed in their duty to provide the people with security and vision. Now the image emphasized the entrenched character of these elites. They must be "weeded out."

A change of direction, however, there may have been in 1935 but settled policy there was not. Following upon the statement of the Jacksonian premise were important caveats. Roosevelt had no wish to "destroy ambition" or to "divide our wealth into equal shares on stated occasions." There was to be no exploration of a new Skidmorian founding. In fact, the thrust of the rest of the speech focuses, as Rauch reminds us, on the general security of the population. But that was only the second part of the premise. There were no proposals for "weeding out" the overprivileged.

Throughout the spring FDR seemed conceptually immobilized. The Supreme Court had put its own stamp of disapproval on his version of a nationalized Jefferson. His advisers were pulling him in different directions. The New Deal apparatchik seemed to be running individually with Frances Perkins pushing her social security bill; Marriner Eccles, his banking bill; Benjamin Cohen and Thomas Corcoran, public utilities. In May Roosevelt complained to a reporter: "I am fighting Communism, Huey Longism, Coughlinism, Townsendism." The tax revision legislation, proposed to Congress in June, was regarded by many observers as a tactical error. But the "soak the rich" plan appeared to raise the president's spirits and, more important, provided a peroration to the January address. Inherited wealth and the corporation took on some of the ideological functions of the Monster Bank of the Jacksonians. The issue implied in the message was one of intergenerational justice: "The transmission from generation to generation of vast fortunes by will, inheritance, or gift is not consistent with the ideals and sentiments of the American people." Such accumulations amounted to "the perpetuation of great and undesirable concentration of control in a relatively few individuals. . . ." There were social-democratic tinges in the message (wealth, especially in a modern economy, was "achieved through the cooperation of the entire community"), but the thrust of the proposal rested on a more Jacksonian framework. A distinction was made between "dynamic" and "static" wealth. The proposed legislation was designed only to control the latter. "Creative enterprise is not stimulated by vast inheritances." As to ongoing income, the message singled out the corporation that had avoided the graduated income tax through the use of subsidiaries and affiliates. Small business was now paying the same rate on net profits as corporations a thousand times their size.[7]

"They loved him for the enemies he had made"

The message on tax revision was an attempt to "weed out" the inequalities of which Roosevelt spoke in January. The congressional log jam had broken, but still FDR had not fully developed the Jacksonian model. In fact, it was in September that Roosevelt in response to the head of the Scripps-Howard newspaper chain's query about "frightened" businessmen, responded that his reform had been substantially completed and that he now expected a "breathing spell" that Roy Howard had pleaded for. Two months later FDR told his speechwriters that he wanted a "fighting speech" for his 1936 annual message to Congress.[8] The address that he delivered is certainly the most sustained, impassioned attack on business ever made by an American president.

The most shocking aspect of the speech was FDR's connection between enemies of democracy abroad and the business elite in America. Throughout the world there was a growing conflict between men of good and ill will. The latter appealed not to "patience" and the "finer instincts of world justice" but to the "twin spirits of autocracy and aggression." The masses of people, "denied full access to the processes of democratic government," follow "blindly and fervently the lead of those who seek autocratic power." In 1932 Roosevelt, speaking in terms of American domestic politics, had continually contrasted the Hamiltonian with the Jeffersonian conceptions of national unity. Both models did have conceptions of national unity but the Hamiltonians had envisioned a country led by "a small group of able and public spirited citizens." The new men of ill will on the international scene believed in "the fantastic conception that they, and they alone, are chosen to fulfill a mission." But these men (unnamed in the address) are far worse than the American Hamiltonians discussed in 1932. They permitted "no opportunity for the people to express themselves" and they had "reverted to the old belief in the law of the sword." Then Roosevelt made the connection between the men of ill will in the world arena and American business: "Within our borders, as in the world at large, popular opinion is at war with a power seeking minority." They, like their counterparts, "engage in vast propaganda to spread fear and discord among the people—they would 'gang up' against the people's liberties." As peace was threatened abroad by the few "who seek selfish power" it is threatened at home by those who "seek the restoration of their selfish power."[9]

The speech itself clearly suffered from hyperbole. It was true that the opposition of business elites had become intense. FDR was correct in saying that those who in 1932 had cried, "Save us, save us, lest we perish" had now organized in opposition to the New Deal. But were the bankers and corporate leaders really now seeking an abandonment of representative government? Were they to be compared to Hitler and Mussolini or their supporters? Roosevelt in the speech had actually asserted that these autocrats seemed to desire a status quo ante ("Shall we say now to the farmer, 'The prices for your products are in part restored. Now go and hoe on your own row?'; . . . Shall we say to the laborer, 'Your right to organize, your relations with your employer have nothing to do with the public interest; if your employer will not even meet with you to discuss your problems and his, that is none of our affair?'"). But the connection between the aims of dictators and business at home was made so directly that Roosevelt had raised the specter of extraconstitutional action on the part of American economic elites. If people, denied full information, were following "blindly and fervently the lead of those who seek autocratic power," American autocrats were attempting to create the same conditions through "a synthetic, manufactured, poisonous fear that is being spread subtly, expensively, and cleverly." And what had the president meant when he had said that the goals of this elite was to "'gang up' on the people?"[10] The speech itself was designed in part to counter the charge that the New Deal itself was a threat to the constitutional order. In his 1935 address Roosevelt had taken pains to emphasize that the recovery was achieved through "tested liberal traditions." Now he charged that business elites would "steal the livery of great constitution ideals to serve discredited special interest." But most significant of all was the return to the apocalyptic language of the inaugural. The threat to the republic itself became the danger once again. Only this time the president faced no elites that had abdicated but those that sought the restoration of their selfish power. What better model to explore than the antielite politics of the Jacksonians?

Five days after the address Roosevelt did just this. Jackson was "like Jefferson," he was following "the fundamentals of Jefferson" in adhering to a "broad philosophy" that decisions should be made by the "average of voters" rather than "small segments of the electorate." Jackson is interpreted as a Jefferson embattled. He was "compelled to fight every inch of the way for the ideals and policies of the Democratic Republic which was his ideal." His opponents were the great elites of the nation—men of "material power," "haughty and sterile" intellectuals, "musty" reactionaries, "hollow and outworn" traditionalists. "It seemed—sometimes that all were against him—all but the people of the United States." According to FDR, Jackson was admired not for his intellect but for his passion. He was "two fisted"; he spoke with an "amazing zeal"; he was "rugged and fearless." As Roosevelt had reminded his audience in his Jefferson Day speech in 1932 about the individualism of American society with a quote from Chesterton, he admitted that "good old Jackson no doubt realized that every red-blooded American citizen considered himself a committee of one." But Jackson had pierced the anarchy of the American political character. Since every "man on the street" and every "man on the farm" knew intuitively of the ideals of which Jackson spoke, he had "roused the people to their fundamental duties as citizens."[11]

If we take a moment to review FDR's efforts to overcome the privatism and individualism in American life, we can appreciate better this effort in 1936. I have noted that in his first campaign for governor of New York he had searched for some ideological basis for collectivism. He had evoked the image of battlefield equality and the legacy that had morally entailed. He had reached for some lowest common denominator of welfare. In 1932 he attempted to nationalize Jefferson with the idea of a concert of interests. After his inaugural he had offered the concepts of neighborliness and pioneering. The Jacksonian turn would not represent the last effort of the president to find some ideological formulation that would transform America from millions of committees of one, but it was a bold, new one despite his assertions that Jackson was simply following Jefferson. For here as never before FDR appealed directly to American passions. He did not urge Americans to stop thinking about political issues but he did urge them to copy Jackson's "passionate devotion" by acting on their historical prejudices against elites. He recommended liberal equivalents to committees of public safety. "Each and every one of you," he told his audience, must "make an inventory in your own community" and "run down statements made to you by others which you may believe to be false. . . . To do this you need no parchment certificate, to do this you need no title." All that was needed was "your own conviction, your own intelligence and your own belief in the highest duty of the American citizen." "History repeats" was the refrain of this speech, and FDR contended that vigilant citizens could again beat back "autocratic and oligarchic aggression" as they had done under Jackson's leadership.[12] During the summer and fall of 1936 Roosevelt outlined the ideological elements of the Jacksonian turn.

In the early days of the campaign FDR redefined the concepts of neighborliness and pioneering to make them more in keeping with the idea of the vigilant citizen. In June at Little Rock he praised the "hardy pioneers" who peopled Arkansas. He reminded the audience that Arkansas would never have existed had not it been for Jefferson, who had "the courage, the backbone" to "act for the benefit of the United States without the full and unanimous approval of every member of the legal profession." He noted that Arkansas had gained statehood in the last year of Jackson's presidency. In his annual message FDR had used the metaphors of youth to describe the determination of Jackson and the Jacksonians. Here he presents westward expansion itself as flowing "with the vigor of a living stream" through the "stagnant marshes" of a seaboard oligarchy. The "life of the pioneer" required "sympathy and kindly help, ready cooperation in the accidents and emergencies of the frontier life." These "neighborly instincts," existing in an environment in which "the personal qualities of the men and not the inheritance of caste or property" were nurtured, reinvigorated the American idea of equality outlined by Jefferson. Jackson was able to stave off an America in its dotage by grasping this pioneering spirit that had been lost in the "older, more conservative East."[13]

With vigilance comes organization. FDR in 1936 returned to the war analogy he flirted with in the 1932 campaign and announced in his inaugural. In his Madison Square Garden speech he closed by announcing: "I am enlisted for the duration of the war." The objections of business to the New Deal were described as enemy propaganda. They were guilty of more than deceit; here were the "old enemies of peace" spreading fear as tyrants had always done throughout history. They had lied when they had said that Jefferson had planned to set up a guillotine. They had lied when they had said that Jackson had planned to "surrender American democracy to the dictatorship of a frontier mob." "Cunning in purpose," they were lying when they said Roosevelt was planning the sovietization of America. "They are unanimous in their hate for me," Roosevelt told a frenzied crowd. And when he said, "I welcome their hatred," he was urging the American people to return that hate. War always involves the dehumanization of the enemy; FDR's speeches never mentioned individuals and always referred to business in abstract, negative terms. The enemy were "forces of selfishness," "enemies of peace," autocrats, "economic royalists," "aliens to the spirit of American democracy," "economic dynasties," "new mercenaries." What did the enemy want? They had grown used to regarding the "government of the United States as a mere appendage of their own affairs." They seek a "new despotism" wrapped in the robes of legal sanction." They seek "to regiment people, their labor and their property."[14]

To meet this challenge FDR in 1936 called up his army, his committees of one. After all, "the average man" confronted the same "problem that faced the Minute Man." But this was not a call for extraconstitutional action. (When the public perceived in 1938 that Roosevelt was making this kind of demand it refused to enlist.) Nor was it a Lincolnian evocation, clothed in Old Testament language, of providential unity. FDR was calling up a Jacksonian army, "a vast army of small business-men, factory workers and shopowners." This was the army he stood poised to enlist in his 1932 "forgotten man" speech. As an army of the petit bourgeoisie of America, it was the army of the majority, what FDR called the 90 percent of the population. To raise it the president appealed to every fear and prejudice the "forgotten man" would entertain. He evoked images of capital as old men in silk hats; he denounced the old conservative East and those who had "fostered class distinctions"; he appealed to the American paranoia over bigness and declared that there was "no excuse for it in terms of industrial efficiency, . . . no excuse for it from the point of view of the average investor, . . . no excuse for it from the point of view of the average business man"; he appealed to the democratic mistrust of the professions (there were men who were "tied together by interlocking directors, interlocking bankers, interlocking lawyers"). He appealed to the American desire for simpler times, times when the "neighborly instincts of the frontier" guaranteed that people were "custodians of their own destiny."[15] In short, FDR continued to take the individualism of the inaugural parade as a given but now instead of seeking a concert of interest through the articulation of the aspirations of the American common man, he sought one through their fears. Indeed this was class rhetoric of a base kind, often vicious and certainly calculating. But the demos that FDR appealed to was not a nation of peasants or workers. The campaigner in 1936 was not a Louis Bonaparte or a Lenin. For in America the demos was composed, to use the president's remarkably astute words, of committees of one.

The petit bourgeois mind in America is so complete (Hartz referred to it as a giant) that FDR in unleashing it and training its attention toward big business created a majority of overwhelming proportions. This army was so ideologically dominant that FDR was able to hurl the ultimate threat to big business. Since they were already "aliens to the spirit of American democracy, . . . let them emigrate."[16] When he continued by saying, let them "try their lot under some foreign flag in which they have more confidence," he was offering more than an assessment of the relative merits for investment in the United States versus abroad. FDR had made big business itself un-American. The corporations and great banks were big when Americans trusted only neighborly capital. Americans wanted freedom, they wanted regimentation. Americans were good Samaritans, they believed in the principle of the "devil take the hindmost." Americans believed in self-government, they believed in government by organized money. There was, so the president implied, nothing American at all about these economic royalists. Why not let them emigrate, why not cast them out after "nine mocking years with the golden calf and three long years of the scourge!"[17]

There were additional reasons, I think, for the sharpness of this Jacksonian turn and FDR's recruitment of committees of one in 1936. No president had a better understanding of the fragility of public space in a liberal society than Roosevelt. He had experienced the difficulties of locating some grounding for principles of public happiness in his first campaign for governor and perhaps most important of all, he had seen the complete disintegration of progressivism in the 1920s. Late in his first administration he had told Tugwell a story that Woodrow Wilson had related to him. Roosevelt was complaining to his adviser about the failure of progressives to give the president loyalty. Wilson had had the same complaint. The remarks may well have been directed to Tugwell himself since Tugwell had just been complaining about the leniency of Johnson's NRA regulations. FDR said that Wilson once told him that conservatives have the "striking power of a closed fist" but progressives "are like a man trying to strike with his fingers spread out stiffly." He could "accomplish nothing and would very likely break his fingers."[18]

"The spirit of the husking bee is found today in carefully drafted statutes"

Roosevelt had certainly made a fist in 1936. But the turn toward Jackson had created as many ideological problems as it had solved. The president had raised a Jacksonian army and in doing so had redefined his reading of Jeffersonian public happiness as pioneering and neighborliness in terms of the vigilant citizen. He had attempted to define the public happiness in terms of a collective hatred toward economic elites. That was what the American public all had in common and he praised Jackson for "rousing" the entire population. Moley had complained that FDR's assertion that there was one issue in the campaign, and that was himself, meant that the election would involve no referendum, no attempt to register a national decision on future policies. All Roosevelt had done was to invite "only an expression of faith in a man." But this observation misses the Jacksonian point. The Jacksonian exemplar requires the president to be the focus of attack by opposition elites. FDR had said of Jackson that the "relentless hatred" directed toward the general was not lost on the people: "They loved him for the enemies he made." In the risorgimento logic of Jacksonian politics leadership is dependent upon the antielite credentials of the politician. The more embattled the leader the more a threat he is to attacking elites, and the more the leader himself takes on the psychological makeup of the common man, who lives himself with "oligarchic aggression." "It seemed," so said FDR in his reading of Jackson, "sometimes that all were against him—all but the people of the United States."[19]

Yet despite the innovativeness of FDR's Jacksonian turn, there remained a problem of major proportions. The Jacksonian exemplar fit up to a point neatly with FDR's own political agenda. It was a means for returning what Roosevelt thought was an unjustified response by corporate elites. It was a solution to his own immediate political problems, including that of his reelection. It was a model that philosophically represented an extension of his revised Jeffersonianism. But the exemplar did fit only up to a point. The success of the Jacksonian exemplar in American politics rests not only with the populist anger it unleashes but also with the strivings both psychological and economic of America's giant petit bourgeoisie. These are men and women who rail against the "exclusive privileges" of the "moneyed interests" so that they can make money. It is true, as Croly argued, that there is a social-democratic tinge to the Jacksonians. The Western democrats' crusade against the "Money Power" did mean that "money must not become a power in a democratic state" and that the spoils system did embody in a corrupt way the idea that public office was "the tangible patrimony of the American people."[20] But these truths should not obscure the fact that the appeal of Jacksonianism rested in part on the world view, if not the greed, of the middle classes. Of what use was a National Bank to an indebted farmer in Kentucky if that farmer could not get hold of its funds? Of what use is the Cumberland Road to a barber in Tennessee? The Whigs tried bravely to educate the petit bourgeoisie in the national idea and the universal benefit of internal improvements. The "moneyed interest" could see the connection between economic nationalism and class interest, the Jacksonians could not, in part because there was none. Consequently they defined nationalism in terms of equal rights and equal laws (and opposition to paper currency and internal improvements).

In short, FDR's problem was how, despite the general fit of the Jacksonian exemplar, to appeal to the economic self-interest of the forgotten man. Jacksonian laissez-faire would not fit with depression politics. Class hatred by itself was only a temporary glue. The president needed a surer, more permanent way to gain the allegiance of the middle class. For this FDR substituted the idea of economic security as the final portion of his revision of Jackson. In the end it would be as unstable a reading of Jackson as was his reading of Jefferson. But the so-called New Deal coalition that it created did produce the intergenerational basis for reform that progressivism lacked. There was, of course, a price, a price that later generations of politicians would have to pay. FDR's defense of economic security was always woven into the fabric of his adopted Jacksonianism. In a campaign speech in Wichita, Kansas, Roosevelt justified security as a defense against economic royalists. Their kind of individualism "hurts the community." It is "individualism run amuck." The welfare state would be the common man's protection against those whose interests were pursued without "any regard to the deep injuries which they were causing the great masses of our people." There was "a school of thought in this country that would have us believe that those vast numbers of average citizens who do not get to the top of the economic ladder do not deserve the security which government alone can give them." Those who held this position were forced to leave Washington in 1933. Now they give "vague lip service to that word 'security' " and at the same time, "are seeking to block, to thwart, and to annul every measure" that was being taken to assure protection.[21]

Marvin Meyers's characterization of the grass roots Jacksonian as a "venturous conservative" fits well the petit bourgeois, who craves advancement and fears failure. Tocqueville had spoken of the narrow range of property differences in the United States and the predominance of the "eager and apprehensive men of small property." They are, he told his European readers, "still almost within the reach of poverty, they see its privations near at hand and dread them; between poverty and themselves there is nothing but a scanty fortune, upon which they fix their apprehensions and hopes." Without the distinction of ranks in society and with the subdivision of hereditary property, "the love of well-being" became "the predominant taste of the nation, . . . the great current of human passions runs in that channel and sweeps everything along in its course."[22]

In 1936 FDR appealed to that fearful side of the great American petit bourgeois class in a curious addendum to his remarks about fearing fear in his first inaugural. In the course of offering extemporaneous remarks in Poughkeepsie just before election day, Roosevelt remarked that one of the few good things about the depression was that it prompted people to "study the future of America. . . . They have been wondering whether we should do this, or that, or the other thing. . . ." Here were remarks quite similar to the experimentation and pioneering themes he had discussed early in his administration. Then, not inappropriately, he emphasized the method itself. "We are reviewing all kinds of human relationships," was what he told Vassar students. Now he suggested that the answers had been found: "Back of it all there has lain, as far as I can see, two very definite thoughts in people's minds." First, was the decision to "retain our American form of government—the democratic system, spelled with a small 'd'—the representative system of government."[23] No matter how close to collapse the American system may have been, the citizenry had reaffirmed its commitment to democratic institutions. There was to be no turn to fascism here, FDR implied. Second, was the decision "to eliminate . . . chances in life, some of the hardships that have come to a lot of people through no fault of their own":

People in the past have gone along with the idea that we could do without a great many things such, for instance, as security. Well, security means a kind of feeling within our individual selves that we have lacked all through the course of history. We have had to take our chance about old age in days past. We have had to take our chances with depressions and boom times. We have had to take chances on our jobs. We have had to take chances on buying homes.[24]

Here in synoptic form was the philosophy of the American welfare state—democracy plus security. In 1936 FDR used human passion to justify it. He used resentment to attack the authority of economic elites and he used the fear of the American middle class to obtain their support for welfare. Morton Frisch in his thoughtful examination of the philosophy of the New Deal argues that "by viewing the welfare state in light of the Lockean-Jeffersonian tradition, one can fairly see what Roosevelt's principles were." The Declaration of Independence spoke of the "pursuit of happiness" and implied that it was "the function of government to provide the *conditions* of happiness," not happiness itself. But FDR's conception of government as devoted to the achievement of the "greatest happiness of the greatest number" transformed the Jeffersonian pursuit of happiness into "well-being." Frisch concludes that "it is *this* fundamental change in emphasis that gives the New Deal its distinctive character as a political movement; for, from now on, government furnishes not only the conditions of happiness, but, to a considerable extent, the enjoyment or possession of material happiness which may be properly called *well-being*. Well-being or welfare is a kind of in-between concept, in-between the conditions of happiness and happiness itself."[25]

It is certainly true that FDR, especially in 1936, altered and widened the American understanding of happiness in terms of the role of the government. But what Roosevelt had done was to provide an alteration in the concept of happiness-private. In the Jeffersonian heyday of the New Deal FDR's concepts of neighborliness and pioneering did offer a new conception of happiness-public, tenuous as it was particularly in light of the fact that the president's commitment to nationalize Jefferson permitted a large dose of Hamiltonianism. The Jacksonian turn continued the experimentation with developing a conception of happiness-public, although of course the populist aspects of the vigilant citizen did give it a new, ugly dimension. But in appealing to the petit bourgeois apprehensiveness about failure, FDR made happiness-private the central motif of the New Deal; and as it turned out happiness-private became the central motif in American liberal political thought. Roosevelt did assert that there was "one sign on his desk" and it read, "Seek only the greater good of the greater number of Americans"; but the nature of his commitment to economic security was made in pursuit of the "love of well-being" on the part of the "eager and apprehensive men of small property." The task of government then was to use the resources of the public sector to promote the private happiness of citizens.

FDR was devoted to eliminating "chances in life." At a press conference in 1935 the president had stated, in response to a Canadian journalist, the "social objective" of his administration. He admitted that the subject was a difficult one to define but he gave this answer:

to try to increase the security and happiness of a larger number of people in all occupations of life and in all parts of the country; to give them more of the good things of life, to give them a greater distribution not only of wealth in the narrow terms, but of wealth in the wider terms; to give them places to go in the summertime—recreation; to give them assurance that they are not going to starve in their old age; to give honest business a chance to go ahead and make a reasonable profit, and to give everyone a chance to earn a living.[26]

These are certainly admirable goals. They are not the kind of goals that demand great sacrifice, but there was in 1935 a utopian quality about them. In fact they still stand today as statement of middle-class utopia. (A 1979 Roper poll asked Americans what they daydream about. At the top of the list was travel, "better job," speculation about the future; at the bottom was being elected to public office, having great power and influence.) But however well-intended are these aspirations, each conceives the government as an agency to fulfill private desire. However much these aspirations exhibit a social-democratic tinge, they are justified in the petit bourgeois spirit of well-being. FDR could be uncannily perceptive in perceiving bourgeois needs, such as in describing the family vacation as a natural democratic right. But he could not avoid closing the possibility of an appeal to the other side of Tocqueville's men of small property. They were as FDR accurately saw, apprehensive, especially so in 1936; but could they be expected to give up their eagerness? They might hate the arrogance of great wealth, but what other class could they expect to emulate? There was no way the president could eliminate the appeal to middle-class avarice—much less middle-class desire for improvement—without framing his programs in terms more social-democratic or in terms more in keeping with the Jeffersonian republican conception of happiness-public.

Whether these tensions were visible to FDR is not clear. They are evident, however, in a speech FDR made in Charlotte, North Carolina, in 1936. The theme of the address is two lines from the Twenty-third Psalm: "He maketh me lie down in green pastures; He leadeth me beside still waters." FDR extolled the psalm: "Green Pastures! What a memory those words call forth!" The psalm was known to every schoolchild and to every person no matter to what church he or she belonged. The president reflected upon the imagery of the psalm. He noted its bucolic terms even though "the ancient psalmist" had available material for a "parable of the merchants' camel train or the royal palace or the crowded bazaar of the East." He noted that the psalmist described happiness "in terms of the simple ways of Nature rather than in the complex ways of man's fabrications." He concluded that perhaps one of the things the psalmist was telling us was that peace is the symbol of ultimate happiness.[27]

The choice of the verses in this psalm was an intriguing one for an American leader. FDR had noted how this psalm formed a part of childhood remembrance and that it was "better known to men, women and children than any other poem in the English language." The lyric then was a part of our civil religion, and FDR suggests that we can learn something from it in our searches for happiness. Simplicity, tranquility, piety— these were what the lyric told us were true happiness. It would be difficult for even the most imaginative leader to find ways to express this notion of happiness in a commercial society, except perhaps a longing for release from the life of the "crowded bazaar." But Roosevelt had made an effort. Yet at this point the speech undergoes a remarkable transition. For green pastures Roosevelt talks about soil conservation and cotton and tobacco price subsidies. For still waters he talks about floods and government efforts at flood control. For those who "work in the mill or in the office" life can still be "a life in green pastures and beside still waters" to the extent wages are raised. The speech concludes: "I trust, therefore, that you will likewise agree that better conditions in the homes of America are leading us to that beautiful spiritual figure of the old psalmist—green pastures and still waters."[28]

The relationship in the Charlotte speech between the concept of happiness contained in the Twenty-third Psalm and that contained in FDR's program for economic security is, needless to say, a tenuous one. Certainly economic security and national prosperity contribute to peace of mind, but this surely is not the point of the psalm. FDR had reached here for a way to broaden the idea of happiness, located a symbol of national import (and one that appealed to middle-class piety as well) but simply translated the psalm, rich in historical and spiritual meaning, into the goals of economic recovery. The speech probably did the president no harm. The psalmic introduction simply served as a new emendation on a campaign theme. Yet to the extent to which the speech offered a new attempt to define happiness for Americans or offered a justification for the New Deal on terms other than the satisfaction of class needs the speech was a failure.

Aside from the potentially unstable class appeal to economic security FDR's Jacksonian turn suffered from the Hamiltonian implications of a welfare state. Hamilton was, of course, never completely democratized in the Jeffersonian formulation of the New Deal. But the creative merger with Jacksonian populism was even more difficult to achieve. Not only is Jacksonianism an antielite political theory, it is a formulation that derives part of its support from the reconstruction of an earlier, more republican era. FDR did his best to establish that the welfare state was ideologically based on the model of the democratic foundings of pioneers. The welfare state was being constructed under the same conditions of "sympathy and kindly help" that the pioneers had exhibited. Their contemporary and counselor, Andrew Jackson, carried these "neighborly instincts" to the White House and "made possible the first truly democratic administration in our history." In 1938 he argued that "the spirit of the frontier husking bee is found today in carefully-drafted statutes. . . ."[29]

But no amount of ingenious symbolism can hide the fact that not only does a welfare state require a Hamiltonian apparatchik to administer it but also that a welfare state was not simply an application of pioneer principles to modern problems. The lawyers who so carefully drew the statutes of the second New Deal were, of course, as talented as quiltmakers and barn raisers. They too, in their own fashion, were as democratically inspired. But Roosevelt's response to that journalist in 1935 exposed the difference. There were six expressions of "to give" in that explanation ("to give them more of the good things in life . . . ; to give" them a greater distribution of wealth; "to give them places to go"). The welfare state was constructed with attention to great detail "for the people" but only in the broad sense of electoral franchise was it created "by the people." The New Deal lawyer stood in relation to his or her client in terms very different from those of the cornhusker.

"We have seen hard-won constitutions first ridiculed and then, section by section, thrown away"

In 1936 the question of whether a Jacksonian-inspired populace was trading one guardian for another—the economic royalist for the government bureaucrat—did not have to be defended by FDR. But it could be raised, and given the premises of Jacksonianism itself one could say that eventually it would have to be raised. When these new guardians implemented policies that pinched the petit bourgeoisie the question would be raised—and when would these policies not pinch given this class's natural eagerness?

Hoover saw and spoke of these contradictions even before the New Deal was in place. In 1936 Landon saw them as well. The pressures of the depression had to a certain extent drawn him near the ideological orbit of the New Deal. Moreover, he was not a figure of the intellectual stature of Hoover. Thus, the campaign to the extent it was waged between Landon and FDR and not between Roosevelt and big business had an inchoate quality about it. Still, given Landon's world view, his speeches do reveal the kind of skepticism about the New Deal that men and women of his type held even in the moment of the president's days of triumph.

Landon conspicuously distanced himself from the party's Old Guard. He kept Hoover and Hearst at a safe distance, began writing his own speeches, exchanged a series of letters with Norman Thomas concerning labor that, while not satisfying the socialist leader, did show flexibility and moderation. On policy matters he pledged to continue the CCC and gave critical support for Social Security. There were several courageous speeches in the campaign, including a defense of academic freedom (in opposition to the Hearst paper editorials) and an impassioned plea for toleration made before an American Legion convention.[30]

The campaign from the Republican side, however, was far from themeless. FDR had drawn the battle lines as Main Street vs. Wall Street, but Landon was not unaware of the enormous importance of the former. He complained that there were "too many businessmen" in his campaign organization, and while his approach to the problem of the depression certainly reflected conservative philosophy it was framed in terms a Rotary member could appreciate. Landon promised to create a cabinet composed of "the most competent executives I can find" and committed himself to a "hard working, painstaking commonsense administration."[31] But it was his acceptance speech in Topeka that is the best example of Landon's attempt to hold onto the American middle. Here his managers had created the parade spirit of the inaugural in its natural setting. Cecil B. De Mille himself worked on the spectacle, which included a day-long event modeled on the celebratory aspects of the American state fair. There was a two-hour parade featuring elephants, choirs, floats, soldiers, bands, drum corps, and the symbols of the prairie—stage coaches, cowboys, and Indians. Landon's speech contained two main themes, which he would repeat throughout the campaign. First, he appealed to Main Street's commitment to the Constitution. Change there could and must be, but it "must come by and through the people and not by usurpation." Second, he repeated the Jefferson formula of American exceptionalism—this must be "a land in which equal opportunity shall prevail and special privilege shall have no place. . . . An America that, for the sake of all mankind—as well as ourselves, shall never lose faith that human freedom is a practical ideal."[32]

Landon's call for a rededication to the Constitution was not simple symbolic recitation. It was directly related to his demand for a commitment to Jefferson, however much Jefferson himself might have been opposed to Constitution worship. But, on this point at least, if FDR had the better of the historical argument (a constitution was for the living in terms of the Jeffersonian exemplar), Landon had been able to construct a connection between constitutional symbolism and Jeffersonianism that made cultural sense. Roosevelt's Madison Square Garden speech was a long and bitter attack on economic elites. By contrast, Landon's rally, while certainly partisan, was highlighted by a recitation:

I believe in our Constitutional form of government—a government established by the people, responsible to the people, and alterably only in accordance with the will of the people. I believe in our indivisible union of indestructible states. I believe in the American system of free enterprise, regulated by law. I believe in the liberty of the individual as guaranteed by the Constitution; I believe in the rights of minorities as protected by the Constitution. I believe in the liberties secured by the Bill of Rights and in their maintenance as the best protection against bigotry and all intolerance, whether of race, color or creed. I believe in an independent Supreme Court and judiciary, secure from executive or legislative invasion.[33]

Certainly FDR would have had no difficulty assenting to Landon's belief system. But this, Landon might have responded, missed his point.

There was something unconstitutional about the New Deal; and thus, while Landon was no red baiter, by implication, there was something un-American about it as well. FDR had compared the opposition of big business to his programs to the rise of authoritarian leaders abroad. Landon drew a different lesson from world affairs. In Philadelphia he told a crowd: "we have seen what happens in nation after nation . . . democracies fall and dictatorships rise. We have seen societies planned and liberties destroyed. And we have seen hard-won constitutions first ridiculed and then, section by section, thrown away." The New Dealers were wielding "the same axe which has destroyed the liberties of much of the old world—an unbalanced budget, inflation of the currency, delegation of power to the chief executive, destruction of local self-government."[34]

At the least, Landon argued, there was Hamiltonianism in the New Deal. There was a "strange new group" in Washington. "They believe in an all powerful executive. They believe in the destruction of states rights and home rule. . . . They believe in the concentration of political and economic authority in the White House." They "fostered monopoly and suspended the antitrust laws." Landon wanted a government that is concerned about the economic rights and opportunities of the average man. He wanted "a government that is also concerned about the pocketbooks of everybody."[35]

The governor clearly had not waged a successful campaign in 1936. But he had fashioned an intelligent and potentially politically effective critique of the New Deal. Landon never defended the economic elites FDR attacked. In fact, unlike Hoover he never offered an explanation for the origins of the depression. His cure for the depression was simply to hire "hard-working" people. He accepted portions of the New Deal in its specifics. His argument, simply put, was that the Constitution was not, as Roosevelt had contended, a device that elites hid behind, but the single most important defense of the middle class. When there were departures from it, people of small property were threatened. Concentrations of economic and political authority tax the person of small property, take away his or her right to be "a lord on his own farm," invade the privacy of the home, have one's "minutest doings . . . scrutinized and regulated," crack "the whip on those individuals who refuse to be led like sheep." Direct your apprehensiveness to Washington, said Landon. As for eagerness, the Republican passed out gummed labels that read, "VOTE FOR LANDON AND LAND A JOB—REGULAR JOBS AT REGULAR PAY." Landon insisted that opportunity still existed in America. The frontier of which he chose to speak was a frontier, not of security derived from apprehensiveness, but a frontier derived from bourgeois venturousness:

A new frontier had been discovered—the frontier of invention and new wants, under our American way of life, men with courage and imagination were free to occupy this new frontier and develop it. They built a greater America. Our people were able to buy the new luxuries, comforts, and conveniences, because they had new purchasing power,—new purchasing power that came not from checks from the Treasury, but from the production of goods.[36]

It was not that the people of small property did not understand or appreciate Landon's arguments in 1936, it was that these people chose to act on the basis of their class apprehensiveness rather than on their eagerness.

7

They Have Retired into the Judiciary

If there is space in the Jacksonian exemplar for a conception of public happiness broader than class hatred, Franklin Roosevelt discovered it in his second inaugural. The speech continued with the attack on elites that characterized his campaign. Inaugurals often afford opportunities for reconciliation after hard-fought battles. But FDR had not reminded the American people that we are all democrats and republicans, and there was no absence of malice in the address. Instead he reminded Americans of their pledge to "drive from the temple of our ancient faith those who had profaned it." He gloried in their recent defeat. "Private autocratic powers" were being brought to "their proper subordination." The election had shattered the belief that these people were "invincible." "They have been challenged and beaten." The president repeated the populist premises of Jacksonianism: "We have made the exercise of all power more democratic; . . . we were writing a new chapter in our book of self-government; . . . The Constitution of 1787 did not make our democracy impotent."[1]

During the 1936 campaign Roosevelt had used the promise of economic security to unite America's "committees of one." The inaugural recast that strategy. FDR offered himself as a Jacksonian Moses, insisting that the election constituted a covenant and warning Americans that they could not now turn back or tarry. As he had done repeatedly during the campaign, the president recalled 1932, when the Republic was "single minded in anxiety." He warns the people not to forget "our covenant" made when we were so "baffled and bewildered." The terms, he insists, involved a "deeper" commitment than ending the "despair of that day." They involved a dedication to wiping out "the line that divides the practical from the ideal." This required "fashioning an instrument of unimagined power for the establishment of a morally better world." The inaugural presents a vision of a nation from the perspective of a leader standing on Mount Sinai. The address includes a series of "I see" descriptions, the most famous of which became "I see one-third of a nation ill-housed, ill-clad, ill-nourished." But FDR also "saw" millions "trying to live on incomes so meager that the pall of family disaster hangs over them day by day, . . . whose daily lives in city and on farm continue under conditions labeled indecent by so-called polite society half a century ago," millions "denied education, recreation, and the opportunity to better their lot and the lot of their children," millions "lacking the means to buy the products of farm and factory. . . ."[2]

From his vantage point FDR also saw the possibilities for American society: national wealth can be translated into a "spreading volume of human comforts hitherto unknown, and the lowest standard of living can be raised far above the level of mere subsistence." He warned that America in 1937 was not "the promised land." In the biblical account of Exodus, the people are described as "murmuring" when there are doubts about Moses' policies. FDR notes in confronting the question, "Shall we pause now and turn our back upon the road that lies ahead?" that many voices are heard. "Comfort says, 'Tarry a while.' Opportunism says, 'This is a good spot.' Timidity asks, 'How difficult is the road ahead?'" Four years ago progress was assured "under the goad of fear and suffering." But today, "dulled conscience, irresponsibility, and ruthless self interest already re-appear." Roosevelt, in outlining the terms of the covenant, allows that "in our personal ambitions we are individualists" but "in our seeking for economic and political progress as a nation, we all go up, or else we all go down, as one people."[3]

In a sense the speech simply reiterated the themes of the 1936 campaign magnified by inaugural rhetoric. But the use of the Exodus metaphor with its subtexts of leadership, covenant, and backsliding revealed the nature of FDR's political situation. Roosevelt had appealed to the apprehensiveness of America's grand petit bourgeoisie, but the very nature of the contract was limited. The approach of the inaugural was to up the ante. A commitment to the creation of a whole new society was implied by the commitment to reduce or remove apprehensiveness. But the "symptoms of prosperity" had already reawakened the other part of the bourgeois character, eagerness. FDR had seen dulled conscience, irresponsibility, and ruthless self-interest on the horizon. "Prosperity already tests the persistence of our progressive purpose." But all FDR could do was to remind Americans of their helplessness just four years ago and of the one-third who still were stricken. But why would the two-thirds care about the rest, especially if dulled conscience had reappeared? FDR's answer involved a reformulation of the pursuit of happiness. We can all remain individualists in our personal ambitions. But as a nation, "we all go up, or else we all go down as a people." Progress then in political and economic terms was to be measured not in terms of "whether we add more to the abundance of those who have too much" but "whether we provide enough for those who have too little." In essence FDR was arguing that the petit bourgeois become social democrats. They did not do so.

"A classic enemy of the people"

The golden calf, however, did not appear from the direction FDR had expected. It was not from dulled conscience that the turn away from the president's promised land originated. Bourgeois eagerness was not the initial source for the refusal of Americans to follow the president to the "happy valley." Actually, this refusal came from that same general disposition, apprehensiveness, from which FDR built his coalition. For when the president's attack on the Supreme Court culminated in his plan for the reorganization of the judiciary in February, the great American petit bourgeoisie exhibited again its class apprehensiveness, this time with a tilt away from the president.

Perhaps skittishness is a better term for the public's state of mind. For despite the ominous warning in the first inaugural and the warning not to look back in the second, FDR had always stayed within the American system. Even this time he insisted that he only wanted men who could give the Constitution a modern interpretation. But 1937 was not 1933, and the reorganization plan seemed to involve something more than stretching the system. The public was not sure—or not completely sure—that this Plan was not somehow different from the many other New Deal plans, and FDR could not convince them that it was not different. There were also many groups, like the Associations to Preserve Our Liberties, that sprang up out of the 1936 defeat and loudly reminded the public that this Plan was different. But most skittish of all were the Democratic senators who could not bring themselves to support the president. Here were men who, at least in a direct sense, were not tied to class apprehensiveness, although as politicians they had to be sensitive to it. Many, however, were, according to Rexford Tugwell "highly sensitized to dictatorship by Hitler and

Mussolini, and Franklin had showed signs, they thought, of suggestive impatience."[4]

There were of course strategic mistakes and fortuitous events that contributed to the failure: the indirectness of the Plan itself (which seemed to make people even more skittish), the president's supreme overconfidence once his decision had been made, the secrecy in the deliberations over the choice of the Plan (which gave the appearance of an attempted coup), a series of political miscalculations over the summer of 1937, the death of Senator Joseph Robinson, the retirement of Willis Van Devanter, the underestimation of Charles Evans Hughes as a politician, the rapidity and dramatic nature of the Supreme Court's own turn.[5] But foremost in the defeat was the president's inability to fashion an ideological defense that would overcome this skittishness.

Rexford Tugwell, who had his own doubts about the Plan, praised FDR for engaging "a classic enemy of the people." The Supreme Court was an ideal opponent in part because its members allowed themselves— had indeed volunteered—to become the defenders of groups and classes whose prestige had "drastically diminished before the depression." Other New Dealers held similar views. The Court was an undemocratic institution, a leftover from earlier more undemocratic eras that had become the last refuge of the economic royalists. While the 1936 democratic campaign did not directly raise the Court as an issue, Landon had done so and he had lost and lost big. Moreover, the populism of the Jacksonian turn had been overwhelmingly supported by the American people. It seemed that an extension of the exemplar—especially given the far more difficult readings of Jacksonianism on other questions—to the Court would be a relatively easy enterprise. For instance, Tugwell felt that the Court had only dignity on its side and "this a President, with all the weapons he commanded, might easily undermine." Once ridicule began, "dignity would melt away." Harold Ickes thought support for the Court was based on prejudice and superstition. God had not declared that when the Court was created, the number nine was to be sacred. All that was needed was to "declare the Court immaculately conceived; that it is infallible; that it is the spiritual descendant of Moses and that the number Nine is three times three, and three stands for the trinity." Donald Richberg in the same vein, complained that people need to be reminded that "putting a black robe on a man" does not make him "a superior variety of human being." FDR himself, in explaining his defeat, wrote in 1941 that "the one major mistake" he had made was that he "did not place enough emphasis upon the real mischief" of the Court when he first presented the Plan.[6] What better framework to move the people away from these vestiges of deference than the cultural figure of Jackson with his attack upon Marshall and "moneyed interests"?

It is true, as FDR admitted, that the speech that proposed the Plan itself did not make full use of the Jacksonian exemplar. The president argued that he corrected his mistake—that is, the failure to place enough emphasis on the real mischief—in the speeches that followed. He also, however, employed a Jacksonian attack on the Court before the election. At a May 31 press conference after the invalidation of the NIRA, he engaged in a lengthy analysis of the case and its political implications. Reading excerpts from letters from an Indiana state association of businessmen ("small—well, they are drug store people") complaining in apocalyptic terms about the invalidation, he emphasized how the NRA was designed to help "little fellows" and "smaller or local men" and how big business had choked them out through oligarchic pricing policies before the legislation. This was the occasion when the president referred to the Court as living psychologically in the "horse and buggy age."[7]

While the president's characterization of the NRA as a program designed to help little fellows was an inaccurate one, his coupling of the attack on the justices as representing antiquated viewpoints with the defense of small business, which many New Dealers regarded as part of the horse and buggy age itself, fully captured the Jacksonian perspective, which celebrated the past while promoting the aspirations of an eager class.

There were also extended comments on the reasoning of the Court generally designed to prick the cover of authority that New Dealers saw as the judges' only defense. FDR compared *Schecter Poultry Corp.* v. *U.S.* to a decision notorious for its faulty extrapolation of American political culture, the *Dred Scott* v. *Sanford* case. He ridiculed the chief justice's comment that "extraordinary conditions do not create or enlarge constitutional power." Legislation in 1917 was "far more violative of the strict interpretation of the Constitution than any legislation that was passed in 1933." The Court had admitted that a delegation of power, declared unconstitutional in the case, could be written to be constitutional. FDR's comment was "get that!"[8]

All the elements for a Jacksonian attack on the Court were in place in 1935 and FDR did return to them in 1937. What was especially well conceived in his press conference comments was the implication that the Court had invalidated NIRA as part of a plot on the part of big capital to regain its strangle hold on "smaller or local men."

When FDR was asked by reporters what should be done with the Court he cagily replied, "we have to decide one way or another. . . ." The secrecy surrounding the unveiling of the Plan nearly two years later was initially interpreted as casualness or even recklessness on FDR's part. Actually all manner of plans had been under consideration during this period. The president rejected the proposal for a constitutional amendment on the basis of his own political cynicism. State legislators could be readily bought. The George Norris measure requiring a greater than majority vote for invalidation of an act of Congress was rejected on the basis of cynicism toward the Court itself. The justices were sure to declare the restriction itself unconstitutional. The president had discussed with Felix Frankfurter and Hiram Johnson a plan to take away the Court's appellate jurisdiction over certain legislation. This plan had a certain appeal to the president. The use of historical analogy was part of his genius as a politician and Jefferson had attempted to exempt his repeal of the midnight judges from review. FDR had come to regard judicial review itself as a usurpation that was justified only by historical acquiescence. But this option too was rejected. When Homer Cummings presented a plan based upon James McReynolds's proposal in 1913 to add a federal justice for each who failed to retire at the age provided by law the president was "enchanted."[9]

Freedom of contract is "the general rule and restraint the exception"

It is necessary in reviewing the "Constitutional Crisis" that FDR precipitated to take a moment to try to assess the actual role that the Court had been playing in the American system in regard to economic legislation. The president's view and that of the New Dealers was that recent decisions represented a "conspiracy" on the part of corporate elites. FDR argued that the Supreme Court had purposefully created a "no man's land" in the area of economic regulation. Since *Lochner* v. *New York* it had invalidated state legislation on the grounds of substantive due process and with *Schecter* invalidated federal legislation in part on the grounds of intrastate commerce. Thus the Court could hardly be said to be upholding a Jeffersonian-Jacksonian view of government at all. In fact, they were in effect rendering government "impotent" in crucial areas (in his fireside chat FDR quoted Harlan Stone's dissent in a New York minimum wage law case to make the point).[10] The Court then was one front in what the president had called the "strike by capital" in 1937.

A closer reading of the Court's decisions, however, does not fully support this interpretation. The NIRA was a notoriously poorly drafted act that was unanimously invalidated by the Court. Hughes was instructing the president and Congress on how to write an emergency measure. In any case the NRA was a political liability to FDR after the Jacksonian turn, and with the scores of lawyers now drafting the legislation of the second New Deal, greater constitutional precision was assured. Actually *Railroad Retirement Board* v. *Alton Railroad Co.*, decided shortly before *Schecter*, seemed to present a more severe threat to the New Deal. Congress had regulated railroads for some time but the majority here concluded that the "fostering of a contented mind on the part of an employee" was too remote from the regulation of interstate commerce to be constitutional. Often overlooked however in *Alton* was Justice Owen Roberts's admission that liability, hours, even compulsory workmen's compensation are constitutionally permissible since they had "a direct and intimate connection with the actual operation of the railroads."[11] The Court then was insisting that a constitutional line existed between interstate and intrastate commerce. The minority position (which became the majority after *National Labor Relations Board* v. *Jones and Laughlin Steel Corp.*) in accepting a "house that Jack built" style of reasoning was willing to obliterate the distinction.

The majority had determined that the National Labor Relations Act was designed in part to "protect interstate commerce from the paralyzing consequences of industrial war." The conservative dissenters in *Jones and Laughlin* mocked the new interpretation of "affecting commerce interstate": "In [*Jones and Laughlin*] ten men out of ten thousand were discharged; in other cases only a few. The immediate effect in the factory may be to create discontent among all those employed and a strike may follow, which in turn, may result in reducing production, which ultimately may reduce the volume of goods moving interstate commerce. By this chain of indirect and progressively remote events we finally reach the evil with which it is said the legislation under consideration undertakes to deal. A more remote and indirect interference with interstate commerce or a more definite invasion of the powers reserved to the states is difficult, if not, impossible to imagine." Almost anything, McReynolds wrote, "—marriage, birth, death—may in some fashion affect commerce." The majority had, I think, the better of the argument in 1937. "Industrial war" had already broken out. But the point to be made in terms of the Plan was that both factions of the Court were applying rules over which they had been disagreeing since the Knight and Shreveport cases.[12]

Lochner v. *New York* was the case that had set up the other post that created what FDR called a no man's land. There is no more infamous decision concerning economic matters for progressives and liberals. Today it is still known for Holmes's dissent about the relationship between the Fourteenth Amendment and Spencer's *Social Statics*. But however heretical it might sound, *Lochner* did not create a no man's land by barring state economic legislation through the due process clause any more than it barred federal legislation through the interstate commerce clause. It is true that the rule announced by George Sutherland in *Adkins* v. *Children's Hospital* was the dominant one. Freedom of contract was "the general rule and restraint the exception," but exceptions were permitted and a considerable amount of state legislation managed to avoid the axe of unconstitutionality. *Lochner* did involve the application of the Lockean theory of contracts (the decision was based upon the individual's "right to purchase or sell labor") while *West Coast Hotel* v. *Parrish*, for instance, adopted a corporate model ("the exploitation of a class of workers who are in an unequal position . . . and relatively defenseless").

But Justice Rufus Peckham in *Lochner* did search for some basis for an exception to freedom of contract. Was the employment like mining or smelting, which would require the exercise of state police power? "In looking through statistics regarding all trades and occupations" the trade of the baker was less healthy than some and more healthy than others. In a fascinating aside on the nature of work, Peckham concluded that it was "unfortunately true that labor, even in any department, may possibly carry with it the seeds of unhealthiness." Was it in the interest of the state to ensure that its population be "strong and robust"? If so, then "not only the hours of employees, but the hours of employers, could be regulated, and doctors, lawyers, scientists, all professional men, as well as athletes and artisans, could be forbidden to fatigue their brains and bodies. . . ." Would limited bakers' hours promote cleaner bakeries? The connection was "too shadowy and thin."[13] The Court de-Lochnerized the Constitution in the 1937 *West Coast Hotel* case, but Roberts, writing for the majority in 1934, had upheld a New York state law regulating retail prices for milk (*Nebbia* v. *New York*) on the grounds that failure to obtain a reasonable return threatened a "relaxation of vigilance against contamination."[14]

In conclusion, the Supreme Court was certainly a troublesome institution for New Dealers but it had not constructed a no man's land for the exploitation of capital. It did have a substantial minority that was not ideologically attuned to the New Deal. Sutherland in dissent after the switch in time complained bitterly that the "meaning of the constitution does not change with the ebb and flow of economic events."[15] But it was not the stable majority coalition that FDR had pictured. Roberts's conference vote supporting the Washington minimum wage law had occurred before the Plan was unveiled. The Court clearly had developed doctrines that had, as Roosevelt argued, made it a superlegislature. But its conception of the right of contract as substantive due process had created rights no more out of line with legislative majorities than it later did in *Griswold* v. *Conn.* or *Roe* v. *Wade.* In fact, the Lochnerized constitution was considerably more flexible in this regard than the current penumbrized Constitution.

Like a "three-horse team"

With the Jacksonian turn, however, Roosevelt gave no quarter to troublesome institutions. Jacksonianism located sovereignty with the people at large. The president had created a Jacksonian army with committees of one in 1936, and now he demanded that the will of this army be accepted. The analogy he employed at the Democratic victory dinner in March captured this new exemplar. The American system was like a "three-horse team": "If three well-matched horses are put to the task of ploughing up a field where the going is heavy, and the team of three pull as one, the field will be ploughed. If one horse lies down in the traces or plunges off in another direction, the field will not be ploughed." He reminded his audience that "in three elections during the past five years great majorities have approved what we are trying to do." Efforts by the president and Congress to meet basic human needs (needs that other countries, even those with parliamentary forms of government, had failed to meet) were being blocked by "judicial pronunciamento." "The language of decisions already rendered," the president concluded, had created "widespread refusal to obey law incited by the attitude of the courts."[16]

Was the Supreme Court, as Tugwell put it in Jacksonian terms, a "classic enemy of the people"? Certainly it had both the structure and aims of an undemocratic institution. Its members were not elected and served terms unlimited by direct democratic method. FDR complained that even with the switch in time "one man—not elected by the people—" could "by a nod of the head . . . nullify or uphold the will of the overwhelming majority of a nation of 130,000,000 people." The original justification of the Plan admitted that life tenure was "assured by the Constitution" but only "to place the courts beyond temptations or influences which might impair their judgments." It was "not intended to create a static judiciary." In later remarks the president contended that "reactionary members of the Court" were "determined to remain on the bench as long as life continued—for the sole purpose of blocking any program of reform." The Court's structure, then, even by FDR's own admission, is related to its major function, at least as that function evolved historically, which is to pass upon the constitutionality of legislation. The president, quoting Holmes and Stone, was willing to grant judicial review in "very clear" cases when unconstitutionality was proved "beyond a rational doubt." But as Stone had stated, according to Roosevelt, the Court had been reaching decisions based on "personal economic predilections."[17]

There were then two related critiques of the Supreme Court from FDR's Jacksonian perspective aside from the issue of elderly justices. In its strongest terms FDR asserted that judicial review was itself a kind of usurpation. For twenty years, the president told the American people in his fireside chat, there "was no conflict between the Congress and the Court." Then in 1803 the Court "claimed the power" to declare legislation unconstitutional and "did so declare it." After a period of restraint the Court "more and more often and more and more boldly" asserted a power to "veto laws passed by Congress." Now the chief justice had the affrontery to declare that "the constitution is what the Judges say it is." There was, the president insisted, nothing in the Constitution that permitted the Court to "thwart the will of the people." A way must be found "to take an appeal from the Supreme Court to the constitution itself." This involved nothing less than dismantling the Court's usurpation as a "third House of the Congress." Contained in the three-horse team metaphor was the assertion that once they have spoken through their president and legislature, the people have a right to "expect the third horse to pull in unison with the other two."[18]

The second critique, more moderate in its populism but still Jacksonian in thrust, involved an assertion about the behavior of particular judges. Here the problem originated with the reactionary members of the Court, a "few men . . . fearful of the future" who would deny us the "means of dealing with the present." When he voiced the more limited critique, the president would quote approvingly of the Court's dissenting block. "And three other justices agreed with him" was the refrain FDR employed to show that the Court had strayed from his interpretation of the "reasonable doubt" principle of constitutionality. Similarly, when he defended his Plan by denying that he would "place on the bench spineless puppets who would disregard the law and would decide cases as I wished them to be decided," he implied support for the concept of judicial review. [19]

Nearly always the president conceded the stronger view but in the structure of intense political rhetoric leaned on or borrowed upon the more radical critique in order to give legitimacy to the former. Let us call the broader attack, the attack on judicial review itself, the institutional usurpation critique; and the more limited attack, the personnel usurpation critique. As the president repeatedly insisted, his position (actually both critiques) was clearly within the boundaries of American political thought. It is extremely difficult to make a historical case for judicial review much before Marshall's decision in the Marbury case. [20] The subject was rarely raised at the convention or even during the ratification debates. It seems to have been discovered almost accidentally by Hamilton in the course of his defense against the antifederalist Brutus in Federalist Paper 78. The first sustained discussion of the Court's power of review occurs as an issue in the conflict between Federalists and Jeffersonians. There was an ideological reason, I think, why the debate occurred as late as it did. Republican theory, Locke included, placed legislative supremacy at the center of its conception of government. The courts, along with the executive, were the primary threats to liberty.

The faith in legislatures underwent severe shocks during the Confederal period, and the Constitution itself reflects an attempt to revise republicanism ("republican remedies for republican defects" in Madison's words). But the founders apparently had not resorted to the courts as a means for dealing with unconstitutional legislative majorities. When they looked for defenses against usurpation by Congress the Federalists found them not in the courts but in state legislatures and in the trial by jury system. During this period it is the antifederalists who are generally the more reliable interpreters of traditional republicanism. Brutus complained that the world had never seen a court "invested with such immense powers" and declared that if the legislature "pass any laws, inconsistent with the sense the judges put upon the constitution, they will declare it void; and therefore in this respect their power is superior to that of a legislature." The Federal Farmer drew a historical scenario of Brutus's fears: "the measures of popular legislatures naturally settle down in time, and gradually approach a mild and just medium; while the rigid systems of law courts naturally become more severe and arbitrary, if not carefully tempered and guarded by the constitution, and by laws, from time to time." He concluded that the judiciary was not the least dangerous branch as Publius would contend, but that "we are more in danger of sowing the seeds of arbitrary government in this department than in any other."[21]

Hamilton, in responding to these concerns in Federalist Paper 78, exhibits his usual ingenuity and subtlety. After dismissing charges about the power of the judiciary by arguing that its separation from the executive makes the judiciary "beyond comparison the weakest of three departments," he states fully the modern conception of judicial review. In a monarchy the judiciary is "an excellent barrier to the despotism of the prince; in a republic it is a no less excellent barrier to the encroachments and oppressions of the representative body." The limited Constitution cannot be preserved unless the courts have the power "to declare all acts contrary to the manifest tenor of the Constitution void." Without this, all the constitutional exceptions to legislative authority "would amount to nothing." Hamilton next turned to the view that the doctrine that the courts have a right to declare legislative acts void would "imply a superiority of the judiciary to the legislative power." While the "interpretation of the laws is the proper and peculiar province of the courts" the power of the people is superior to that of both the courts and the legislature.

Lest one conclude that Hamilton provides support for FDR's institutional usurpation argument, however, Publius goes on to define exactly how popular superiority can be asserted. Since the Constitution is an expression of the people's will, "it is binding upon themselves collectively" until "by some solemn and authoritative act, annulled or changed the established form." The amendment process then is the mechanism that permits popular control of judicial review. Hamilton, returning to his argument that the power of the judiciary is limited, contends that the courts are likely to assert their power only when "infractions . . . had proceeded wholly from the cabals of the representative body."[22] In summary, Publius argues a series of seemingly inconsistent propositions: the court is an excellent barrier against legislative encroachments but it is the weakest branch of government; the court has a "proper and peculiar province" to interpret the Constitution but is not superior to the legislature—in fact both branches are inferior to popular authority (although the latter is bound to accept the court's interpretation until the Constitution can be amended). The essay holds together to a certain extent, however, as long as one accepts two of Hamilton's central assumptions: legislatures cannot be relied upon not to infringe upon, and the courts can be relied upon to uphold, the Constitution.

It seems as if Hamilton's interest in judicial review is derived in part from his national vision and his distrust of democracy even in its republican form. As Publius, Hamilton had said in effect that the Constitution is what the people say it is; but he had so constructed his position—by denying the legislature final or coequal constitutional review and by limiting popular review to the difficult process of constitutional amendment—as to mean that the Constitution is what the judges say it is. Those who did not share Hamilton's ideological position in general did not accept his position on judicial review. In response to the Sedition Act and in defense of the Judiciary Act of 1802 the Jeffersonians either attacked the principle of judicial review altogether (Roosevelt's institutional usurpation critique) or offered their own interpretation of the doctrine. The latter was not exactly the same as FDR's personnel usurpation critique. Roosevelt's second critique can in fact be subsumed under Hamilton's position, which after all assumed judicial restraint. Jefferson himself regarded the courts as an agency of federalist guerrilla war: "They have retired into the judiciary as a stronghold. There the remains of federalism are to be preserved and fed from the Treasury; and from that battery all the works of republicanism are to be beaten down." Repeatedly Jefferson asserted that judicial review as Hamilton, then the Federalists, outlined it, "would place us under the despotism of an oligarchy." His response was to argue that each branch of government had "equally the right to decide for itself what is its duty under the Constitution."[23] This coordinate theory was revived by Jackson as indicated in his 1832 message: "The Congress, the Executive, and the Court must each for itself be guided by its own opinion of the Constitution. Each public officer who takes an oath to support it as he understands it, and not as it is understood by others. . . . The opinion of the judges has no more authority over Congress than the opinion of Congress has over the judges, and on that point the President is independent of both."[24]

The coordinate theory then says that the constitution is what *each* department of government says it is. This seems to have been Lincoln's position as well. If "vital questions affecting the whole people are to be irrevocably fixed by decisions of the Supreme Court . . . the people will have ceased to be their own rulers, having to that extent practically resigned their Government into the hands of that eminent tribunal."[25] Reconstructionist Republicans considered many plans to restrict the power of judicial review. These ranged from a court-packing plan, a larger than majority margin to declare acts unconstitutional, a limitation on the types of acts susceptible to review. Progressive reformers attacked the Hamiltonian theory as well. Michael Kammen notes that the keyword in the debate became "usurpation" and "the most egregious flaw seemed to be unbridled judicial review."[26] In 1912 Theodore Roosevelt made the Supreme Court an election issue. Comparing the threat to public order resulting from new industrial conditions to that of the crisis of the Civil War, he cited Lincoln as an authority. Lincoln had appealed to the people against the judges "when the judges went wrong."[27] La Follette attempted to solve the most difficult problem with the coordinate theory by proposing a constitutional amendment that would permit Congress to override the Court by repassing laws with a two-thirds majority. LaFollette's plan was a major issue in his campaign for the presidency in 1924.[28]

FDR's critiques then had been offered commonly throughout American history. His Plan, as he himself noted, was not a historically novel one. In general he seemed to accept the Hamiltonian conception of judicial review, if reluctantly, and made the case for personnel usurpation, the lesser of the usurpation critiques. He had as an ideological resource not only the statements and positions of Jefferson and Jackson but nearly every presidential exemplar including Lincoln and Theodore Roosevelt.

"Who is to save us except the Courts?"

Why then, tactical errors aside, did Roosevelt fail? The answer lies, I think, in consideration of Tugwell's assertion that the Supreme Court was a classic enemy of the people. In each of the periods under which judicial review was portrayed as usurpation, a governing elite in the two branches of government had charged that the Court had become a stronghold for discredited or challenged forces in American politics. This was the substance of Jefferson's charge that the Federalists had "retired into the judiciary." It formed the basis of the abolitionist attack before the Civil War, when the Court was attacked as an agency of the slave conspiracy. It became the critical motif in the 1890s, when the charge was made that the Court refused to accept the legislation of populist and reformist legislatures.

In this sense the Supreme Court has historically been indeed an enemy of the people. Yet, at least as perceived in American culture, the Court has not been an enemy of the people in the way that the Bank of the United States was. For the eager petit bourgeois that Jackson led could not see the Bank as an institution that operated in its interests. The latter-day Jacksonians that FDR had recruited seemed to have immediately seen that the Court could further or at least protect their interests. Of course this was supposed to be the Rooseveltian point. The personnel usurpation critique emphasized the role that the Court could play as part of the three-horse team. But if the president could change the direction of the Court in ways other than simply filling new appointments, the president could be in the position of usurper. This was precisely the language that the Judiciary Committee used to assess the Plan: "Today it may be the Court which is charged with forgetting its constitutional duties. Tomorrow it may be Congress. The next day it may be the Executive. If we yield to temptation now to lay the lash upon the Court we are only teaching others how to apply it to ourselves and to the people when the occasion seems to warrant." The Committee concluded that the "American system" was "immeasurably more important, immeasurably more sacred to the people of America . . . than the immediate adoption of any legislation, however beneficial." The report ended with a quote from George Washington warning of usurpations.[29]

It must be remembered that the reactions of the senators, with a few exceptions, were never enthusiastic. It was the intensity of popular concern, which was immediate, that emboldened the senators. Soon it seemed as if every American had discovered reasons for supporting the Court. Oswald Villard worried about the opportunities for blacks with a Court that could be packed "so that no Negro could get within a thousand miles of justice. . . ." Southerners worried about the consequences for white supremacy without the Court. "Voices cry from every Confederate grave," wrote one constituent. A Detroiter despaired about the fate of Jews. "Currents of feeling sweeping middle-class America" emerged over law and order and property rights. In March the *New Republic* had felt compelled to deny that the sit-down strikes were "duplicating the conditions that existed in Italy before Mussolini's march on Rome." The historian James Truslow Adams summarized all these concerns: "If a president tries to take away our freedom of speech, if a Congress takes away our property unlawfully, if a State legislature . . . takes away the freedom of the press, who is to save us except the Courts?"[30]

"Who is to save us except the Courts?" Americans, bourgeois all, had a class interest in the Court or at least a certain psychological disposition derived from their class position that made them skittish about the Plan. Marx in his indictment of the European bourgeoisie argued that when their interests were threatened the middle classes were quite willing to forsake democracy for order. Suffrage, freedom of speech and of association—all the fundamentals of constitutional democracy were cast aside when a threat to class domination was imminent. In a sense the degree to which Americans rallied in support of the Court in 1937 (and to a certain extent in other periods as well) indicates the American equivalent of the European bourgeoisie abandonment of democracy under conditions of class stress.

There are of course important differences in the analogy, and they are ones that Marx would not have likely accepted. The Court may be the functional equivalent of Bonapartism but the substantive nature of each is quite different. The Court represents protection against legislatures and threats from majorities in general but it also represents those interests through the context of the rule of law. Herein lies the answer to Robert Dahl's observation that the Court poses a quandary in American political culture: "As a political institution, the Court is highly unusual, not least because Americans are not quite willing to accept the fact that it is a political institution and not quite capable of denying it; so that frequently we take both positions at once."[31] The function of the Court then in terms of judicial review is eminently a political one—that is, to frustrate majorities when they challenge the direct interests of minorities. The nature of this political function is to be carried out in legal terms. Another difference involves the class composition in America itself. To the extent that America represents a case that comes as close as empirically possible to the concept of embourgeoisiement, a class disposition is transformed into a national disposition and of course a class ideology becomes—not quite automatically but without significant problems of translation—a part of American political thought.

FDR showed in 1936 with his Jacksonian turn how overwhelming support can be created out of class appeals based upon bourgeois apprehensiveness. In a Marxist sense Roosevelt's campaign represented an appeal to one section of a class against another. This insight, as important as it is, is valuable only to the extent to which one holds on to the consequences of the American ideological world. Intraclass appeals in the context of a society without successful competing class ideologies assume the character of class conflicts in a traditional Marxist sense. To ignore the reality of this kind of class appeal misses the entire nature of American politics. But the intraclass structure of the Jacksonian turn in 1936 is revealed in the court battle. Landon had seen intuitively this ultimate intraclass dimension in the campaign when he attempted to make devotion to the Constitution and an independent judiciary a central feature of his own appeal. Economic elites were more than apprehensive over the president's programs. Landon argued that it was in the interest of the "little fellow" to be apprehensive about FDR's obsession "with the idea that it had a mandate to direct and control American business, American agriculture and American life." When the Court declared his methods to be unconstitutional, he "actually attempted to bring the court in disrepute." As we saw, FDR's Jacksonian turn was so effective in appealing to middle-class apprehensiveness in terms of economic security that the intraclass aspect never emerged. On the other hand, FDR's belief that "the people are with me," which he held to throughout the battle, misunderstood the intraclass nature of the coalition he had built.

FDR's Jacksonian army refused to chase the retreating enemy into the enclaves of the courts. It would, as other armies did as well, stand before the gates of the Court and hurl charges of usurpation. It might bang loudly against the door. It might encamp for a long siege. It might even permit forays into the enclave itself. But when a full-scale onslaught is ever ordered, the army deserts and deserts in large numbers. The reason why it does lies in part in that the committees of one realize that they themselves may find themselves some day in that enclave themselves. Of course the enclave is not impervious to the army of any generation. Members of its ranks enter, often one by one, until the defeated forces become a minority even here and with the passage of time disappear. There the enemy is finally defeated as if in a war of attrition.

FDR, speaking shortly after the battle was lost, complained that these wars of attrition were too costly:

It cost a Civil War to gain recognition of the constitutional power of Congress to legislate for the territories.

It cost twenty years of taxation on those *least* able to pay to recognize the constitutional power of Congress to levy taxes on those *most* able to pay.

It cost twenty years of exploitation of women's labor to recognize the constitutional power of the States to pass minimum wage laws for their protection.

It has cost twenty years already—no one knows how many more are to come—to obtain a constitutional interpretation that will let the Nation regulate shipment in national commerce of goods sweated from the labor of little children.

The president insisted that we "should no longer be permitted to sacrifice each generation in turn while the law catches up with life. We can no longer afford the luxury of twenty-year lags."[32] But if his army would not advance, it is hard to imagine any that would no matter how appealing the promised land on the other side might be portrayed.

"On a thousand fronts"

Roosevelt's attempt to influence the primary elections in 1938 (the "purges") further illustrated the limitations of the Jacksonian exemplar. The president had for some time dreamed of a realignment of the party system along the lines of pure Jacksonian theory with "liberal" forces on one side and the party of reaction on the other. The court battle had painfully confirmed FDR's belief that "America requires that one of its parties be the liberal party and the other be the conservative party." The historical Jacksonians were of course attached to a party as diverse as FDR's but the president believed ideologically that the history of representative government had always revealed "two general schools of political belief," one that believed in "the wisdom and efficacy of the great majority of the people" and one that wished to rely upon "a small minority of education or wealth."[33]

This style of thought FDR had elaborated through both his Jeffersonian and Jacksonian phases. It provided the theme for both campaigns. The "purge" then simply involved a rationalization of American politics, an effort to make political structure consistent with the phenomenology of representative politics. It was in fact, even more. It was in the summer of 1938 that Roosevelt systematically began to use the word "liberalism" in ways other than as a generic substitute for progressivism or reform. Liberalism now was what the New Deal had done. His June fireside chat on the upcoming primaries continued the generic use of the label. Liberals are those who believe that we "can solve our problems . . . through democratic processes instead of Fascism and Communism." Herbert Hoover, Al Smith, and the targeted Democrats would certainly accept this definition. But the president elaborated. "The liberal school of thought recognizes that new conditions throughout the world call for new remedies." These remedies were set forth in the 1936 Democratic platform. Foremost was the belief that "under modern conditions government has a continuing responsibility to meet continuing problems . . ."[34]

FDR's latest philosophical imagination aside notwithstanding, Democratic voters seemed to be unwilling to decide in the primaries to create a liberal party on the president's or anyone else's terms. America as a nation of villagers seemed to be the reality in 1938. In 1933 the New Dealers had been able to direct at least in broad terms this Jeffersonian reality. In 1936 FDR had created a sense of common purpose based on Jacksonian principles. Each village and each villager in their apprehensiveness had in common anger at economic elites. But in 1938 Jeffersonianism, not necessarily opposed to the president's definition of New Deal liberalism, crowded out the rationalization proposed. When he traveled around the country, ostensibly as FDR had put it to get a "look-see" at the current state of the nation, the president attempted at every stop to connect the concerns of America's villagers to his agenda. In Marietta, Ohio, he reminded his audience that the government was helping the "average man, woman and child" on "a thousands fronts." At Covington, Kentucky; Oklahoma City; Fort Worth, Childress, and Amarillo, Texas; Pueblo, Colorado; Barnesville, Georgia; Greenville, South Carolina; Morgantown, Berlin, Shamptown, Salisbury, and Annapolis, Maryland, the president reviewed the impact of the New Deal on local communities: help to farmers in Kentucky, flood control in Texas, reforestation in Colorado, roads and electricity in Georgia, parcel post in Maryland. "We are getting over a selfish point of view," he told a crowd in Pueblo, Colorado, "we are thinking of all our problems in national terms." At each stop in the "purge," he reminded audiences that the benefit to each local community benefited each other. Even Texas, "a great empire in itself," needed to be looked at from a "national angle" in order to get away from "spotty prosperity" and to achieve "universal prosperity."[35]

Here was FDR a few years after the crisis presenting the achievements of a nationalized Jefferson. In truth, the benefits of which the president spoke appeared more Hamiltonian than Jeffersonian, but Roosevelt's failure in 1938 seemed to result less from an anti-Hamiltonian attack on the New Deal than a miscalculation of the extent to which the traditional Jeffersonianism of America had been altered.

FDR may have hoped that a national party responsive to the will of a national party leader and the interests of a national electorate would further transform America along national lines. If so, he underestimated how Jeffersonian in both ideology and structure the Democratic Party remained. Senator Walter George and FDR may not have spoken the same language but Georgia voters still returned the incumbent. The South may have been committed to the principles of democracy, not feudalism, which FDR compared to fascism. But in South Carolina the New Deal senatorial candidate accused Cotton Ed of "voting to let a big buck nigger sit next to your wife or daughter on a train." In other parts of the country local questions seemed to determine primary outcomes: corruption in Pennsylvania and New Jersey, a state pension plan in California, labor in Michigan and Texas. In Maryland Senator Millard Tydings made the intervention his local issue: "Maryland will not permit her star in the flag to be 'purged' from the constellation of the states."[36]

By the fall of 1938 both the Jeffersonian and Jacksonian exemplars that FDR had so imaginatively employed were exhausted as sources of political persuasion. Neighborliness as a political sentiment had drifted back to localities, albeit sheltered by the Hamiltonian structures of the New Deal. As for pioneering, even Hopkins noted that Americans seemed "bored with the poor, the unemployed and the insecure." A group of congressmen in the spring of 1938 pleaded with Stephen Early to convey to the president, "for God's sakes, don't send us any more controversial legislation."[37] The "New Faces" of the Republicans (eighty-one House seats and eight in the Senate) were about the task of doing some pioneering on their own. Relief appropriations were reduced, investigations were initiated, programs were terminated. The president conceded when he had to (the Federal Theatre Project was thrown to the new pioneers) but still attempted to hold to Jacksonian pleas. In his 1939 Jackson Day speech he used the rhetorical devise of "put[ting] in a call for General Andrew Jackson." The former president chided FDR: "And as for me, son, my Democrats licked old Nick Biddle when we didn't even have a majority in the Senate and had few votes to spare in the House. Tell your fellows to learn how to count. Some of you Democrats today get scared and let the other fellows tell you you've lost an election just because you don't have majorities so big that you can go to sleep without sentries."[38] Yet despite the ghostly presence of Jackson, the New Deal was itself dead.

8

Black Easter and Other Lincolns

J ust after the Supreme Court fight, the *New Republic* observed that it was "obvious that the New Deal is cracking up pretty fast."[1] After the 1938 elections one columnist concluded that the president could not run for a third term even if he so wished. The *New Republic* had even begun analyzing the potential of presidential aspirants in 1940. But FDR had not yet explored the use of a remaining presidential exemplar. He had available to him the Lincolnian model in the crisis of 1932–33. As I have attempted to show, while the president made some use of the war analogy in these years, for the most part he pursued his own reading of Jefferson. Events in the Pacific and in Europe made the Lincoln exemplar again a possibility. This time FDR seized the opportunity.

"The Second Father of Our Republic"

But imitating Lincoln was no simple task, for there were many Lincolns to draw from and some to avoid. One aspect of the Lincoln exemplar was developed immediately after his death. This is the "Black Easter" Lincoln, the man who, through his vision of America as an indissoluble union, suffered and died for the cause that many did not understand as fully as he. Lincoln was the "savior" of America as Washington had been its founder. The biblical rhetoric that the Civil War president had employed to justify the conflict was now used to describe the fallen leader. One Northern minister, noting that the assassination had taken place on Good Friday, concluded that "it is no blasphemy against the Son of God that we declare the fitness of the slaying of the second Father of our Republic on the anniversary of the day on which he was slain. Jesus Christ died for the world, Abraham Lincoln died for his country."[2]

There was also another use of the Lincoln exemplar that emphasizes

Lincoln's modest origins. Here was a Lincoln as a child of the frontier, prairie lawyer and people's politician. This interpretation has at least three major readings. One had been developed during Lincoln's career. Lincoln was portrayed as a man who was self-made in the new Whig tradition of Harrison and Tyler. "Honest Abe, the Rail Splitter" was essentially an antipolitical politician who stood for the Whig principles of individual advancement and the tariff. In his campaign for state legislature in 1832, Lincoln discussed ambition (later a frequent topic in all readings of the president): "Every man is said to have his peculiar ambition. . . . I have no other so great as that of being truly esteemed of my fellow-men, by rendering myself worthy to many of you. I was born, and have ever remained, in the most humble walks of life. I have no wealthy or popular relations or friends to recommend me. My case is thrown exclusively upon the independent voters of the country. . . ." The slavery question continuously crowded out Lincoln's contribution to Whiggery but as Richard Hofstadter has concluded, Lincoln's class background and party affiliation "enabled him to speak with sincerity for Jeffersonian principles while supporting Hamiltonian measures."[3]

Another version of the frontier leader also focused on the president's origins, but, rather than emphasizing the distance Lincoln had traveled, spoke of the advantages of his beginnings as a man of the people. Here is the Lincoln of democratic folk, a model that fits far better the Jacksonian democracy that Lincoln had actually deserted. William H. Herndon's biography, published in 1889, still remains the best representative of this view.

Lincoln's law partner claimed that he wrote the biography to take the memory of Lincoln away from the "nice sweet smelling gentlemen." Herndon's Lincoln was born in a "stagnant, putrid pool," the son of white trash and the illegitimate daughter of a Virginia planter. Herndon even raised doubts about Lincoln's own paternity. The young Abraham is foremost a man's man regaling his cronies with exploits of strength and carousing and dirty jokes. He is an avid reader but, according to Herndon, his studies were limited to a few books. He brooded over religious questions but Herndon emphasizes his anticlericalism. He is a young man of "restless ambition," but his energy is often unfocused and he is given to forgetfulness and a "certain lack of discipline." In fact, Herndon suggests that the style of lawyer that Lincoln represented was fast becoming an anachronism in Illinois. The courts were becoming "graver and more learned"; courtroom pyrotechnics and oratory were now not always enough to win cases. And so, Herndon implies, Lincoln was drawn into politics. In the biography it is Herndon who subscribes to the *Chicago Tribune, New York Tribune,* and the *Charleston Mercury* and *Richmond Enquirer,* reads Fitzhugh's *Sociology* and corresponds with Sumner, Greeley, Philips, and Garrison. "Lincoln himself never bought many books" but he did discuss issues with his partner. But it was Lincoln who warned Herndon: "Billy, don't shoot too high—aim lower and the common people will understand you. They are the ones you want to reach—at least they are the ones you ought to reach."[4]

However shocking Herndon's Lincoln may have been to nineteenth-century sensibilities, especially religious ones, the biography supplemented rather than eroded the Lincoln Black Easter exemplar. Lincoln's modest origins, even the question of his and his mother's paternity, fit both with the American Horatio Alger myth and with the mysteries surrounding the biological origins of all mythological heroes. Lincoln's height and even his homeliness mark him off from other men. His jokes only show his democratic origins and connection to American folk or, even more heroic, are poignant expressions of his sorrow. His dreams and portents are not the expressions of a superstitious man but demonstrate instead an extreme sensitivity concerning his own fate. Even the contention that he was the village atheist is reinterpreted as proof only of his populism—he was always politically opposed by priggish Springfield ministers—and/or proof of a deeper and broader religious vision than nineteenth-century sectarianism.[5]

This is not to say that Lincoln the prairie lawyer did not historically leave open a critical Lincoln literature. During the Civil War the Northern president was alternately portrayed as a buffoon and as a diabolical Napoleonic usurper. Writing in 1904, Elizabeth Mary Meriwether made use of the Herndon Lincoln in her assessment of Lincoln as the frontier bully, the very opposite of the Black Easter Lincoln:

Is it insanity or pure mendacity to liken a man of this nature to the gentle and loving Nazarene? Who for an instant can imagine Jesus swinging a bottle of whiskey around his head, swearing to the rowdy crowd that he was the "big buck of the lick?" Or with whip in hand, lashing a faithful old slave at every round of her labor? Who can imagine Jesus sewing up hog's eyes? What act of Lincoln's life betrays tender-heartedness? Was he tender-hearted when he made medicine contraband of war? When he punished women caught with a bottle of quinine going South?[6]

Albert Bledsoe, the editor of the *Southern Review,* borrowed upon W. H. Lamon's biography of Lincoln to reach an assessment remarkably similar to contemporary psychological studies of the Great Emancipator: Lincoln's success "has been the wonder of all nations . . . perhaps the wonder of all ages" but it was the outcome of a "ruling passion" not based upon a love of freedom or hatred of oppression but rather a thirst for personal distinction. Without a faith in God, "the one thought . . . which haunted and tormented his soul, was the reflection that he had done nothing, and might die without doing anything, to link his name and memory forever with the events of his time."[7]

Perhaps the most significant of these critiques, however, is Edgar Lee Masters's *Lincoln: The Man*. Masters's Lincoln is quite different from the Lincoln of Carl Sandburg's immensely popular *Prairie Years* published three years earlier. Yet both men are poets and the image of Lincoln they create out of this imagination can tell us much about the complexity of this exemplar. Both Masters and Sandburg attempt to create cultural syntheses from the frontier lawyer and Black Easter Lincolns. The political significance of origins is renewed. Both writers emphasize the humble nature of Lincoln. Here is Masters's description: "Living was in every way indecent. The cabins were filthy, and rats and vermin abounded. Men and women undressed before each other; and the children were cognizant of the most intimate relationships carried on within a few feet of where they slept, including the hired man or the stranger guests. The food was vile. . . . Much whiskey was drunk; and all weird superstitions abounded concerning the moon, the flight of birds, the bringing of a shovel into a room, which meant near death; and there were ghosts and witches about, whispering in dark corners, or flying over the roofs. In this sort of cabin was Abraham Lincoln born . . . in no wise fit to be called the home of a human being." As for the president's father, Thomas Lincoln had "all the indicia of poor Southern white . . . he was sprung from the lowest stratum of American life . . . rather than labor to rise . . . he preferred the woods and loathsome poverty, rats, cold and filth."[8]

Sandburg too emphasizes cramped quarters but here is his description: "The one-room cabin now sheltered eight people to feed and clothe. At bedtime the men and boys undressed first, the women and girls following and by the code of decent folk no one was abashed." In the cabin Nancy Lincoln read "mystic Bible verses . . . over and over for their promises." For food there was deer, turkey, ducks, nuts, fruits, and honey. Frontier life was not a harbor for the indigent but a beehive of activity: "clearing land for crops, cutting brush and burning it, splitting rails, pulling crosscut saw and whipsaw, driving the shovel plow, harrowing, spading, planting, hoeing, cradling grain, milking cows, helping neighbors at house-raisings, log rollings, cornhuskings, hog killings." As for Thomas Lincoln, he "worked hard and had a reputation for paying his debts." He moved to provide a home for his family and to avoid slavery.[9]

Masters draws such a negative image of Lincoln's poverty (the Lincolns are a kind of American lumpen peasant class) that no positive political consequences can lead from it. Lincoln's early life eliminates the possibility of development to a humane leader or political theorist. His learning is too limited, his ambition untempered, his reasoning overpowered by superstition. For Masters, Lincoln is the model demagogue (in fact, he compares him to Robespierre) whose driving force is cruelty, ambition, and ruthlessness. As for political thought, Lincoln, "armed with the theology of a rural Methodist . . . crushed the principles of free government . . . he evolved out of the superstition of Pigeon Creek into a career in which he dramatized Jehovah as a celebrant of horrible doctrines of sin and atonement. . . . Tragic pity and comprehensiveness did not belong to his mind; and thus his thinking went no farther than to say, 'Thus saith the Lord.' He saw Jehovah ruling the insane scene because he rules it." It enrages Masters that Lincoln has been placed in the American political tradition. "Lincoln was not Jefferson's son. He was Hamilton's." He was a "centralist," a "privilegist," an "imperialist." Lincoln's precedent had already been used in the Philippines; Wilson "did many of the things, and with Lincoln as his authority for doing them." Who knows when in the future, "a few men deciding what is a cause of war . . . may, as Lincoln did, seal the lips of discussion . . . ?"[10]

Sandburg's Lincoln, on the other hand, is nourished by the generosity and openness of a vigorous frontier community. His boyhood and adolescence are Tom Sawyer-like. There is the timeliness of the seasons and the work that fit so perfectly with the rhythm of bucolic life. In the young Lincoln "sleep came deep to him after work outdoors." Pigeon Creek had its share of sorrows (Nancy Lincoln died from "milk sickness") but it also had schoolmasters paid by parents in venison, animal skins, and ham; girls with corn silk hair to kiss; preachers on the circuit; friendly neighbors and friendly fist fights.

The adult Lincoln fashions his political theory from the boisterous populism of Illinois democracy. Sandburg passes over Lincoln's career as a railroad lawyer. And he does not dwell upon legislative politics at the state capital. The stump is the essence of democratic politics and it is Lincoln speaking at state fairs and party rallies, responding to hecklers and crowds partly resembling a circus and partly a camp meeting that receives the most attention. The citizens who come to hear Lincoln and other politicians also come to talk. When a young woman in Rushville taunted Lincoln with a black baby doll, he responded, "Madam, are you the mother of that?" Men yelled that they would fight any man who voted for a candidate. From these experiences there came an appreciation of a word—"democracy": "Tongues of politics played with it. Lincoln had a slant at it. 'As I would not be a slave, so I would not be a master. This expresses my idea of democracy. Whatever differs from this, to the extent of the difference, is no democracy.' "[11]

Both depression biographies, however, had some difficulty connecting their portrayal of Lincoln with their assessments. For Masters, "the Lincoln mind puzzles the student at every step." Masters admitted that Lincoln was a poet who "hypnotized" Americans as he had ideologically defeated Douglas with his "touch of genius." If Masters cannot quite explain Lincoln's achievements as a political theorist given limited literacy, Sandburg cannot quite explain the president's greatness in terms of the vigorous but provincial vision of Illinois democracy. He resorts to the theme of the "strange friend and friendly stranger." Lincoln, after all, was in but not of the communities he represented: "He was loose-jointed and comic with appeals in street-corner slang and dialect from the public square hitching posts; yet at moments he was strange and far-off as the last dark sands of a red sunset, solemn as naked facts of death and hunger. He was a seeker."[12]

"Roosevelt is Grim / Quotes Lincoln"

The liabilities of the Lincoln exemplar were as clear in 1938–39 as they had been in 1932–33. It was not just that Lincoln had been a Republican or that FDR was from Dutchess County, New York, not New Salem, Illinois, or that Hyde Park was a whole world away from Pigeon Creek. Roosevelt could manage these differences as he cleared new ground for new policies. He had done as much in his employment of the Jackson metaphor. The towering liability was that Lincoln—any biographer's Lincoln—had become sui generis in American culture. There was, of course, only one Jefferson as well. But since most Americans naturally spoke in Jeffersonian dialect, the exemplar was the national language. And of course every corporate chief executive officer carried Hamiltonian yearnings in his breast. Admittedly, Jackson was a rarer ideological persona but copies of populist protest had already appeared sporadically before FDR appropriated the exemplar in 1936.

Lincoln was different. The Black Easter Lincoln and its various supplements, however iconoclastic some were intended, had created an image of a leader unlike any accorded by Americans. No event in American history even approached the tragedy of the Civil War. Generational memories were still orally transmitted, as FDR himself illustrated in 1938 when scores of veterans from both armies arrived in Gettysburg to participate in the dedication of a federal memorial. Lincoln had provoked and justified that war and his speeches, memorized by schoolchildren, outlined the principles of the regime under conditions under threat of disintegration. To draw upon Lincoln then as an exemplar required not only a crisis as extreme as civil war (and save revolution or invasion, no more cataclysmic event exists for a nation state) but also required the exploration of symbols of redemption and unity rarely employed with such force in American political culture. Failure to convince Americans of the symmetry with a current crisis and a Lincolnian resolution could raise questions of usurpation, questions that are submerged in the Black Easter interpretation and a major part of the critical tradition regarding Lincoln. Roosevelt, particularly after the court battle and the purges, was especially vulnerable on this point.

During FDR's Jacksonian turn Lincoln had been used as a supplement to the populism of the general. In his 1935 press conference on the Court, Roosevelt mentioned the Dred Scott decision and Lincoln's opposition to it. In 1936 he had noted that Lincoln could not have come from "any class that did not know, through daily struggle, the grim realities of life. . . ." Part of his 1938 Jackson Day address was devoted to Lincoln as a man "scorned for his uncouthness, his simplicity, his homely stories and his solicitude for the little man." Lincoln's enemies were similar to Jackson's—and Roosevelt's: "gold speculators in Wall Street," "a minority unwilling to support their people and their government unless the government would leave them free to pursue their private gains."[13]

During the 1938 primaries FDR made direct comparisons to Lincoln post factum. In 1787 there was a "grave danger that the states would never become a nation." "In the time of Lincoln . . . a tragic division threatened to become lasting." In 1933 another "test" had come. In 1940, however, a new use of Lincoln emerged. At the Jackson Day dinner Roosevelt announced that he planned to talk to his audience not only about Jackson but about Lincoln as well. The purpose of examining past leaders was not to advance the cause of party. "Yes, the devil can quote past statesmen as readily as he can quote Scriptures." The purpose was to examine "the motives behind leaders of the past" to see how they completed "the big job that their times demanded to be done."[14]

The president cited three personal heroes in addition to Jackson. Jefferson made the list, of course. But there was uncharacteristic criticism of the Sage of Monticello from the president. Jefferson was "a hero to me despite the fact that the theories of the French revolutionists at times overexcited his practical judgement." If Jefferson's radicalism was to be noted and condemned, Hamilton, the negative exemplar of the New Deal, was now added to the ranks of FDR's heroes: "he is a hero because he did the job which then had to be done—to bring stability out of chaos of currency and banking difficulties." Lincoln was the next hero. He had preserved the union and made possible the "united country that we all live in today."[15]

This Jackson Day speech represented something of an anomaly in FDR's traditional use of the event. It is a transitional address in Roosevelt's move toward the Lincoln exemplar. Jackson had been a perfect theme for these speeches. He was very much a partisan symbol and from 1936 on FDR had been able to employ Jacksonian populism to create the unique class base of the second New Deal. But these same assets had become clear liabilities by 1940. In fact, after 1941 the Jackson Day address itself was abandoned entirely. The Rooseveltian peroration on Jacksonian middle-class apprehensiveness as the basis for a new social contract had eroded on all sides. Rexford Tugwell's comment about farmers in 1938 (they "had a treaty with the New Deal, but it was a very limited one") held for the political situation in general.[16] The "new faces" of the Seventy-sixth Congress, men like Robert Taft and John Bricker, had moved offensively and were attempting to use that same apprehensiveness for their cause. As significant, moreover, was the growing threat from abroad. By January 1940 FDR could no longer concentrate on domestic concerns, using the international situation as a metaphor to attack corporate elites as he had done in 1936. A European war had begun; just months later Norway, Denmark, Holland, Belgium, and France were to fall to the Nazis. The Jacksonian exemplar, with its class appeals, thrived on division. What FDR needed was unity, hence the selection of heroes that contributed to unity, men who "did the job which then had to be done."

Jefferson's radicalism was in 1936 a figment of aristocratic imagination. In 1940 FDR carefully separated himself from this failure of Jefferson's "practical judgement." Jackson is praised for saving "the economic democracy of the Union for its westward expansion." And Hamilton, while he may always have had a bureaucratic presence in the Jefferson-Jackson New Deal, had never been positively acknowledged. But Hamilton was a nationalist and in 1940 the president, despite his comments about the devil's quoting, looked where he could for support. In fact, in September Roosevelt returned once more to the Jefferson-Hamilton debate and acknowledged the "high motives and disinterestedness of Hamilton and his school." He would not openly betray Jefferson but he admitted this time that only "if government could be guaranteed to be kept always on the high level of unselfish service suggested by Hamilton there would be nothing to fear." The argument is the same as that in 1932 and 1936 but there is a sympathy now for Hamilton's effort to create a tradition of national service. Lincoln was the remaining hero discussed. FDR dismissed partisan affiliation: "I do not know which party Lincoln would belong to if he were alive in 1940 . . . a new party had to be created before he could be elected President." In any case, Lincoln was "the legitimate property of all parties—of every man and woman and child in every part of our land."[17]

The addition of Lincoln to the list of New Deal heroes (the introduction, written in 1941, to the 1938 volume of official addresses cites a "liberal party" throughout American history that begins with Jefferson and included Jackson, Lincoln, Theodore Roosevelt, and Wilson) represented only one aspect of an ideological change that began in 1940. The Lincoln exemplar was used far more thoroughly than as a general legitimating device. The cultural openings that Lincoln had personally created were consciously studied and copied. The shift from "Doctor New Deal" to "Doctor Win the War," as contained in the slogan the president recommended to the popular press, reflected a series of options carefully selected, at least as far as events permitted.

In 1936 FDR had, after some hesitation, adopted the leadership style of Jackson. In 1939–40 the comparison with Lincoln was carefully nurtured. When a group of students arrived for a meeting at the White House in the spring of 1940 to complain about the guns and butter problem, the president halted the barrage of criticism by asking one questioner, "Young man, I think you are very sincere. Have you read Carl Sandburg's Lincoln?" When the man answered negatively, Roosevelt responded thus: "I think the impression was that Lincoln was a pretty sad man because he could not do all he wanted to do at one time, and I think you will find examples where Lincoln had to compromise to gain a little something. He had to compromise to make a few gains. Lincoln was one of the unfortunate people called a 'politician' but he was a politician who was practical enough to get a great many things for his country. He was sad because he could not get it all done at once. And nobody can." Here is a very different Roosevelt from the Jacksonian demands of the second inaugural and the exclamations of "now" in the court fight. Privately he had referred to college pacifists as "shrimps"; publicly he took on the role as the suffering leader.[18]

Robert Sherwood, the author of the popular broadway play *Abe Lincoln of Illinois*, was hired as a speechwriter late in 1940. Viewing the film version of Sherwood's play, FDR had requested copies of two of Lincoln's speeches from the debates with Douglas. On election eve, as part of a nationwide radio program, Carl Sandburg offered an emotional eulogy to Lincoln and closed with his support for Roosevelt. Sandburg implied that this election was much like the one in 1864, Lincoln was much like the prophet Samuel, and FDR was much like Lincoln. The Lincoln biographer spoke as an independent who belonged to "no political party, no faction, no political group open or secret," who recognized Franklin Roosevelt, as earlier generations recognized Lincoln, as "not a perfect man and yet more precious than gold." On election day Stephen Vincent Benet published a poem in the *New York Post* that spoke of leaders who knew "the tides and ways of the people / As Abe Lincoln knew the wind on the prairies." One was "A country squire from Hyde Park with a Harvard accent, / who never once failed the people / And whom the people won't fail."[19]

There were doubters. Raymond Moley, now a political enemy of the president, complained that college youth were being bombarded with "new cliches": capitalism has failed, a dollar spent is a dollar earned, Congress is terrible, and Roosevelt is greater than Abraham Lincoln. Herbert Hoover noted that it was no coincidence that both Earl Browder and FDR claimed Lincoln as "a founder of their faiths." Both attempts were unfounded: "The spirit of Abraham Lincoln has not joined the New Deal." Wendell Willkie during an election campaign visit to Springfield denied that either he or the president deserved comparison to Lincoln. But the press as a whole had begun to explore the analogy on their own. Max Lerner in the *Nation* asked, "How much Lincoln does Roosevelt have in him?" Proof of the success of the attempted parallel can be found in *Time*'s tribute to Roosevelt as "Man of the Year" in 1942, in which the comparison to Lincoln was accepted.[20]

How correct was the Lincoln-FDR leadership analogy? The parallels in themselves were only broadly suggestive without further ideological support. The United States was not in the midst of a civil war. While the debate about intervention was widespread it carried none of the intensity of that of 1864 or even 1860. FDR spoke of the "troubled times" in the past when Lincoln "year after war-torn year . . . sheltered in his great heart the truest aspirations of a country rent in twain."[21] Such was really not the case with the president eighty years later. The inevitability of war seemed a common assumption, but still most Americans hoped to avoid it. Both Willkie and FDR were the peace candidates in 1940, with Willkie charging first that FDR was an appeaser and then that Roosevelt was secretly leading America to war. When he said in Boston at the end of October that "your boys are not going to be sent into any foreign war" FDR may have said so reluctantly and under electoral pressures. But the point is that the statement hardly showed Lincolnian leadership at least as understood by the mythic readings, even though Lincoln himself had been infuriatingly vague about his reaction to secession through his inaugural, a point perhaps that led later to the kind of charges that would suggest that Pearl Harbor was Roosevelt's version of Fort Sumter.

In more general terms, Roosevelt's leadership in foreign policy did not seem to support the slightest claim to the kind of action required by the Lincoln exemplar. It is true that he campaigned for the League of Nations in 1920, but his reaction to Hearst's demands in 1932 did not parallel Lincoln's to Greeley. The rationale of the Good Neighbor policy was vaguely isolationist and FDR made no principled stand against the Neutrality Acts until 1939. When his 1937 quarantine speech received negative reaction he abandoned the statement; his reactions to the crisis in Munich could fairly be termed as appeasement.[22] Perhaps the most successful foreign policy address FDR had delivered was his 1936 Chautauqua speech, and that had been a vivid and emotional antiwar statement. Lincoln's career was hardly without its inconsistencies but from his early addresses to the Senate debates one can establish a conception of his developing vision on the slavery question and the Union. It is difficult to do so with Roosevelt.

Sherwood did his best to defend the 1860 parallel. He noted Lincoln's opposition to war in 1848 as a Whig and his early indifference to slavery. Not until "Lincoln saw that the spirit of slavery was spreading— from Missouri to Kansas and Nebraska" did he turn from an "appeaser into a fighter." In this respect "Lincoln's attitude in the years before the Civil War paralleled the development of the attitude of the whole American people in the years before 1940." Sherwood's statement was itself something of a confessional. He too had been an isolationist and an "appeaser" until 1939. (*Idiot's Delight*, written in 1935, was an antiwar play.)[23] If FDR had been so as well he still kept good company with Lincoln.

Roosevelt's new speechwriter had a point, especially if stated somewhat differently. The parallel to Lincoln was literally awkward and even fictitious. But the attempt to create the parallel itself indicated a change in the president's ideological direction and a pledge of Lincolnian leadership. The adoption of Lincoln certainly had immediate partisan objectives but it also suggested a burden that FDR had implied he would undertake. "Judge me by the standards of Lincoln" involved a risk and a certain element of moral responsibility. Moreover, it now rested with Roosevelt to make a case for action as Lincoln had done.

Roosevelt's successors, with the possible exception of Kennedy, have attempted to use the Lincoln exemplar in specific ways, especially as a precedent for independent executive action. Lincoln himself modeled his conception of the presidency on far broader concerns. Henry Clay was his real exemplar, despite his assertion that all honor was owed to Jefferson. Clay inspired Lincoln not only for his judgment and ideals but also for his ability to cast a "spell . . . with which the souls of men were bound to him. . . ." Lincoln's "House Divided" speech in 1858 had cast its own spell over the nation, one that propelled him to the presidency and, arguably, the country to civil war. The Lincolnian conception of crisis involved not simply the recounting of a danger to the republic but an evocation of a peril in terms of a larger pattern of trial, retribution, and redemption. The central metaphor of Lincolnian theory, a house divided, is derived from the Pharisees' questioning of the sources of Jesus' healing power. Jesus' response, "Every kingdom divided against itself is brought to desolation; and every city or house divided against itself shall not stand," is an extremely complex statement that explores the nature of belief, faith, and motivation. Confusion, desperation, and fear are the consequences of conflict and division, attitudes that Lincoln himself used to describe the failure of the nation to contain slavery. FDR had reconstructed this same consequence of confusion and fear ("nameless, unreasoning, unjustified terror" that is the result of a "generation of self-seekers" who have "no vision") in his first inaugural. The Lincoln exemplar contends that a people pays a price for ignoring its common heritage and tolerating evil. "Satan cannot cast out Satan" was the New Testament lesson that Lincoln had applied, and here Roosevelt reminded the nation that "when there is no vision the people perish." "Small wonder that confidence languishes," he continued, for it thrives only on moral principles ("honesty," "honor," "sacredness of obligations," "faithful protection," "unselfish performance"). But "restoration" is possible. The fear will be worth the price if it "teaches us our true destiny."[24] Of course the path to redemption requires a rededication that is severe enough to establish a purity of spirit.

As I have indicated, FDR had not pursued the full consequences of the Lincolnian exemplar in 1933 despite his stirring evocation in the inaugural. Now in returning to this crisis exemplar he turned to the gray days of 1933. Instructing Samuel Rosenman about the tone of the fireside chat that became known as the arsenal of democracy speech, he said, "I tried to convey to the great mass of American people what the banking crisis meant to them in their daily lives. Tonight, I want to do the same thing, with the same people, in this new crisis that faces America."[25]

Here was FDR's own "crisis" in 1940. And here at an ideological level lay a genuine parallel to Lincoln's crisis. Scholars differ in assigning a date by which Roosevelt had concluded that war was inevitable just as scholars differ about Lincoln's frame of mind regarding armed conflict. Lincoln probably did believe in 1858 that the problem of slavery could be resolved by "peaceful ballots" rather than "bloody bullets." Rosenman believes that not until the fall of 1941 did FDR believe that American participation was unavoidable.

But the problem that both Lincoln and FDR faced was in a broad sense a heritage of the Jeffersonian mind. For both slavery and Nazi conquest challenged American beliefs in pluralism. There was a widespread belief in antebellum America that slavery was wrong. The belief that fascism was an evil was even less contested. The question in both cases was how in terms of national policy could the evil be resisted. Lincoln forcefully attacked this "declared indifference" in his Peoria speech in 1854 and made it a recurrent theme in the great Senate debates. Roughly, he used three lines of argument. He appealed to the self-interest of white citizens. He reminded his audience at Peoria that the opportunities in the territories would be diminished with the spread of slavery. "Slave States are places for poor white people to remove from, not remove to. New free States are the places for poor people to go to, and better their condition."[26] He insisted that if slavery was a moral wrong, indifference was not a suitable policy. Douglas "could not say people have a right to do wrong." And finally, he argued that the major reason for the evil of slavery rested with the fact that it directly contradicted the moral base of the American regime. Lincoln found this base to rest with the Declaration of Independence. If slavery was accorded any status higher than necessity, the "first precept of our ancient faith" was repudiated. In his famous Springfield address Lincoln concluded that conflict would not cease "until a crisis shall have been reached and passed." America could not "endure permanently half slave and half free."[27]

FDR employed not only Lincolnian vocabulary but Lincolnian arguments in his third-term acceptance speech in Chicago. Roosevelt spoke before a convention in a decidedly churlish mood. Delegates expected Willkie to be a strong opponent; FDR's fiction of a draft (replete with lines written for Alben Barkley) wore thin especially after a futile but nasty challenge by James Farley; a bitter fight over the vice-presidential nomination preceded the address. But all the elements of the upcoming campaign and the ideological arguments offered the year before Pearl Harbor were evident in the speech. It was to a certain extent the ideological equivalent to Lincoln's Peoria address.

There were two tasks necessary to the safeguarding of American institutions. One involved the "united effort of the men and women of the country to make our Federal and State and local Governments responsive to the growing requirements of modern democracy." The president noted that this effort had sometimes been called "social legislation," sometimes "legislation for human security," sometimes it had been labeled "a wider and more equitable distribution of wealth in our land." FDR did not mention forgotten men or economic royalists in 1940. New Deal legislation was described simply as the result of a "growing sense of human decency." This sense was "confined to no group or class"; it was an "urge of humanity" that could "by no means be labelled a war of class against class." It was a "war in which all classes are joining in the interest of a sound and enduring democracy."[28]

Jackson then was formally abandoned in 1940. FDR claimed that much still needed to be done in terms of human decency but now the task was entrusted to "poor and rich alike." There were still enemies. "Appeaser fifth columnists" charged the president with "hysteria and warmongering." But these were men and women who were unwilling to extend the principles of human decency to the democracies of the world. In the height of the Jacksonian period of the New Deal, Roosevelt had declared that economic royalists were "aliens to the spirit of democracy." "Let them emigrate," he had told the crowd at Madison Square Garden. In 1940 he spoke of "selfish and greedy people" whose desires for money led them to "compromise with those who seek to destroy all democracies everywhere, including here."[29]

Lincoln had once asserted that the civil war was a "people's contest."[30] FDR did not in 1940 call for armed conflict. The other task of which he spoke involved military readiness. But he did claim Lincoln as the authority for the truth that democracy can thrive only when it lists the devotion of the common people. More generally, all the basic principles of the Lincoln exemplar were in place. If human decency was a principle of America's national identity, "our credo—unshakable to the end," then indifference to "free peoples resisting . . . aggression" was not possible. People do not have a right to do wrong. The ethical choice was "moral decency versus the firing squad."[31]

In September the president repeated Lincolnian themes. He reiterated his pledge of no foreign wars except in cases of attack to a Teamsters Union convention, but he reminded labor leaders that it was in their self-interest to "loyally cooperate" in the task of munitions making. "In country after country in other lands, labor unions have disappeared as the iron hand of the dictator has taken command. Only in free lands have free labor unions survived."[32] On registration day for selective service he announced that "we cannot remain indifferent to the philosophy of force now rampant in the world." To the Jeffersonian-Jacksonian principles of "equal rights, equal privileges, equal opportunities," Roosevelt added "equal service." At the time of the adoption of the Constitution, nine of thirteen states required universal service. Then little training was needed; "the average American . . . brought with him his musket and powder horn." Thus while the draft did not represent "a new and unchartered trail in the history of democratic institutions," the contemporary need for longer training did serve democratic ideals: "Universal service will not only bring greater preparedness . . . but a wider distribution of tolerance and understanding." It would "bring an appreciation of each other's dignity as American citizens." In October, drawing the first numbers for the draft, the president referred to "our democratic army."[33] At the University of Pennsylvania he reminded scholars of the fate of books under dictatorships as he also did at a dedication of three new schools in New York. In a letter read at the World's Fair on the seventy-fifth anniversary of the ratification of the Thirteenth Amendment, he noted the irony that in just three-quarters of a century there were now forces that would "return the human family to that state of slavery" from which emancipation came through the Thirteenth Amendment.[34]

"In his hands our traditions are not safe"

Self-interest, a people's war, the immorality of indifference—these arguments were repeated throughout the campaign of 1940. Opinion polls did suggest a sympathy for FDR's new Lincolnism.[35] People were concerned about the fate of the world's peoples; they were concerned about the military security of the United States. They seemed to have appreciated national as well as individual self-interest in a free Europe and they were willing to provide aid to meet these concerns. They were not yet convinced, however, of the necessity of war itself. Perhaps neither was FDR himself. But his immediate political situation required a delicacy that made the complete presentation of the Lincoln exemplar difficult.

The president confided to many that Willkie was the strongest candidate he had faced in a presidential election. Not that the Republican candidate did not have his problems. His August acceptance speech theme of unleashing the bourgeoisie ("Only the strong can be free and only the productive can be strong") was outstripped by world events. His early attacks on Roosevelt as an appeaser had been effectively rebutted by the president, so much so in fact that Roosevelt continued to reply to them after Willkie changed his tactic. FDR's Madison Square Garden speech, itself a reversion to the Jacksonian exemplar in the campaign, thrilled the audience with its repetition of "Martin, Barton, and Fish" on national defense. Willkie was also hardly the darling of the Republican right wing. The Willkie clubs reflected the strategy of treating the Republican Party "as an allied but somewhat alien power."[36] But by mid-October Willkie's campaign seemed to have mounted a real challenge. And that challenge was based in part on the liabilities of the Lincoln exemplar.

After September Willkie did not move toward a Douglas position, and after Pearl Harbor he was the polar opposite of a Vallandigham. But the Republican candidate attempted to assume the role of the peace candidate, and the only peace candidate, in 1940. In Kansas he said, "I warn you—and I say this in dead earnest—if, because of some fine speeches about humanity, you return this administration to office, you will be serving under a totalitarian government before the long third term is finished." Three days later in Los Angeles, he told a crowd: "I hope and pray that he [FDR] remembers his pledge [no American participation in foreign wars] better than he did the one in 1932. If he does not, you better get ready to get on the transports. . . ." At the end of October he predicted that should FDR be elected, America would be at war in six months.[37]

Willkie, early in the campaign, had attempted to make the third-term issue a major feature of his strategy for election. FDR had hoped to run as a Lincoln against Hitler.[38] Willkie's shift toward an isolationist position sharpened his third-term argument because in part it focused upon the liabilities of the Lincoln exemplar that Roosevelt himself had chosen. I have mentioned the critical strand in Lincoln interpreters. While, of course it is difficult to determine if this critique was explicitly part of the American mind when it contemplated Lincoln, it is possible to say that the employment of the Lincolnian exemplar does signal crisis, sacrifice, and the most demanding leadership. The equation of Lincoln with war and a war led against opposition is an inevitable part of the Lincoln symbol. Thus while the Lincoln exemplar among the general population probably contains no details about the Civil War president's suspension of habeas corpus and his appropriation of money unauthorized by Congress, by its very nature it does provide an opening for a critique.

FDR's "oratory, as defender of democracy conceals the fact that by his own meddling in international politics he encouraged the European conflagration. . . ."[39] The organized isolationist forces in 1940 were a disparate group, including Communists, Midwestern progressives, and ethnic groups with their own specific loyalties and animosities. The Willkie position permitted a common focus on FDR's use of executive power. The specter of dictatorship that formed a central part of New Deal opposition could now be raised not against New Deal policies, which Willkie found had risen to the level of a general consensus in 1940, but against participation in foreign wars. Willkie gained the support of Hiram Johnson, nearly gained support from Joe Kennedy, received (and rejected) support from Father Coughlin, gained support from Charles Lindburgh. But Willkie's real catch was the powerful, charismatic labor leader John L. Lewis, who had been sparring with Roosevelt for several years. It is not clear exactly why Lewis felt driven to support a corporate lawyer. The answer lies partly in Lewis's own Midwestern and immigrant background, his competitive relationship with FDR, his penchant for the big gamble (the CIO president closed his speech with a promise to resign if Roosevelt was reelected). But Lewis did appear to genuinely feel that the independence of labor would be seriously threatened by war mobilization, and that a "personal craving for power" rather than a concern for the worker was the driving force of FDR's policies. His October 25 speech before a national radio audience warned that the president's reelection "may create a dictatorship in this land." The address probably represented the psychological crest of the Willkie campaign.[40]

Willkie's shift from internationalist to isolationist is taken as a classic case of electoral opportunism. Willkie himself, when asked by Senator Gerald Nye after the election if the Republican candidate still believed that the United States would be at war by April, responded by admitting that his prediction was "a bit of campaign oratory." Yet the fear of war in the fall of 1940 did permit Willkie to directly confront the New Deal in ways that neither Hoover nor Landon had been able to do. In general, FDR had responded to charges that he would or had subverted the American system by exposing the attack as a disguised attempt at class domination. They only "seek the restoration of their selfish power" was the theme of the 1936 campaign. But to the extent to which the president had attempted to employ the Lincolnian exemplar of unity, such responses were not available.

Willkie raised the parallel to European dictatorships early in the campaign. At Coffeyville, Kansas, he vividly described the bombing of London: "Gas and water mains are ripped open, houses are blown to pieces, women and children lie dead. . . ." But something more was under attack in Britain, and that was the "philosophy of democracy." Willkie paid tribute to this small town by autobiographically recounting his experiences as a history teacher at Coffeyville High School. He had "learned much more than I taught": "I learned that democracy is not what we call the government. Democracy is the people. At school we learned these things. We got our first lessons in how to get along with others; we learned also gratitude; we learned how to play fair and we tasted the excitement of competition within the rules. We learned the meaning of companionship as well as the meaning of self-reliance and also in Sunday school and church we learned other things, and many other things in this Western country."[41]

The Coffeyville speech was of course part of the politician's traditional obeisance to the small town, one that both Hoover and Landon had also enacted. Willkie too was attempting to capture the Jeffersonian mind for his campaign. But Willkie gave a special cast to this strategy. Hoover had praised the morality of Main Street only to warn against nostalgia for its economic and political forms. Landon focused upon rural and small-town commitments to constitutionalism and free enterprise. For Willkie the small town was the repository of "freedom," "equality," and "democracy." The philosophy of democracy was nurtured and taught and preserved across generations at this level. "Our mothers taught us to be honest, polite, to be pleasant and kind . . . our fathers to be brave. . . ." The New Deal spoke in the language of democracy and portrayed themselves as "great 'defenders' of democracy," but its proponents are all "cynics who scoff at our simple virtues . . . and govern us with catchphrases." They have used relief money to manipulate votes; they "terrorize" their opponents by leaking untruths to newspapers; they "purge—

they purge and purge" those who try to be independent of the "New Deal machine." Because they do not trust in a philosophy of democracy they "have concentrated power in their own hands." FDR "may not want dictatorship" but "in his hands our traditions are not safe." He had "declared forty emergencies in the past seven years."[42]

In Peoria, Willkie argued that whenever democracies had existed in history—"the ancient Roman republic or Sparta, or Athens"—they fell when economic chaos came. So too in Germany, when economic breakdown occurred the people turned to a paper hanger because their democratic system would not work. Where was FDR when Germany fell? Willkie asked. He answered, FDR was attacking the Supreme Court: "He tore this country, this great united people to pieces when he might have exercised leadership." The policies of the New Deal set an example for the world and Willkie contended that Léon Blum modeled his policies on Roosevelt's and "took France to its wreckage."[43] Later in the campaign he suggested that not only had Roosevelt's policy failures promoted dictatorship abroad but that FDR himself was following a path toward dictatorship. Since he had been in office he had repeatedly declared emergencies (the count now was at sixty-seven) and "seized more power." "I will leave it to any student of our time whether this pattern I have described is not the pattern and the exact pattern of the decline in democracy in every country in the world where democracy has passed away." Now he was asking for more power, the violation of the "unwritten law" that prohibits a third term. This was a government that "treats our Constitution like a scrap of paper." This was a man who referred to an ambassador of the United States as "my ambassador." "Pretty soon it may be 'My Generals.' . . . After a while it will be 'My People.'"[44]

While Roosevelt was trying to argue that the choice the American people faced was a commitment to a world of democracies versus one of dictatorships, Willkie was contending that perhaps the president was on the side of the latter. He was casting himself as the "indispensable leader," a "tactic used by tyrants throughout history and the world today." Those who opposed the New Deal needed no such urging, but for those who had doubts Willkie repeated the 9 million unemployment figure as well as the suspicion that the current crisis in international affairs was, unlike the depression, avoidable. Could the president be trusted? Willkie's Jeffersonian "philosophy of democracy" suggested that Americans rely on themselves rather than on indispensable leaders.

FDR recoiled before this ideological assault. In a letter to Rosenman he complained that those who "most loudly cried dictatorship against me would have been the first to justify the beginnings of dictatorship by somebody else."[45] He planned five major campaign speeches between October 23 and November 2. For one, which was incorporated into his Cleveland address, he wrote notes for his writers to state why "FDR could not be a dictator, etc."[46] It would have been a fascinating debate had the president continued to pursue the Lincoln exemplar in the face of Willkie's Jeffersonian-inspired one. But FDR did not do so. Not only did he pledge that "your boys are not going to be sent into any foreign wars" but he largely although temporarily abandoned Lincoln to return to Jefferson and Jackson again.

In Brooklyn FDR returned to his 1936 response to his critics. The opposition might employ all manner of arguments, but their "only common philosophy and common purpose" was to get rid of the New Deal because their real aim was based upon their fear of "losing their own selfish power." It was the Republican leadership that had no faith in the people. They "hate democracy because it is Christian" and "they oppose Christianity because it preaches democracy." They had no conception of true public happiness because they "measured prosperity only by the stock ticker." Roosevelt was the candidate who fought for the "rights of the little man."[47]

The Brooklyn speech claimed that the forces opposing the New Deal might be unscrupulous but motivations did not come "necessarily from wickedness" but rather from a "sub-conscious resistance to any measure that disturbs the position of privilege." But in the present situation there was something "evil" about these natural attempts to reassert class privilege. There was an "unholy alliance" based upon "secret understanding" between "the extreme reactionary" in the Republican party and the "extreme elements of this country." Their "common ground" apart from a "common will to power" was an "impatience with the democratic process to produce overnight the inconsistent dictatorial ends that they, each of them seek."[48]

Louis Hartz in *The Liberal Tradition in America* reported the discovery of a nearly invincible ideological tactic on the part of those with Whiggish sentiments after their unsuccessful battles with the Jacksonians. The strategy, according to Hartz, involved invoking an element of "charm" (the possibilities for individual advancement) along with an element of "terror" (the penalties for rejecting the American system). Hoover had used this Whiggish formula magnificently in 1928 but found that the terror from the depression was far greater than his own about the consequences that would occur from a departure from the American system. Landon too raised that specter in 1936 but found that FDR had fully developed his own conception of terror (economic elites were poised to "gang up" on the people). Now in 1940 Willkie offered his own version of Whiggish terror, suppressing the element of capitalist economic protest in favor of the terror of war as a consequence of abandoning the morality of Jefferson and accepting the "cynicism" of the New Dealers. FDR's ideological response in returning to Jackson added another interpretive layer to his own version of the terror that he had constructed in the last election.[49]

In 1936 Roosevelt too had suggested a connection between the opposition and the men of "ill will" abroad, the same connection that Willkie was now making between FDR and foreign dictators. But in 1936 while he welcomed the hatred of American elites FDR did not confront the men of ill-will abroad. In his Jacksonian return late in 1940 he took on both. There are always subterranean forces in a campaign that find expression in comments by figures that the candidate himself is not directly responsible for. Harold Ickes's characterization of Willkie as the "barefoot boy from Wall Street" was a nicely turned phrase designed to show Willkie's alleged class loyalties. There were also other forces much nastier. Pamphlets asserted that Willkie's sister was the wife of a Nazi navy officer. (She was married to a U.S. naval attaché stationed in Berlin.) A Democratic senator claimed that the grave marker on the Willkie family plot bore the German spelling of "Wilcke." There was open speculation as to which candidate Berlin "preferred."[50] FDR of course did not participate in any of these activities, but he did connect the fate of the New Deal more directly to those "men of ill will" abroad.

In Cleveland FDR layed out the "charm" of his own ideological position. Employing the "I see" structure of his second Jacksonian inaugural he presented a picture of a vibrant, even social-democratic America:

I see an America where factory workers are not discarded after they reach their prime. . . .

I see an America whose rivers and valleys . . . are protected as the rightful heritage of all of the people.

I see an America where small business really has a chance to flourish and grow.

I see an America of great cultural and educational opportunity for all its people.

I see an America where the income from the land shall be implemented and protected by a Government determined to guarantee to those who hoe it a fair share in the national income.

I see an America with peace in the ranks of labor. [51]

This future was under threat from "evil forces" at home and abroad. There were forces within our national community composed of men "who call themselves American but who would destroy America." Those who voted against the New Deal were those who "in this as in other lands" hoped to "weaken democracy," to "destroy the free man's faith in his own cause." Those who doubted our foreign policy are "those who are doubters of our democracy." [52]

There emerged in the final days of the campaign a neat oppositional symmetry in the ideological arguments of both candidates despite the fact that both candidates had given in to opportunism on the question of American participation in the war in Europe. Willkie compared FDR's motives and tactics to those of European dictators. FDR compared Willkie (or at least the groups supporting him) to European dictators. Both arguments managed to evoke their share of terrors: a president who could not be trusted with American traditions, who regarded the constitution as a scrap of paper; and a reactionary opposition that had allied itself secretly with the far left in an unscrupulous attempt to achieve its dictatorial ends. Those who threatened democracy in both instances spoke as defenders of democracy.

"A nation is like a person"

FDR won the argument. But immediately Willkie pledged support for Roosevelt and moved to an internationalist position. FDR had in the last weeks of the campaign portrayed the conflict in Europe as a class war. Immediately he returned to the Lincolnian model of national unity. It would be slightly over a year before America was to be a major participant in world war but in the next eight weeks the president would have completed the application of the Lincoln exemplar to the international crisis.

The December 29 fireside chat began with the assertion that it was not a speech on war but national security: "the purpose of your President is to keep you now, and your children later, and your grandchildren much later, out of a last-ditch war for the preservation of American independence. . . ." While Roosevelt admitted that there was a risk of war in making America "the great arsenal of democracy" the action was justified because "we and our children will be saved the agony and suffering of war which others have had to endure." He repeated his Boston campaign pledge: "there is no demand for sending an American expeditionary force outside our borders. There is no intention by any member of your government to send such a force. You can, therefore, nail any talk about sending armies to Europe as deliberate untruth."[53]

Yet despite these disavowals, the arsenal of democracy speech was very much the ideological equivalent of Lincoln's Springfield address. Lincoln had declared that the government "cannot endure permanently half slave and half free," that the discord in the nation would "not cease until a crisis shall have been reached and passed." FDR too spoke of crisis, one as great as that of 1860 and 1932. Lincoln had argued that Douglas's "care not" policy could not maintain a status quo. Roosevelt stated the belief of some that "wars in Europe and in Asia are of no concern to us." He spoke of those "who want to see no evil and hear no evil, even though they knew in their hearts that evil exists." But the Nazi goal was world conquest. If Britain fell, Hitler would turn to this hemisphere. The United States "would be living at the point of a gun. . . . To survive in such a world we would have to convert ourselves permanently into a militaristic power on the basis of war economy. The U.S. was threatened with a modern form of slavery." The Axis proclamations were correct: "there can be no ultimate peace between their philosophy of government and our philosophy of government."[54]

A week later, in his annual message to Congress the president repeated his argument in military-political terms. The threat of war facing the country was unlike any except the Civil War. FDR defended various American military actions in the past but admitted that even in World War I there was "only a small threat of danger to our own American future." But today "the future of all the American Republics is in danger." Without the protection of the British Navy, the United States would not immediately be subject to invasion, but only because strategic bases would be required to facilitate troop landings. Thus the first phase of the invasion would occur in Latin America through the activities of "secret agents and their dupes" just as it had already occurred in Norway. No negotiation is possible, despite those who "with sounding brass and tinkling cymbal preach the 'ism' of appeasement," for "no realistic American can expect from a dictator's peace international generosity. . . ."[55]

So imminent is the crisis that must be reached and passed in his image of the world situation that Roosevelt also declared what amounted to war aims:

The first is freedom of speech and expression—everywhere in the world.

The second is freedom of every person to worship God in his own way—everywhere in the world.

The third is freedom from want . . . everywhere in the world.

The fourth is freedom from fear . . . everywhere in the world.[56]

The "four freedoms," included in the Atlantic Charter and repeated throughout the war, are often interpreted as part of FDR's Progressive heritage. The president had "picked up Woodrow Wilson's fallen banner, fashioned new symbols and programs to realize old ideals of peace and democracy. . . ."[57] Indeed, FDR had already begun to elaborate a defense of America's participation in the world war as part of his attack on the isolationists and the charge that America had been drawn into the conflict by munitions dealers. In his annual message he had compared Versailles and Munich. The former, while imperfect, was "far less unjust than the kind of pacification that occurred in 1933." A week after the election he praised the "young men of 1917 and 1918" who helped preserve "those truths of democracy for our generation." A year later he spoke of those who had questioned the sacrifice that had been made. "What did it get you? What was there in it for you?" veterans had been asked. The "cynics and doubters" did not know what we now know. Sacrifices were made "to make the world safe for democracy."[58]

But FDR himself had more in mind in his elaboration of the four freedoms than a vindication of Wilsonianism. In July a reporter had asked what were the president's long-range peace objectives. Roosevelt had obviously given the issue some thought, and in a long reply he compared the current international situation to that of 1776. Americans had been searching for some form of government "in order to check tyranny by individuals, kings, barons or whatever it might be—conquerors—and to assure certain individual rights." FDR continued, "Well, I call it almost an American invention because while it had been talked about philosophically by various writers before 1776 we were the first people to put it into effect. Other countries followed." Today this American invention was threatened by a new form of government set up by conquerors. "It is called by different names; probably the easiest name, as a symbol, is the corporate state." FDR admitted the efficiency of the corporate state and admitted that "a large number of Americans" were "willing to consider, because of efficiency, the corporate state." But the price for efficiency was the loss of "four freedoms." He continued by outlining these freedoms: freedom of information, freedom of religion, freedom of expression, freedom from fear. The reporter asked about a fifth, "freedom from want—

free trade, opening up trade." The president replied: "Yes, that is true. I had in mind but forgot it. Freedom from want—in other words, the removal of certain barriers between nations, cultural in the first place and commercial in the second place. That is the fifth, very definitely."[59]

When the president dictated the close of his annual message months later to his secretary, Rosenman was impressed with the way the "words seemed to roll off his tongue as though he had rehearsed them many times over."[60] The first formulation was clearly Jeffersonian in inspiration. The American invention in 1776 was the key to understanding the current crisis of democracy. The reporter's Wilsonian addition was casually accepted. By December "freedom from want" had been transformed into the New Deal goal of economic security. As Jefferson had been used as the ideological foundation of the early New Deal his theories were now used as the goals of war. But as there were strains in using Jefferson for Hamiltonian ends in 1932–33 there would be strains in using Jefferson for Lincolnian ends in 1940–41. Of course, as I have indicated, Lincoln himself employed Jefferson for his war aims as well. Certainly Lincoln was confronted with the paradox more intensely and more often. The Civil War always had its critics. But FDR too could not escape the contradiction involved in employing Jeffersonian freedoms, however modified by New Deal values, for a challenge that required unity, centralization, and national sacrifice.

The two exemplars are artfully merged in the third inaugural. Lincoln as well as Washington are presented as symbols of unity and order. "In Washington's day the task of the people was to create and weld together a Nation. In Lincoln's day the task of the people was to preserve that Nation from disruption from within." FDR announced that his task was to save the Nation from "disruption from without."[61]

Lincoln's great contribution to political thought centered around his admonition, stated as early as the Lyceum address, that time was the great destroyer of free government. The "jealousy, envy, and avarice incident to our nature . . . so common to a state of peace, prosperity, and common strength" no longer "lie dormant." Only a conscious, rational rededication to the principles of the regime can defend against the "silent artillery of time."[62] Roosevelt had begun to explore this theme in his third-term campaign. "Remember 1932" was of course important as a simple campaign slogan, but it also served as an occasion to remind Americans that it is in the memory of crisis that a people prolongs its freedom. In the inaugural, the president declared that "the lives of nations are determined not by the count of years, but by the lifetime of the human spirit."

A man's life was "three score and ten; a little more, a little less." But the life of a nation is determined by "the measure of its will to live."[63]

The central metaphor of the inaugural was the assertion that a nation was "like a person." The metaphor has a long tradition in political thought, and all its variations from Plato's to the medieval concept of a "great chain of being" to Hobbes's mechanistic interpretation are designed to emphasize unity and order as the central aims of politics. The Lincolnian interpretation that a nation could not be divided on basic principles, it could not remain "half slave and half free," was generally consistent with the claim that there are certain elements of a political system that cannot be subject to pluralism. The house divided metaphor that I have discussed, of course, evoked an image far more complex than that of the literal one of a dwelling. Lincoln himself had experimented with the more literal aspects of architectural imagery before he focused upon the biblical source.[64] Roosevelt's formulation takes on Hegelian tones. A nation, like a person, has a body that must be "fed and clothed and housed." A nation has a mind that "must know itself" and understand the "hopes and needs of its neighbors." But most of all a nation, like a person, has a soul, "something deeper, something larger than the sum of its parts." This aspect of a nation was the most important of the three and requires "the most sacred guarding of its present." A nation that loses its spirit loses its will to live, and FDR asserted that since the spirit of America was "born of the multitude of those who came from many lands" and represented the culmination of democratic struggle from the "ancient life of early peoples" it must speak to other nations—"the enslaved, as well as the free."[65]

Roosevelt was very much aware of the claims that fascism represented a "New Order." He had attacked this idea in his acceptance speech, charging that "tyranny is the oldest and most discredited rule known to history" and that the rise of dictatorships was "only a relapse, a relapse into ancient history." Robert Sherwood discussed Anne Lindburgh's best-seller *The Wave of the Future* with the president and remarked, "I certainly wish we could use that terrible phrase. . . ." FDR had replied, "Why not?" and included the Lindburgh argument in the address: "There are men who believe that democracy, as a form of government and a frame of life, is limited or measured by a kind of mystical and artificial fate—that, for some unexplained reason, tyranny and slavery have become the surging wave of the future—and freedom is an ebbing tide."[66]

The third inaugural claimed that the United States was, to use

Hegelian language, a world historical nation. This of course was not a new assertion. But now America as "novus ordo seclorum" was interpreted in global terms even more far-reaching than the Wilsonian "make the world safe for democracy." For, unless the spirit of America defeated the spirit of tyranny, the spirit of America would perish although the nation's "body and mind" might live on for a while "constricted in an alien world." Here was a position as demanding and crisis ridden as Lincoln's house divided interpretation of the problem of slavery. But if the spirit of America must become absolute, the spirit itself was a spirit of localism, pluralism, political restraint, and freedom. The spirit was "written into the Magna Carta, the Mayflower Compact, the Declaration of Independence, the Constitution." The spirit of America spoke through "our daily lives," through the processes of governing in "the sovereignties of 48 states," through our "counties," "cities," "towns," and "villages." It is true, of course, that there are principles and practices that so affront the nature of a free people that they cannot be tolerated. If fascism (and chattel slavery in Lincoln's time) did not qualify as the outer limit of pluralism then no principles and practices could ever do so. But one can still ask if in Roosevelt's formulation the American spirit that was to protect freedom had become so generalized and so absolute as to become detached from the actual life of a free society, which after all is one in which many voices speak.

In the months before Pearl Harbor the president repeated his commitment to Jeffersonian ends. He repeated the four freedoms, reminding his audience that should America fail these would "become forbidden things" for centuries. He told labor leaders that should fascism fail to be stopped "trade unions would become historical relics and collective bargaining a joke." He assured farmers that "there is no call to plough up the plains." He commended the savings stamp approach to the financing of defense: "It is national and it is homey at the same time." He asked what a Jeffersonian America would look like if Hitler were to defeat Britain: "Will our children, too, wander off, goose-stepping in search of new gods?" He distinguished between "obedience and loyalty." "Obedience can be obtained and enforced in a dictatorship by the use of threat or extortion or blackmail. . . ." Loyalty, on the other hand, was far different. "It springs from the mind that is given the facts, that retains ancient ideals and proceeds without coercion to give support to its own government."[67]

A little more than a month before Pearl Harbor, FDR, in extemporaneous remarks to teachers in Dutchess County, vividly restated the principles of a Jeffersonian America. He described the debate over consolidated school districts. The debate had taken "a long time but it was a far better method than one in which some dictator would have said to the town of Hyde Park fifteen years ago, 'You have got to have one.'" This was the method of the so-called New Order. But here "we like to do things, talk about them, fight about them among ourselves, say some pretty awful things to each other and finally work things out." He praised the experimental genius of American Federalism. New ideas had been tried in localities and states and if they worked they were "extended to the body politic of the United States." He urged teachers to take students to county courthouses and police stations, to the district attorney's office, to behind the cage of a bank and to the backs of department stores. If we have obtained a knowledge of our economics and politics at home we get an interest in the politics and economics of the country at large. This process too took a long time. The president closed by reminding his audience if "[I] try to get people to do things too fast, or do them my way, I hope you people will be the first to tell me to 'go way back and sit down.'"[68]

But what of those who did question when given the facts, who complained that decisions were being rendered too fast? Here the spirit of America spoke of "appeasers," "defeatists," "back stairs manufacturers of panic," "propagandists, defeatists and dupes, protected as they are by our fundamental civil liberties. . . ." In an April press conference he responded to those who questioned the feasibility of Lend Lease thus: "Now, I don't call that good Americanism." Those who asked for negotiation were referred to as "Vallandighams."[69] In August the president paused in the middle of a press conference. He pulled out Sandburg's *Lincoln: The War Years* and read two quotations. One, made in 1862, was a complaint that "the people have not yet made up their minds that we are at war with the South." The other was reported to take place a year later. It too was a complaint directed toward McClellan and his supporters: "They have no idea that the War is to be carried on and put through by hard, tough fighting, that it will hurt somebody; and no headway is going to be made while this delusion lasts." FDR noted what he called an "interesting parallel. . . . Lincoln's belief that this country hadn't waked up to the fact that they had a war to win, and Lincoln saw what was going on." When a reporter asked how his lead ought to read, the president answered: "I'd say, 'President Quotes Lincoln—And Draws Parallel.'"[70] In September he told the nation that those who ask for negotiation "ask me to become the modern Benedict Arnold. . . ." Then there was the language of totality: "single-mindedness," "no divisions of party or section," "total effort," "weapons of freedom," "total defense," "deep duty," "the battle lines of democracy."[71] In March, after the passage of Lend Lease, the president formally declared that the "great debate" was over: "It was not limited to the halls of Congress. It was argued in every newspaper, on every wave length, over every cracker barrel in all the land; and it was finally settled and decided by the American people themselves." Now that the decision had been made there was to be an "end of any attempts at appeasement in our land; the end of urging us to get along with dictators; the end of compromise with tyranny and the forces of oppression." The decision "is binding on us all. And the world is no longer in doubt."[72] All honor to Jefferson.

9

Which Roosevelt Do I Imitate?

A month after FDR died, Dwight Macdonald delivered a very unelegiac assessment of the president. After quoting from some sentimental reactions of American citizens, he concluded that Roosevelt's status as "the Father especially of the left-of-center section of American society" was an "unhealthy state of affairs, both politically and psychologically." Macdonald complained that FDR had been out of ideas at least since 1937 and that by the time he died he had "emerged as the Commander-in-Chief, the implacable executioner of the Enemy Peoples." While he was sorry to see anyone die, "one must regard Roosevelt's death as a gain."[1] Nearly thirty years later William Leuchtenburg described FDR in the same terms of ambivalence that makes up the Freudian conception of a father. However much his successors tried they would never be able to excel their father. "No president could ever again introduce the welfare state. None, after the Constitution was amended, could ever again serve as long as FDR. None, in an atomic age, could anticipate fighting a world war through to the kind of victory achieved in 1945. None could be the first to lead the country out of isolation into a United Nations and a dominant role in world affairs."[2] Thus, concluded Leuchtenburg, presidents and presidential aspirants were caught in a prisoner's dilemma. If they did not walk in FDR's footsteps they would be accused of walking in Hoover's. If they did so, they lost any chance of establishing their own claim to recognition. Leuchtenburg chronicled the nimble uses to which Roosevelt had been employed since Truman and claimed that the FDR shadow was slowly becoming fainter.

What is FDR's legacy as a presidential exemplar? Have his ideological "sons" gradually freed themselves of his grip? One way to answer these questions is to review Roosevelt's achievements and failures in terms of the concept of the exemplary presidency.

"The foundation of all social morality"

In Chapter 1 I outlined three functional aspects of the exemplary presidency. Roosevelt used presidential exemplars to justify each of his major policy initiatives. However to the point his critics' charges were, FDR nevertheless built the first structures of the welfare state and attracted an entire generation of liberal nomenklatura in the name of Jefferson when his advisers nearly to a man or woman preferred other exemplary figures. The Jacksonian turn provided new initiatives, including the "soak the rich" tax plan, the achievements of the second hundred days and the Supreme Court reorganization proposal. The appropriation of Lincoln, with which the president flirted in the midst of the 1933 crisis, was reserved for the task of moving the country away from isolationism.

Especially intriguing is the manner in which FDR's public persona seemed to change with the movement from one exemplar to another. Of course the same smile and glasses and cigarette holder and hat worn just slightly rakishly off center were always there. But the Jeffersonian Roosevelt used his own class background to imitative advantage. FDR as country squire could never be completely changed to FDR as Sage of Hyde Park (in fact, a Republican election truth squad once distributed photographs to the press of Roosevelt's "farm" in Dutchess County). While FDR could not and never attempted to portray himself as the Enlightenment figure from Virginia, he did use Jefferson's cosmopolitanism and aristocratic life to emphasize class empathy as a moral choice. The patrician as democrat (Richard Hofstadter's later description of Jefferson), implied Roosevelt, was a personality type that deserved special moral attention because simple identification with one's class of birth was the easy and natural decision.

This is the image that the presidential aspirant created in his St. Paul address. Jefferson, the tidewater aristocrat, had understood "the yearnings and the lack of opportunity, the hopes and fears of millions." He had risked the ostracism of his own class in the election of 1800, as FDR had learned from Bowers's biography, to create a party based upon "common participation" and led by "men and women who understand the hopes and fears of millions of their fellow human beings."[3] The implication, of course, was that Hoover, a man of modest origins, had felt a need, as Hamilton had, to identify with and support "certain sections of the Nation." Throughout 1933 and 1934 the president pursued this image by reminding cadets not to forget the "average run of folks" and cultivate friendships beyond "your own class and profession" and reminding college graduates of the need for "building up, not a class, but a whole community." It is easy to see the inner condescension in this position and I will in a moment speak to the new Hamiltonianism of the generations of welfare apparatchik, but the imitative use of Jefferson on this point was certainly an inventive achievement on FDR's part.

When Roosevelt called up his Jacksonian army, the image of the patrician democrat was replaced by the imitation of Old Hickory. Jackson had not been admired for his intellect, FDR had told his audience, but for his rugged fearlessness. The president reminded Americans that Jackson had been the object of the "relentless hatred" of elites but that the people had "loved him for the enemies he made." So too had Roosevelt welcomed the hatred of his enemies, who by definition were also the enemies of the people.

Robert V. Remini in his political biography of Jackson described a "fierce, choleric old man who rumbled and growled and made a great deal of noise as he went about the business of the presidency,"[4] but it was his aged ferocity that highlighted the risorgimento that Jackson led. His chronological age connected him with the youth of the republic, the central ideological motif of the new democracy. Roosevelt appreciated the psychic bond that Jackson had forged with the people, noting that Old Hickory had presided over a "rebirth" of the pioneering spirit that had been dissipated by the "older, more conservative East." That FDR himself was an Easterner, and as much a descendant of a conservative gentry that one could find in America, was papered over by the Jacksonian imitation. However much that true descendant of pioneers, Alf Landon, might attempt to call forth his own ideological formulation of a "new frontier," it was FDR who, like Jackson, had engendered class hatred and hence the love of the people.

Remini also notes the affection so many Americans had for Jackson. They sent him gifts of cheese and canes and hats that suggested an emotional attachment to him that "exceeded that of any previous president, including Washington and Jefferson."[5] FDR too in his Jacksonian turn had—Machiavelli's advice notwithstanding—managed to have the people love him. One could respect Jefferson or a Jeffersonian president (even Lincoln had not been loved until Black Easter) but that is a different bond of affection. To the extent that a president hopes to be loved he or she must undergo the difficult and dangerous imitative process through FDR and back to Jackson.

When he finally turned to Lincoln in 1939, Roosevelt created a new mask. There was the Lincolnian dolefulness that he presented to the visiting college students in 1940. But more significant, the Lincolnian Roosevelt required a different relationship with the American people. Lincoln had been "ahead" of the populace. He was more farsighted in his appreciation of public sentiment, however understandable public opinion might be at any moment. In fact, it is the Black Easter Lincoln that is prescient and therefore substantially enigmatic in relation to the public. But too much mystery does not hold power in a democracy. In elections the Lincolnian leader may retain an element of ideological mystery as Lincoln himself had done in 1860, but he must couple it with an educative function. FDR saved this role for the most part until after the election, although his acceptance speech had Lincolnian touches, and actually returned to Jackson in the fall of 1940.

As imaginative as they were (and we should not overlook the difficulties FDR himself encountered in selecting and developing each), these imitative performances can be fully appreciated only by reviewing them in the context of the hermeneutic aspect of the exemplary presidency. Here, in terms of scope and ideological inventiveness, it is unlikely that any other president will ever rival Franklin Delano Roosevelt.

The chart below illustrates in general terms the basic exemplars carved out of American political culture. In 1932 FDR was faced with the dual appropriation of Jefferson by American political parties. Hoover had brilliantly recast the Jeffersonian symbol into corporate terms. The Democratic Party platform in 1932 closed with the Jeffersonian motto, "equality for all; special privileges for none." But the Jeffersonian Democrats, having retreated to electoral enclaves as the opponents of the hegemonic party, affirmed their interpretation of the verities of the Jeffersonian exemplar: a modestly conceived presidency, a balanced budget and defense of the states, an attack on governmental "extravagance," and a return to a wet society. After scavenging through the remnants of symbols of progressive reform in his gubernatorial campaigns, FDR, as early as his prenomination "forgotten man" speech, developed a new reading of Jefferson. The Apostle of Freedom had always had a vision of a national community (counteracting the "Jeffersonian Democrats" who had accepted the adage that all politics is local) but it could be built only "from bottom to top and from top to bottom" (counteracting the carefully constructed Hooverian-Hegelian vision of Jefferson). Of course it is difficult to say whether this inventive reading would have been hermeneutically successful without the cataclysms of a Great Depression, but then the political theorist-regime actor always is subject to fortune. The depression did in fact support the Roosevelt reading in that the crisis afforded

Presidential Exemplars Before FDR

	Washington/ Hamilton	Jefferson	Jackson	Lincoln
Human nature, undirected	Negative	Positive	Positive	Negative
Attitude toward government, general	Positive	Negative	Negative	Positive
Presidential model	Positive, independent	Negative, partisan	Positive, partisan	Positive, independent
Ideological base	National elites	Local elites	"Eager" petit bourgeoisie	National coalition led by elites
Ideological enemy	Jacobin democracy	National elites	All elites ("designing politicians" / "moneyed corporations")	Local elites/ sectional interests
Ideological appeal, negative	Fear of anarchy; desire for deference	Fear of "monocrats"; threats to liberties	"Apprehensiveness"; resentment	Amoralism; self-interest
Ideological appeal, positive	National strength; prosperity	American exceptionalism	Democratic reform	Unity through recommitment
Vision of authority	Centralized, deferential	Decentralized, deferential	Decentralized, participatory	Centralized, participatory
Leadership personality	Republican hero	Movement leader	Partisan combative	Jeremaic
Exemplars, specific and general	Cincinnatus; British aristocracy; men of property	Sydney, Locke; alert citizenry	Jefferson; republican hero resurgent	Clay; "our fathers," republican and biblical referents
Moment of opportunity	Search for order, political stability, economic growth	Decentralization as creedal affirmation	Risorgimento	National emergency

the governor the opportunity to supplement the national Jefferson with Lincoln and the wartime Wilson. Hoover has "either forgotten or does not want to remember the infantry of our economic army."

The real challenge to Roosevelt's reading of Jefferson actually came after the election. Faced with the severe deteriorization of the whole economic fabric of the country in the terrible winter of 1932–33 (FDR critics still insist that the president-elect shared in the responsibility for this deepening crisis), Roosevelt could have more easily turned to Lincoln. He did not do so. With the significant exception of the first inaugural, the New Deal, often fitfully and with hosts of contradictions, pursued the implementation of a national Jefferson. Critics like Zinn and Conkin, who emphasize the opportunities missed by what we have referred to as the new reading of Jefferson, should consider the legacy that could have been left had FDR followed the Lincoln exemplar of the first inaugural with its threat to pursue a course of "temporary departure" from the normal balance of the Constitution.

The Jacksonian turn may have been the most opportunistic reading by FDR of an exemplar but it was also his most inventive. There may have been a natural lineage between Jefferson and Jackson in an ideological and historical sense, but the Jacksonian risorgimento had to be considerably revised to meet FDR's goals of reelection and social democracy (to the extent to which these goals in 1936 were intertwined). It was the new reading of Jackson that broke open the Democratic Party so that it might be reconstructed. Al Smith may have begrudgingly accepted that 1932 was a replay of 1800, but he refused to accede to 1936 as a replication of 1828. It was "all right" for him if FDR and the New Dealers wanted to "disguise themselves as Norman Thomas, or Karl Marx or Lenin" but he would not permit them to "march under the banner" of Jefferson or Jackson.[6] Of course the party was less transformed than put together with larger parts despite the protests of the "Jeffersonian Democrats." Still, in 1936 FDR had plucked the essence of the Jacksonian risorgimento. Jacksonianism was based upon the fears and desires of Tocqueville's men of small property. FDR saw that in 1936, properly manipulated by apprehensiveness, these men would have a class interest in a social democracy quite different from that envisioned by the original Jacksonians. Thus he fostered in the name of Jackson a class war, albeit an electoral, liberal, and pre-Marxist one.

When he adopted a reading of the Lincoln exemplar in 1940, FDR assumed as many risks as he had in 1932 and 1936. The critical Lincoln tradition historically raised questions of dictatorship and personal ambition, questions that had already been raised about FDR himself in the Supreme Court fight. Moreover, it was one ideological achievement to argue successfully, as Lincoln had done, that there were mystic chords that made America one nation; it was quite another to assert pax Americana as the logical progression of the American idea in history. But again this FDR did, admittedly at first cautiously and with the usual turns and twists that seemed to always occasion his selection of a new exemplar.

FDR's brilliance in accepting and partially discarding presidential exemplars was much more raggedly reflected in the public policies of the New Deal. Men like Raymond Moley could not or would not move from Jefferson to Jackson, or like Arthur Morgan could not accept the current interpretive exemplary implementation; and they had to be discarded and replaced by new recruits. Others like Rexford Tugwell and Frances Perkins and Henry Wallace had exemplary visions always somewhat at odds with Roosevelt. Through deft bureaucratic maneuvering they sought to put their own reading on New Deal programs and their implementation. Policy entrepreneurs like Lilienthal, Johnson, Hopkins, and Flanagan were able to partially independently construct programs based upon their own interpretive readings of exemplars. Thus if the Roosevelt-inspired exemplars clashed ideologically against one another on many occasions, their refractions among the New Deal apparatchik often took on even more contradictory dimensions. Nearly every New Deal program from NIRA to the Fair Labor Standards Act was administered by competing and often warring Hamiltonian, Jeffersonian, and Jacksonian bureaucrats.

There is a sense then—and I shall return to this point again—that the Roosevelt exemplar upon examination can be deconstructed to at least three past exemplars. A regime actor who intends to follow the path of FDR must ask, "Which Roosevelt do I imitate?"—The FDR who embraced the Jeffersonian implications of the inaugural parade? The FDR who welcomed the hatred of the money changers? The FDR who insisted that the world could not exist half slave and half free? In this sense the task of a presidential aspirant, to the extent to which he or she wishes to come to terms with the FDR exemplar in some fashion, is to examine the interpretive contribution that Roosevelt gave to each of his exemplars and if he or she chooses, to continue to work backward ideologically.

But there is a sense also in which the achievements in FDR's use of past exemplars constitute a stable synthesis and this is one, as both Macdonald and Leuchtenburg suggest in different ways, in which it can be said the Roosevelt exemplar can be accepted or rejected in toto. There are, I think, two ways in which the FDR exemplar can be approached from this perspective. One is to assert that the connecting link between 1933 and 1936 and 1940 is indeed the Jeffersonian exemplar. After all, Jacksonian democracy has always been justified as an extension of Jeffersonianism, and the war aims did involve a reinterpretation of Jeffersonian principles. Thus, the New Deal can be seen as twentieth-century Jeffersonianism, the "foundation of all social morality" with FDR as "the source of enduring strength" and a contemporary liberal as one who "measures politics by the memory of Franklin Roosevelt."[7]

"The ghost of Hamilton"

The problem, however, with this interpretation of the Roosevelt exemplar is that the bulk of the Jeffersonian initiatives conceived by the New Deal were disappearing institutionally by 1938 and had been transformed ideologically by FDR himself by 1936. I have noted in chapter 4 how even in Jefferson's own political theory the concept of public happiness had been ambiguously conceived, and how according to Arendt the concept did crystalize in his conception of a ward system for America. FDR did give the Jeffersonian idea a fresh and imaginative reinterpretation in 1932–34 through the concepts of neighborliness and pioneering. And we saw how these initiatives gave birth to all sorts of new local communities, often serendipitously and through the sufferance of the New Dealers. It is true that the labor movement or the greenbelt towns or Arthur Morgan's vision of the Tennessee Valley Authority, or all together, were not ward systems. But they did have the remote chance of becoming their functional equivalents. All of these Jeffersonian-inspired inventions died or were transformed, and it was FDR himself who ideologically altered them with his Jacksonian turn. The vigilant citizen, the new ideological motif of the second New Deal, may have contained an element of happiness-public as class hatred, but FDR had refocused the goals of the citizen and the government toward a new kind of happiness-private, the love of well-being.

The New Deal from its inception had always had proponents of a Washington-Hamiltonian interpretation. Some took their referents from their experience as war managers in the Wilson administration, some from their experience as organizational and professional technocrats, some from their experience as social scientists.[8] The NRA, despite the fact that it had some unexpected Jeffersonian aspects, represented the ideological and institutional base for a new Hamiltonianism. When the NRA was discarded in 1935, however, the new Hamiltonians had not really lost ideological control of the New Deal, although even they would not have expected it to emerge victorious through the Jacksonian exemplar.

I have tried to suggest how complex this struggle between Hamiltonian and Jeffersonian solutions was throughout the New Deal. FDR's own commitment to nationalize Jefferson always implied treading close to Hamilton. Likewise, although not quite so closely, those who supported a Hamiltonian solution through a democratized Hamilton risked verging toward Jefferson. This complexity is exquisitely illustrated in Henry Wallace's 1934 book, *New Frontiers*. Wallace's defense of and further prescriptions for the New Deal were consistently phrased in terms of the official Jeffersonianism of the period. Wallace spoke of the tradition of explorers and pioneers in America and showed how the New Deal represented its culmination. "Social inventors need to become politicians, not only in the fine sense of the word, but in a practical sense." Jefferson had been right about the public-spiritedness of farmers. There was "something wooden and inhuman" about a government interfering in "a definite, precise way with the details of our private and business lives." Hamiltonians had since the days of the Constitution attempted to use government for the benefit of the "aristocratic few." "Smaller men who sit at home attending quietly to their own business . . . do not realize the extent to which we have always had private control of government." But it is interesting that Hamilton is mentioned much more frequently than Jefferson in *New Frontiers*. Wallace suggested that although "we may not like it" there was no way to loosen the Hamiltonian grip by the farmer's traditional "devil-baiting" of the railroads, the middlemen, Wall Street. Only by "changing the rules" and boldly deciding to go in "new directions" despite the "sacrifices" involved, could these Hamiltonian "ghouls" be exorcised.[9]

In *New Frontiers* the Jeffersonian vision had still been eloquently evoked: Wallace spoke of the impact the AAA would have on localities: "every community can become precious in its own right." Children will not try to escape as they grow up. They will look ahead to the possibility of enriching the traditions of their ancestors. They will feel it is a privilege to learn to live with the soil of the neighbors of their fathers. Such communities will be "strung like many-colored beads on the thread of the nation and the varied strings of beads will be the glory of the world." Wallace thought of the AAA as "essentially a graded hierarchy of New England town meetings with responsible, democratically selected people dealing with the hard facts of just quotas at every step."[10]

By mid-1935 Wallace was still thinking in Jeffersonian-Hamiltonian terms but with a different reading. He told a group of Louisiana farmers that in the historic battles between states rights Jeffersonians and nationalist Hamiltonians, the latter had captured the government and were forcing farmers to "pay through their nose" by selling goods on an open market while buying in a protected one. "The ghost of Hamilton" was still "abroad in the land" and the programs of the AAA were a historically new weapon in the age-old American battle. "The processing tax is the farmer's tariff, the marketing agreements and licenses are the farmer's corporation laws." The AAA could be employed "to obtain and to use governmental powers comparable with those already used by corporations." Wallace insisted that Jefferson had always been "the practical statesman" and he would have understood that this was the "only sensible alternative" to those who tilled the earth. [11] One can see here that in a very short period of time the commitment to creating a national Jefferson had slipped to a commitment to creating a democratic Hamilton.

What the New Dealers rarely saw was how easily the democratic Hamilton could revert both institutionally and ideologically to a new aristocratic Hamilton and thus be subject to a Jeffersonian-Jacksonian challenge from different directions. For the great programs of the second New Deal that created the American welfare state, justified in terms of a Jacksonian interpretation of well-being, were Hamiltonian-inspired structures designed to create rights "already used by corporations." An unforeseen aspect of the ghost of Hamilton in New Deal was that the FDR exemplar had created a new vision of the presidency. The Washington-Hamilton model had always been committed to an expansive and independent conception of presidential power but always to protect propertied and conservative interests. Whether he had nationalized Jefferson or democratized Hamilton, FDR had created a new model of the presidency, one that Lincoln employed but that was available only in special circumstances—one that in different ways Theodore Roosevelt and Wilson had attempted to create. The FDR exemplar may not represent a plebiscitary presidency but it does offer a popularly based and powerful one that seeks as much as possible to portray itself ideologically superior to Congress.

There are then three possible interpretations of the FDR years as an exemplary presidency. One suggests that the Roosevelt presidency is really a series of separate exemplars, admittedly inventively reinterpreted. The presidential aspirant or president then either ideologically runs with that interpretation or reinterprets it. Another suggests that a presidential aspirant or president focus upon the Jeffersonian base of the

FDR years and ideologically evoke and/or revise it. A third suggests that a presidential aspirant or president aim at the Hamiltonian aspects of the New Deal and run ideologically with or against it.

"Adding story to story"

It is easy to see then how complex is the shadow of FDR that Leuchtenburg attempted to describe. It is certainly not true that Truman was a Martin Van Buren (although in some respects he was), or John F. Kennedy a Lincoln (although, again, in some respects he was) or Richard Nixon a Hamilton (although in some respects he was as well). The exemplary presidency is more complex and often more inchoate than this. Moreover, space does not permit in this volume a complete analysis of the uses of the FDR exemplar. But some exploratory comments are possible, and I can center them around the three interpretations of the Roosevelt exemplar outlined above.

Whatever Truman's personal assessment of FDR may have been, his presidency followed along the general lines of the Roosevelt exemplar. The Fair Deal was portrayed partly as a simple extension of the New Deal and partly to emphasize that "I had some ideas of my own."[12] Commentators who tended to take the former view referred to the programs as a warmed-over New Deal if in opposition or applauded the president for attempting to uphold the Roosevelt legacy. Thus Thomas Sancton in the *Nation* described Truman's 1949 State of the Union message as "magnificent as a restatement of the entire Roosevelt program" while the Alsops questioned the Fair Deal's "intellectual content," noting that there was no attempt to "alter the pattern of American society." Rather Truman "simply sees his health and housing, education and labor policies and all the others as convenient ways of helping large groups of citizens, not essentially very different from the veteran's bonus after the first World War."[13]

The Alsops' own political aims aside, there was a great deal of truth in their critique. For in 1948 Truman had run for election largely upon the Jacksonian exemplar that FDR had reinterpreted. The plain speech (the complaints about the do-nothing Congress), the class rhetoric (the assertion in the acceptance speech that the tax bill "helps the rich and sticks a knife in the back of the poor"), the emphasis on the need for security were all a replay of the exemplar of 1936. In many ways Truman made a better Jacksonian persona than FDR had and of course the electorate responded. But even more so than in 1936, the citizenry was responding to bourgeois apprehensiveness, this time arising from a concern that the security belt of the New Deal might be threatened. Truman's pitch in terms of this concern was perfect: "All I ask you to do is vote for yourself, vote for your family." Thus the Jacksonian component of the FDR exemplar provided for a margin of victory but not a mandate for a second (or third) New Deal. In fact, the ideological flaccidity of the Fair Deal as a New Deal legacy had already begun to show. The Alsops saw it. The New Deal as a Jacksonian movement had always been predicated upon class interests and private happiness. To the extent to which those interests were now essentially preservative (polls showed little concern for new welfare initiatives save the postwar problem of housing), the movement became more clearly a collection of interest entitlements administered Hamiltonianally.

But what really confronted the Truman presidency and *all* post-FDR presidencies with a unique challenge was the legacy of the Roosevelt use of the Lincoln exemplar. Roosevelt had spent his whole career attempting to create openings in American political culture. In the adoption of the Lincoln exemplar he sought to close up alternative visions. The application of the Lincoln exemplar to tensions with the Soviet Union was a relatively simple ideological task. The Nazis had been defeated but the world was still half slave and half free. But the use of FDR-Lincoln was ideologically neutral in terms of partisan politics in America. Socioeconomically the Republicans could not really present a New Deal or even a Fair Deal, but they could compete ideologically in terms of the FDR-inspired interpretation of Lincoln. Moreover, since the transition from antifacism to anticommunism was made under a Democratic administration, and under the protest of the party's left, the question of Yalta and China and Alger Hiss gave the Republicans a certain initiative. Unlike FDR, Truman had been unable or unwilling to abandon the Jacksonian persona and hence his Cold War Lincolnianism was not only an unstable ideological mix but also permitted Republicans to connect the Democratic Jacksonian president to "popular frontism." Most troubling in the long run, however, was the fact that the apocalyptic structure of the Lincolnian exemplar (of which Truman's inaugural address is a perfect illustration) is incapable of resolution under the constraints of the atomic age. Winning and losing may have been difficult enough ideological categories in regard to Antietam or even Guam. They provided the basis for incoherency in the context of an exemplar that permitted none when applied to the Berlin airlift or Korea. Still, as Lincoln had spoken of the peoples' war, the opposition to communism could be pursued systematically and ruthlessly at home. And this both parties and presidents and presidential aspirants have done since FDR.

It is easy to overlook the fact that the 1952 Republican challenge had so many of the earmarks of 1936, 1940, or even 1944. Like Landon and Willkie and Dewey, Eisenhower had campaigned on the promise to unleash the American bourgeoisie. Later he would offer the standard for the assessment of his presidency as the extent to which the programs of FDR had been rejected. But aside from the ideological complications of the Cold War, which were beginning to assume Peloponnesian proportions, the success of the Eisenhower presidency depended upon a set of factors unavailable to previous GOP challengers. The unique status of Eisenhower as war hero permitted him to raise Hooverian type objections to the New Deal without raising bourgeois apprehensiveness to negative proportions. Ike's boyhood persona was as barefoot as Willkie's but the supreme commander had never served Wall Street. Like Washington, Eisenhower could speak for business interests once removed. While he never had a Hamilton (although both Charles Wilson and George Humphrey could perform that basic role), the war hero did manage to reconstruct the Federalist presidency under modern conditions.

The key here, of course, is the qualifier, "under modern conditions." Eisenhower and the "new Republican" intelligentsia were at least intuitively aware of the Hamiltonian liabilities of Hoover, however much Hoover might have spoken in praise of Jefferson. Thus there emerged in the Eisenhower years the ideological slogans of "middle-of-the-road" and "dynamic conservatism." Arthur Larson, speechwriter, nicely clarified this position, which began to emerge by 1956. The "New Republicanism" was a mean between the principles of 1896 (note how 1928 is wisely avoided) and 1936. Larson emphasized tactical advantage as the key to ideological hegemony: "in politics—as in chess—the man who holds the center holds a position of almost unbeatable strength."[14] To this strategy Eisenhower largely held, accepting higher minimum wage legislation and increases in Social Security and certain public works projects such as the highway system and the St. Lawrence Seaway. Thus, despite Eisenhower's self-described standards of rolling back the New Deal, his administration—perhaps even more so than Truman's—rationalized and extended it. But what is more significant, the Eisenhower administration locating itself in the center, which at this historical moment meant pursuing the interests of the American corporate elite as far as the general public would permit, solidified the Hamiltonian tendencies of the New Deal itself.

There was so much ideological ingenuity in regard to the FDR exemplar in the Kennedy administration that it is difficult to even note it in a short space. Moreover, it is not clear that such inventiveness would not have imploded (as it did for Johnson) had the administration lasted for more than its one thousand days. It is true, as Leuchtenburg notes, that JFK sometimes chafed at the constant comparisons to FDR that were made by the New Deal intelligentsia that saw itself as returning from the exile of the Eisenhower years. But his repeated insistences that he was not an FDR and that the problems of the 1960s were different from those of the 1930s (more difficult, he argued) did not prevent him from quoting Roosevelt more than one hundred times while he was in office. Clearly Kennedy did not adopt the FDR exemplar in the in toto sense described above. In fact he defeated Hubert Humphrey, who had taken this position in the primaries. He did, however, employ the exemplar in more complex and innovative ways a couple of which can be noted here. He gave a new vigor and excitement to Cold War politics by imitating the martial cadences of the Lincoln exemplar to different purposes. Here was an Alcibiadean president who introduced an element of res publica into the peoples' war aspect of the exemplar. Kennedy's concept of national service, as epitomized in the concept of the Peace Corps, combined an institutional outlet for citizen participation that was more productive than McCarthyism with a vision of a humane pax Americana and its educational, medicinal, and agricultural citizen soldiers. Of course, this new Lincolnianism propelled the administration into a series of frightful international crises, one of which carried the world to the brink of nuclear war.

Kennedy's domestic policies are generally regarded as a failure in part because of a recalcitrant Congress. Yet there was ideological innovation here as well. Both Theodore Sorensen and Arthur Schlesinger had some difficulty describing just what the "New Frontier" was. Schlesinger referred to the New Frontierman "like Rexford Tugwell in another age." JFK himself is reported to have asked, "who is the Raymond Moley of this administration?"[15] But while, like the New Dealers, the New Frontiersman would "try anything," Schlesinger noted a certain disdain for moralism, a coolness, a mood that reflected the belief that things must be done because they were "rational and necessary" rather than because they were "just and right." There were fewer invocations of "the people" although he reminds his readers that these characteristics "should not be exaggerated. . . . In the thirties idealism was sometimes declared, even when it did not exist; in the sixties, it was sometimes deprecated, even when it was the dominant motive."[16]

This peculiarity of tone can, I think, be traced to the Roosevelt exemplar. The New Frontier as ideological mood—if not a program—was instituting aspects of the bourgeois mind in much the same way that the New Deal had done in 1935–36. The difference, of course, is that by 1936 FDR was able to build a successful electoral coalition out of the tilt toward bourgeois apprehensiveness while JFK found a much more ambivalent turn of mind. The New Frontier perfectly reflected the sentiment of the early sixties as the nation was poised between liberal reform and bourgeois eagerness. Kennedy attempted to appeal to both. He promised to get the country "moving again"; he promised to restore America's sense of "historic purpose." He encased both in the Rooseveltian imagery of pioneering, carefully noting that the motto of the frontier was not " 'Every man for himself' but 'All for the common cause.' " And the New Frontier in power continued to straddle. There were tax cuts for business to get the country moving again and liberal reforms. JFK had his Jacksonian moment against U.S. Steel but there was much talk about the New Economics and the need for a new "qualitative" liberalism. The president shows appreciation for the delicate nature of this ideological balance in his comment: "I go to the Chamber of Commerce and talk about what we are doing for business—and they sit on their hands. I go to the UAW and warn them about the necessity for restraint—and they cheer every word. . . . It's all political and emotional."[17]

It is impossible to tell if the civil rights question and/or the pursuit of detente would have pulled Kennedy away from the balance he had struck in 1960 or if his brother would have created a new Jacksonianism in 1968. In any case, it was Johnson who held responsibility for this uncertain legacy and it was Johnson who perhaps more than any president since FDR pursued that exemplar in his own time. There are enormous differences of course between 1965 and 1933 but the first 100 days of the Johnson administration show many of the same features of the Jeffersonian Roosevelt. There was the same flurry of activity, the same chaotic planning, that corresponded to the early FDR years. George Reedy reports the casual furiousness of a Johnson demanding a speech and a program on a problem that attracted his interest. There was that redefinition of equality of opportunity, the same reopening and resigning of a new social contract. There was that same conception of a battle to be won on all fronts at once. What politician in our own historical moment would speak of a "total victory" over poverty? But most significant of all were the immediate growth of Jeffersonian structures, some anticipated, some unintended, many tolerated by sufferance. And, of course, there is the story of their same collapse and dismemberment and the same survival of Hamiltonian remnants in Medicaid, Medicare, and Social Security legislation.

War had ended New Deal reform as it had ended progressive reform but Johnson tried (unsuccessfully) to keep both goals alive. Perhaps more than the New Deal, the Great Society had used martial metaphor although clearly the battles were to be carried out on Jeffersonian CAP (Community Action Program) fronts. When Johnson turned to justifying a real war, however, he turned less to the FDR-Lincoln than to the Jefferson-Jackson exemplars. His Chicago 1966 "Nervous Nellie" address cited the 1937 FDR of the quarantine speech and insisted upon a kind of Jeffersonian appeal to reason as an alternative to the fighting. The famous Johns Hopkins speech repeated the accumulated wisdom of Cold War liberalism, which indeed had its Lincolnian aspects, but asserted that the "only path for reasonable men is the path of peaceful settlement." To that end Johnson proposed a very Rooseveltian economic program for reformed aggressors, one that would "dwarf even our TVA." The New Deal imagery was vivid and apparently heartfelt ("a dam built across a great river," "the sight of healthy children in a classroom," "an end to the bondage of material misery") but it could not be merged easily with the determination necessary to wage a war. [18]

The Roosevelt exemplar involved hermeneutic interpretation of three presidents and, as were argued, drew upon a fourth. In the Nixon administration one sees for the first time since FDR elements of an attempt to create a different combination. This new arrangement is not entirely clear in part because of the enigmatic qualities of Nixon as a regime actor and the difficulties entailed in combining the exemplars themselves. Nixon appears to have been psychologically driven by his childhood poverty and provincial status. On occasion he would speak favorably about the legacy of the New Deal ("my father thought he [FDR] was doing something about the Depression") but in general his Horatio Alger self-image turned him against the New Deal—so much so, in fact, that the most common positive orientation he offered toward Roosevelt as an exemplar seems to be related to his assessment of the president's tactical skills. For instance, he privately told aides before his 1968 inaugural that part of the secret of FDR's success lay in the fact that he would "kick the hell out of someone else and tell the American people they're great."[19] There was then a natural Jacksonianism in Nixon's basic political disposition: a distrust of Eastern elites, a hatred of the power derived from privilege, an empathy for an America as a nation of villagers, a belief in the liberating force of capitalism. As we noted, FDR had taken these sensibilities and pushed them in social democratic directions. Even JFK, Nixon's bitter rival, had carefully managed to sustain at least a part of that orientation. Perhaps it was because of Nixon's generational status as postwar politician (as George Will suggests),[20] perhaps it was his experience as a minor New Deal apparatchik (although Johnson's similar experience did not have this effect), perhaps it was simply the nature of local political opportunities that led Nixon to so firmly reject the Roosevelt interpretation of Jacksonianism. Significantly, the Republicans had finally developed their own counterpart to Jacksonian dispositions in the early postwar period. Anti-communism had all the elements of the Jacksonian appeal (the communists and their sympathizers were the elites) and it held the possibility as well of deconstructing the New Deal on these antielitist grounds. It was in this environment that Nixon flourished as a politician. The hyperbole of this era seemed unbounded, and Nixon is probably correct when he contends that his senatorial prosecution of Hiss sealed his fate with the American left.

Nixon then became the Jacksonian on the Eisenhower ticket, the point man for these sentiments as Ike pursued the center and vaguely solidified the Hamiltonian aspects of the New Deal. In the years between 1960 and 1968 Nixon searched for new exemplars only to return to Jacksonianism again with the concept of the "silent majority." His appreciation of the 1936 FDR in strategic terms was direct, his interpretation shrewd and inventive. He is reported to have said that Roosevelt understood that "in order to have friends you must have enemies." Nixon has been analyzed psychologically enough, but it is worth suggesting the intricacy of a psychic identification with exemplars on the basis of the animosities they fostered. But in truth Nixon was more truly a Jacksonian in important respects. FDR's Jacksonian turn seems to have been the result of part pique and part calculation. While Nixon was always anxious to demonstrate his Machiavellianism, he did believe he was developing a more natural Jacksonian coalition. The Roosevelt coalition was assembled by "pandering to bloc votes"—labor, big-city machines, minorities, and the South. By contrast, the new American majority appealed to "national needs that cut across the narrow self-interest of each bloc . . . the needs of the individuals within each of those old blocs to have a rebirth of personal freedom . . ."[21]

But the Nixon years exhibited more than an inverted FDR-Jacksonianism. The Eisenhower administration had almost backed into a Hamiltonian reinterpretation of the New Deal. Nixon saw the possibilities of an explicitly designed Hamiltonian welfare state, a New Deal stripped of Jeffersonian excrescences and managed by an enlightened corporate elite. Nixon's repeated references to Disraeli uncover this orientation, but only in part. For what was Nixon conserving by reform except middle-class entitlements? His critics implied that he was really a Louis Bonaparte but any fascistlike tendencies (such as his studied support of hard-hat violence) seemed to derive more from the Jacksonian element. Disraeli had employed the Tory formula of reaching to the poor for a coalition. Nixon simply reached down to the American middle and to the working class that had been even further converted to embourgeoisment by the turmoil of the sixties. The Nixon years may have represented the fulfillment of the Hamiltonians' dream, but one had to ask (and ask Reagan did in 1976) what were the Nixon conservatives conserving? Alonzo Hamby raises this point: "In many respects, the neoconservatism he would adopt was simply the old liberalism of the 1940s and 1950s, as espoused by Truman or Kennedy at the working level. . . ."[22]

Still, with all these caveats noted, the systematic transformation of the New Deal, bereft of Jeffersonian impulses, consciously restricted to the middle class and administered by a sober corporate elite was the reformer's nightmare come true even if the Nixon critics could never admit that it was their own formulation that was at its center. Of course, Hamilton has never been completely without effective challengers in the American political tradition and consequently many of the rationalizing initiatives were never fully completed. Moreover, there was that Jacksonian element, however much turned away from liberal reform, that always contained explosive elements. In foreign policy, however, Nixon was able to bring the Washingtonian-Hamiltonian presidency toward its full potential. The Cold War had already moved America toward a kind of Roman counsel system with the Senate often observing executive actions. Nixon, who did have a new vision of global politics, created an executive-centered foreign policy coalition that promised "a generation of peace" based upon a complex set of stratagems that both the public and Congress were expected not fully to comprehend.

The "breach of faith" not only ended all this ideological innovation but created a focus for an ideological reevaluation for the Washington-Hamilton presidency that Nixon had extracted from the FDR exemplar. But the Ford-Carter presidencies showed an independently conceived effort to intuit aspects of a Jeffersonianism that occasionally were pre-Rooseveltian, at least in their sensibility. The Ford presidency was so short lived, so encrusted with the Nixon apparatchik, so soon beset with a challenge of a newly devised exemplar in Reagan, so limited by Ford's own unreflective Midwestern Republicanism that it ideologically collapsed more naturally than almost any other administration. But the central ideological idea of the Ford years, if there was one, involved grasping upon the theme of the president as a national healer. Lincoln had, of course, pursued this concept in his second inaugural, but despite the Black Easter Lincoln tradition of interpretation, it must be noted that he had made the effort after half a million people had died. Nixon raised the theme of lowering voices early in his first term but his own kind of Jacksonianism never permitted it as a more than rhetorical flourish. Ford, set in a position determined by Machiavellian fate, at least was in a position to credibly develop the concept.

It was Jimmy Carter, however, who took his own version of this theme through the primaries and attempted to create from it a new Jeffersonian conception of the presidency. His presidency involved an intriguing search for a new kind of liberalism, at least partially independent of FDR's national Jefferson, that included an appreciation of the delicate nature of caring (derived in part from his religious conviction) along with an appreciation for the hidden potential still left in American culture. There was also a belief, clearly felt, that Americans were threatened by a corruption of the spirit that had to be confronted. As is almost invariably the case, the malaise of which Carter spoke was in his own heart as well, but his efforts to explain symptoms and search for solutions left Americans puzzled and not a little angry.

There were, of course other factors that prevented the success of his presidency as well, most notably Carter's own penchant for engineering as social engineering and his failure to find an apparatchik that he could mold or at least use the way FDR did. But most Jeffersonian of all was Carter's foreign policy, his most glaring failure, a failure all the more glaring because he seemed not to be forgiven by the American people. The Carter foreign policy was republican in ways that Americans had not seen since Wilson and perhaps since Jefferson's administration itself. Involved was not just the emphasis on human rights and the persistence at Camp David, but the general belief that American foreign policy could and had to be exceptional just as the country itself was. A foreign policy based upon peace, reason, and a sense of justice was Jefferson's vision— and Carter's. But as Jefferson had to contend with a European war so had Carter to face the consequences of Iran and Afghanistan. The problems associated with America held hostage were the same as that of the Embargo Act. Henry Adams's assessment of the fall of Jefferson describes the same fate that befell Carter: the administration "which had made peace a passion could lead to no better result than had been reached by the barbarous system which made war a duty. . . . Jefferson's popularity vanished, and the labored fabric of his reputation fell in sudden and general ruin."[23]

Ironically, it was Ronald Reagan who returned to the Roosevelt exemplar. Critics have long fumed over the president's repeated references to FDR but it was Reagan who literally copied, in a direct inverted sense, Roosevelt's use of Jackson in 1936. FDR had appealed to bourgeois apprehensiveness; Reagan appealed to the other frame of the same mind, eagerness. The positions of both, of course, were encased in the language of freedom. Roosevelt had spoken of the "princes of property" who would "gang up" against the people's liberties as they sought the "restoration of their self power." Reagan as early as 1964, when he established himself as a presidential aspirant, contended that the very essence of self-government was under threat from those elites who referred to "the free men and women of this country as masses." FDR had suggested that economic royalists were in league with foreign dictators; Reagan in "The Speech" spoke of elites who would "make a deal" with "slave masters."[24] But both men were appealing to class sentiment: FDR, the concern about economic security; Reagan, the concern about economic advancement. FDR's "forgotten man" was at the bottom of the economic pyramid; Reagan's forgotten American was a suburbanite "working sixty hours a week to support his family and being heavily taxed for the benefit of someone else." They were the same men often literally, and for both, FDR and Reagan had promised a "rendezvous with destiny."

There was more in 1936 to FDR's appeal than economic security, although it is hard not to overemphasize Roosevelt's class appeal; and there was more in Reagan's appeal as well. All the attributes of the Jacksonian leader that Marvin Meyers described were called forth by FDR and now again by Reagan: a new birth (this one capitalistic rather than social democratic); a movement led by a leader whom people loved whatever faults might be exposed; an enemy that was implacable but beatable because the people had finally risen. But it must also be remembered that the same grip on the American mind that seemed viselike in 1936 fell away abruptly in 1938 as it had done in 1840. For the American middle, unless conditions change radically, is in essence still of two minds. Apprehensiveness, as Tocqueville argued, is a class condition and to a great extent in America it is a national one as well. There will come a point—if we have not already reached it—at which the Jacksonian army will refuse to advance and then will disperse, awaiting another call from another general.

There are interpretations of the FDR exemplar not yet tried or deserving of renewed efforts, and there is also the possibility of recovering interpretations of exemplars before the Rooseveltian interpretation. But to the extent to which the exemplary presidency of Franklin Roosevelt represents the exemplary presidency in general as a mode of governance, future presidents will indeed always remain the children of FDR however much they seem to reject their father. There is of course another possibility, one raised by one of FDR's own exemplars. Lincoln once spoke of a person of the future who saw "no distinction in adding story to story, upon monuments of fame, erected to the memory of others" and who scorned "to tread in the footsteps of *any* predecessor, however illustrious." And it is in this sense that Americans would do well to appreciate the exemplary presidency.

Notes

Chapter 1: Exemplary Governance

1 Franklin Delano Roosevelt, "Is There a Jefferson on the Horizon?" *New York Evening World* (December 3, 1925), reprinted in Basil Rauch, ed., *The Roosevelt Reader* (New York: Rinehart, 1957), pp. 43–47; Claude Bowers, *Jefferson and Hamilton* (Boston: Houghton Mifflin, 1925).

2 William E. Leuchtenburg, "The Achievement of the New Deal," in *Fifty Years Later: The New Deal Evaluated*, ed. Harvard Sitkoff (Philadelphia: Temple University Press, 1985), p. 211.

3 Herbert Croly, "The Great Jeffersonian Joke," *New Republic*, June 9, 1926.

4 FDR, "Is There a Jefferson on the Horizon?" p. 47.

5 See Rexford Tugwell, *In Search of Roosevelt* (Cambridge: Harvard University Press, 1972), chap. 4; Raymond Moley, *After Seven Years* (New York: Harper, 1939), chap. 8; Frank Friedel, *Franklin Roosevelt: Launching the New Deal* (Boston: Little, Brown, 1973), pp. 60–82; Arthur Schlesinger, Jr., *The Coming of the New Deal* (Boston: Houghton Mifflin, 1958), pp. 583–88; Richard S. Kirkendall, "FDR and the Service Intellectual," *Mississippi Valley Review* 49 (December 1962): 456–71.

6 Howard Zinn, ed., *New Deal Thought* (Indianapolis: Bobbs-Merrill, 1966), p. xxviii; James MacGregor Burns, *Roosevelt: The Lion and the Fox* (New York: Harcourt, Brace, 1956), p. 475.

7 Arthur Schlesinger, Jr., *The Politics of Upheaval* (Boston: Houghton Mifflin, 1960), p. 647; Louis Hartz, *The Liberal Tradition in America* (New York: Harcourt, Brace, 1955), p. 262.

8 Burns, *Roosevelt: The Lion and the Fox*, p. 331.

9 Examples include Edward S. Corwin's classic, *The President: Office and Powers* (New York: New York University Press, 1957); Joseph E. Kallenbach, *The American Chief Executive* (New York: Harper and Row, 1966); and Richard Pious, *The American Presidency* (New York: Basic Books, 1966).

10 Clinton Rossiter, *The American Presidency* (New York: Harcourt, Brace, 1960); Robert S. Hirschfield, "The Power of the Contemporary Presidency," in *The Power of the Presidency*, ed. Hirschfield (New York: Aldine, 1982), pp. 317–35. Also see Robert Gilmour, "The Institutionalized Presidency: A Conceptual Clarification," in *The Presidency in Contemporary Context*, ed. Norman C. Thomas (New York: Dodd, Mead, 1975).

11 This perspective is probably the dominant approach to the presidency. Richard Neustadt, *Presidential Power* (New York: Wiley, 1980), has been especially influential. Textbooks adopting this approach include Thomas Cronin, *The State of the Presidency* (Boston: Little, Brown, 1975); Erwin Hargrove, *The Power of the Modern Presidency* (New York: Knopf, 1974). Also see James MacGregor Burns, *Presidential Government* (Boston: Houghton, Mifflin, 1965); Godfrey Hodson, *All Things to All Men* (New York: Simon and Schuster, 1980); George C. Edwards, *Presidential Influence on Congress* (San Francisco: Freeman, 1980); Lee Seligman, "Gauging the Public Response to Presidential Leadership," *Presidential Studies Quarterly* 10 (Summer 1980): 427–33.

12 James David Barber, *The Presidential Character* (Englewood Cliffs, N.J.: Prentice-Hall, 1972). Major studies of individual presidents from a psychoanalytical perspective include William Bullit and Sigmund Freud, *Thomas Woodrow Wilson* (Boston: Little, Brown, 1967); and Doris Kearns, *Lyndon Johnson and the American Dream* (New York: Harper and Row, 1976); Betty Glad, *Jimmy Carter* (New York: Norton, 1980); Fawn Brody, *Thomas Jefferson: An Intimate History* (New York: Norton, 1974) and *Richard M. Nixon: The Shaping of His Character* (New York: Norton, 1981).

13 Larry Berman, *Planning a Tragedy: The Americanization of the War in Vietnam* (New York: Norton, 1982); Maeva Marcus, *Truman and the Steel Seizure Case* (New York: Columbia University Press, 1977); Leslie Gelb and Richard Betts, *The Irony of Vietnam: The System Worked* (Washington, D.C.: Brookings, 1979); Ruth Morgan, *The President and Civil Rights: Policy-Making by Executive Order* (New York: St. Martin's, 1970).

14 See the essays by Edwards and Wayne in George C. Edwards III and Stephen J. Wayne, eds., *Studying the Presidency* (Knoxville: University of Tennessee Press, 1983).

15 Two recent collections of American political thought illustrate the significance of presidential contributions. Kenneth Dolbeare, *American Political Thought* (Chatham, N.J.: Chatham House, 1984) includes thirty-one entries, six of which are selections of American presidents (Adams, Madison, Jefferson, Lincoln, Wilson, Franklin Roosevelt). Michael B. Levy, ed., *Political Thought in America* (Homewood, Ill.: Dorsey, 1982) contains seventy-seven entries, twenty-nine from speeches and writings of presidents (Adams, Jefferson, Madison, Jackson, Lincoln, Wilson, Hoover, Franklin Roosevelt, Harry Truman, Lyndon Johnson). Also see Morton Frisch and

Richard Stevens, eds., *The Political Thought of American Statesmen* (Itasca, Ill.: Peacock, 1973) for an anthology that attempts to focus upon the theoretical achievements of American politicians, and Philip Abbott and Michael Riccards, eds., *Reflections in American Political Thought* (New York: Chandler, 1973).

16 Kenneth Thompson, *The President and the Public Philosophy* (Baton Rouge: Louisiana State University Press, 1981), p. 4.

17 Robert Bellah, "Civil Religion in America," reprinted in *Beyond Belief* (New York: Harper and Row, 1970), pp. 168–89; Dante Germino, *The Inaugural Addresses of American Presidents: The Public Philosophy and Rhetoric* (Lanham, N.Y.: University Press of America, 1984), p. 36.

18 James Ceaser, Glen Thurow, Jeffrey Tulis, and Joseph Bessette, "The Rise of the Rhetorical Presidency," *Presidential Studies Quarterly* (1981): 158–72.

19 Hartz, *The Liberal Tradition in America.* Hartz identifies the liberal consensus as a commitment to individualism, progress, rationalism, constitutionalism, and capitalism.

20 See Bert A. Rockman, *The Leadership Question* (New York: Praeger, 1984), pp. 49–59; and Erwin C. Hargrove and Michael Nelson, *Presidents, Politics, and Policy* (Baltimore: Johns Hopkins University Press, 1984), pp. 59–65, for the problems facing a president on this point.

21 Donald J. Devine, *The Political Culture of the United States* (Boston: Little, Brown, 1972); Seymour Martin Lipset, *The First New Nation*, rev. ed. (New York: Norton, 1979), pt. 2; Samuel P. Huntington, *American Politics and the Promise of Disharmony* (Cambridge: Harvard University Press, 1981), chap. 2; Charles Elder and Roger Cobb, *The Political Uses of Symbols* (New York: Longmans, 1983), pp. 85–112.

22 Peter Karsten, *Patriot Heroes in England and America: Political Symbolism and Changing Values Over Three Centuries* (Madison: University of Wisconsin Press, 1978); Ralph Ketchum, *Presidents Above Party: The First American Presidency, 1789–1829* (Chapel Hill: University of North Carolina Press, 1984).

23 Gary Wills, *Cincinnatus: George Washington and the Enlightenment* (Garden City, N.Y.: Doubleday, 1984); Karsten, *Patriot Heroes*, p. 97.

24 William Ober Clough, ed., *Intellectual Origins of American National Thought* (New York: Corinth, 1961), p. 219.

25 Wills, *Cincinnatus*, p. 115.

26 Theodore Roosevelt, "The Autobiography" in *The Works of Theodore Roosevelt*, vol. 20 (New York, 1925), p. 416; Woodrow Wilson, *Leaders of Men*, ed. T. H. Vail Motter (Princeton: Princeton University Press, 1952); Richard Nixon, *Leaders* (New York: Warner, 1982); Jeffrey Tulis, "On Presidential Character," in *The Presidency in the Constitutional Order*, ed. Joseph W. Bessette and Jeffrey Tullis (Baton Rouge: Louisiana State

University Press, 1981), p. 310. Also see Erwin C. Hargrove, *Presidential Leadership; Personality and Political Style* (New York: Macmillan, 1966), who defines presidential leadership models in terms of "ego integration" (p. 3).

27 Wilson, *Leaders of Men*, p. 23.
28 James David Barber, *The Presidential Character* (Englewood Cliffs, N.J.: Prentice Hall, 1985), pp. 77ff.
29 Karsten, *Patriot Heroes*, p. 88. Jefferson, in his first inaugural, spoke of "our first and great revolutionary character," whose services to the republican cause "entitled him to first place in his country's love," *The Life and Selected Writings of Thomas Jefferson*, ed. Adrienne Koch and William Penden (New York: Modern Library, 1944), p. 325.
30 See George Fitshugh, "Bonaparte, Cromwell, and Washington," *DeBow's Review* 28 (February, 1860): 139–54. Washington was also used as a symbol for American profascists: see John P. Diggins, *Mussolini and Fascism: The View from America* (Princeton: Princeton University Press, 1972), p. 118.
31 William Leuchtenburg, *In The Shadow of FDR: From Harry Truman to Ronald Reagan* (Ithaca: Cornell University Press, 1983).
32 I use the term in a limited and analogical sense especially as described by Hans-Georg Gadamer, *Truth and Method*, 2nd ed. (New York: Seabury, 1975), pp. 263–64.
33 Calvin Coolidge, *Have Faith in Massachusetts* (Boston: Houghton Mifflin, 1919), p. 186.
34 Calvin Coolidge, *America's Need for Education* (Boston: Houghton Mifflin, 1925), p. 35. For an analysis of Coolidge on this and related points see Thomas B. Silver, "Coolidge and the Rhetoric of Revolution," in *Rhetoric and American Statesmanship*, ed. Glen E. Thurow and Jeffrey D. Wallin (Durham: Carolina Academic Press, 1984), pp. 111–22. Also see James David Barber's analysis of Coolidge's classicism as autobiographically based upon his experiences at Amherst as an undergraduate, *Politics by Humans* (Durham, N.C.: Duke University Press, 1988), pp. 8–77.
35 Leuchtenburg, *In the Shadow of FDR*, p. 187.
36 See the Binghamton, Buffalo, and Jamestown speeches for FDR's attempt to revive the memory of progressive reform, *Public Papers and Addresses of Franklin D. Roosevelt*, 13 vols. (New York: Macmillian, 1938), (1928–1932). On the use of Jefferson in the New Deal see Merrill D. Peterson, *The Jeffersonian Image in the American Mind* (New York: Oxford University Press, 1960), pp. 355–76. The appropriation of the Lincoln exemplar was probably even more self-conscious; the effort included the addition of two Lincoln biographers as speechwriters. See Alfred Haworth Jones, *Roosevelt's Image Brokers* (Port Washington, N.Y.: Kennikat Press, 1974) and chapter 8 of this volume.
37 The quest for the "real" Jefferson, or any of the presidential exemplars, is

not irrelevant to its use in American political culture. There are interpretations that so violate principles that they are dismissible. On the other hand, the relationship between the historical Jefferson and patina of Jefferson as symbol is not easily separable. As Peterson argues, it is the ambiguities and contradictions in the historical Jefferson that creates in American history the "protracted litigation, negotiations and hearings, trials and appeals in endless number, on Jefferson" (*The Jeffersonian Image in the American Mind*, p. 446).

38 Marvin Meyers, ed., *The Mind of the Founder* (Hanover, N.H.: University Press of New England, 1981), p. 350.

39 Henry Cabot Lodge, *Alexander Hamilton* (1898; reprint, New York: Chelsea, 1980), p. 90.

40 *The Federalist Papers*, ed. Clinton Rossiter (New York: New American Library, 1961), no. 67, p. 407.

41 *The Federalist Papers*, no. 68, p. 414; no. 70, p. 423; no. 72, pp. 437, 438.

42 Michael Riccards, *A Republic If You Can Keep It: The Foundation of the American Presidency, 1700–1800* (Westport, Conn.: Greenwood Press, 1987), p. xiii.

43 Peterson, *The Jeffersonian Image in the American Mind*, p. 69.

44 Arthur Schlesinger, Jr., *The Age of Jackson* (Boston: Little, Brown, 1945).

45 Edward Pessen reviews the findings of the "entrepreneurial" school in *Jacksonian America* (Homewood, Ill.: Dorsey, 1969), pp. 384–93.

46 J. B. S. Hardin, ed., *Rendezvous with Destiny: Addresses and Opinions of Franklin Delano Roosevelt* (New York: Dryden, 1944), p. 85.

47 See Andrew A. King and Floyd Douglas Anderson, "Nixon, Agnew and the Silent Majority: A Case Study in the Rhetoric of Polarization," *Western Journal of Speech Communication* 35 (Fall, 1971): 243–55, and the 1981 State of the Union message in which Reagan focused upon the "troubles" caused by the "mass of regulations imposed upon the shopkeeper, the farmer, the craftsman, professionals . . ." (*A Time for Choosing: The Speeches of Ronald Reagan, 1961–1982* [Chicago: Regnery, 1983], p. 252).

48 Marvin Meyers, *The Jacksonian Persuasion: Politics and Belief* (Stanford: Stanford University Press, 1957). Also see John William Ward, *Andrew Jackson: Symbol for an Age* (New York: Oxford University Press, 1962).

49 Andrew Jackson, "Farewell Address" in *Messages and Papers of the Presidents, 1789–1897*, 20 vols. (New York: Bureau of National Literature, 1896), 3:305.

50 On this aspect of Lincolnian discourse, see Glen E. Thurow, *Abraham Lincoln and American Political Religion* (Albany: State University of New York Press, 1976) as well as Harry Jaffa's classic, *The Crisis of the House Divided* (New York: Doubleday, 1959).

51 Two critical accounts emphasize this point: Gary Wills, *Inventing America* (New York: Vintage, 1979), pp. xiv–xxiii; and Edgar Lee Masters's eccen-

tric but undeservedly neglected *Lincoln the Man* (New York: Dodd, Mead, 1931).

52 See John Milton Cooper, Jr., *The Warrior and the Priest* (Cambridge: Harvard University Press, 1983), pp. 159–60, 306–7.

Chapter 2: The Story Teller and the Theorist

1 *Public Papers and Addresses of Franklin D. Roosevelt*, 13 vols. (New York: Macmillan, 1938), p. 798.

2 *The State Papers and Other Public Writings of Herbert Hoover*, ed. William Starr Myers, 2 vols. (Garden City, N.Y.: Doubleday, 1934), 2: 282.

3 Marriner Eccles, *Beckoning Frontiers* (New York, 1951), p. 95.

4 *Public Papers, FDR* (1928–1932), pp. 684–92.

5 *Public Papers, FDR* (1933), p. 368.

6 Arthur Link, "What Happened to the Progressive Movement in the 1920's?" *American Historical Review* (1959).

7 Frank Freidel, *Franklin D. Roosevelt: The Ordeal* (Boston: Little, Brown, 1954), p. 250.

8 *Public Papers, FDR* (1928–1932), p. 20.

9 Samuel I. Rosenman, *Working with Roosevelt* (New York: Harper and Row, 1952), p. 52.

10 *Public Papers, FDR* (1928–1932), pp. 30–31.

11 Ibid., p. 37.

12 Ibid., pp. 29–30.

13 Ibid., p. 43.

14 Ibid., pp. 40–41, 44.

15 Ibid., p. 59.

16 Herbert Hoover, *American Individualism* (Garden City, N.Y.: Doubleday, 1923), p. 24.

17 Ibid., pp. 7–8.

18 *Public Papers, FDR* (1928–1932), p. 68.

19 Ibid., pp. 68–69.

20 Hoover, *American Individualism*, p. 9.

21 *Public Papers, FDR* (1928–1932), pp. 70, 72.

22 Eliot A. Rosen, *Hoover, Roosevelt, and the Brains Trust* (New York: Columbia University Press, 1977), p. 40.

23 Martin L. Fausold, *The Presidency of Herbert Hoover* (Lawrence: University Press of Kansas, 1985), p. 25; David Burner, *The Politics of Provincialism* (New York: Knopf, 1968), p. 207; Joan Hoff Wilson, *Herbert Hoover, Forgotten Progressive* (Boston: Little, Brown, 1975).

24 William Appleman Williams, *The Contours of American History* (Cleveland: World, 1959), p. 426.

25 Ellis W. Hawley, "Herbert Hoover and American Corporativism, 1929–

1933," in *The Hoover Presidency: A Reappraisal*, ed. Martin L. Fausold and George T. Mazuzan (Albany: State University of New York, 1974), p. 102.

26 Hoover, *American Individualism*, pp. 1–2, 6–7, 12.

27 Ibid., pp. 8–9.

28 Ibid., pp. 24, 30.

29 Ibid., pp. 53–54, 59–60.

30 Ibid., pp. 37, 43.

31 Leon Samson, *Toward a United Front* (New York, 1935), p. 17.

32 Hoover, *American Individualism*, pp. 39–40.

33 Ibid., p. 32.

34 Ibid., pp. 28–30.

35 Ibid., p. 43.

36 George Santayana, *Dominations and Powers* (New York: Scribner's, 1951), p. 311.

37 Robert H. Zeiger, "Labor, Progressivism and Herbert Hoover in the 1920's," *Wisconsin Magazine of History* 63 (Spring, 1975): 206.

38 *State Papers, Hoover*, 1: 490; David E. Hamilton, "Herbert Hoover and the Great Drought of 1930," *Journal of American History* 68 (March 1982): 850–75.

39 Herbert Hoover, *Memoirs of Herbert Hoover*, 2 vols. (New York: Macmillan, 1952), 2: 200; *New York Times*, August 12, 1928.

40 Kent Scofield, "The Public Image of Herbert Hoover in the 1928 Campaign," *Mid-America* 51 (October 1969): 285.

41 Page Smith, *As a City Upon a Hill* (New York: Knopf, 1966), pp. 206–7.

42 Cited in Leo Marx, *The Machine in the Garden* (Oxford: Oxford University Press, 1964), p. 138. Jefferson's commitment to this pastoral vision was itself ambiguous; see Richard K. Matthews, *The Radical Politics of Thomas Jefferson* (Lawrence: University of Kansas Press, 1984), pp. 48–50.

43 Herbert Hoover, *The New Day: Campaign Speeches of Herbert Hoover* (Stanford: Stanford University Press, 1928), p. 50.

44 *New York Herald Tribune*, August 22, 1928.

45 Hoover, *The New Day*, pp. 59–60.

46 Ibid., p. 60.

47 Ibid.

48 Ibid.

49 Ibid., p. 85.

50 Ibid., p. 142.

51 Ibid., pp. 110–11.

52 Hoover, *Memoirs*, p. 202.

53 Fausold, *The Presidency of Herbert Hoover*, p. 29.

54 Hoover, *The New Day*, p. 155.

55 Ibid., p. 162.

56 Ibid., p. 157.

Chapter 3: Is There a Jefferson on the Horizon?

1 Martin L. Fausold, *The Presidency of Herbert C. Hoover* (Lawrence: University Press of Kansas, 1985), pp. 72–77; Albert U. Romasco, *The Poverty of Abundance* (New York: Oxford University Press, 1965), pp. 24–38.

2 *The State Papers and Other Public Writings of Herbert Hoover*, ed. William Starr Myers, 2 vols. (Garden City, N.Y.: Doubleday, 1934), 1: 500–504.

3 Herbert C. Hoover, *The Memoirs of Herbert C. Hoover*, vol. 2 (New York: Macmillan, 1952).

4 *State Papers, Hoover*, 2:194.

5 Ibid. 1:569.

6 Ibid., pp. 470, 264, 250.

7 *Public Papers and Addresses of Franklin D. Roosevelt*, 13 vols. (New York: Macmillan, 1938), (1928–1932), pp. 624–27.

8 Ibid.

9 *The Essays of William Graham Sumner*, ed. Albert Galloway Keller and Maurice R. Davies, 2 vols. (New Haven: Yale University Press, 1934), 1:171. Raymond Moley accepts responsibility for the phrase but appears oblivious to the nature of its ideological source (*After Seven Years* [New York: Harper, 1939], pp. 9–10).

10 See Rexford Tugwell, *The Brains Trust* (New York: Viking, 1969), pp. 49–50, for the context of Smith's reaction.

11 *Public Papers, FDR*, (1928–1932), p. 628.

12 Ibid., pp. 628–29.

13 Ibid., p. 631.

14 Ibid., pp. 639–40.

15 Ibid., p. 645.

16 Ibid., p. 646.

17 Ibid.

18 Tugwell, *The Brains Trust*, pp. 103–5, 109, 127.

19 *Public Papers, FDR* (1928–1932), pp. 646–47.

20 Ibid., pp. 648–50.

21 Ibid., pp. 672, 678.

22 Herbert Hoover, *Addresses Upon the American Road* (New York: Scribner's, 1938), pp. 76, 46.

23 Arthur Schlesinger, Jr., *The Crisis of the Old Order* (Boston: Houghton Mifflin, 1957), p. 426; Rexford Tugwell, *In Search of Roosevelt* (Cambridge, Mass.: Harvard University Press, 1978), pp. 172–80. Also see Moley, *After Seven Years*, pp. 57–60. Elliot A. Rosen argues that the persistent contentions that FDR read a speech he did not fully understand is the result of the "country squire" thesis about the candidate's intellect and motivations (*Hoover, Roosevelt, and the Brains Trust* [New York: Columbia University Press, 1977], pp. 357–61).

24 *Public Papers, FDR* (1928–1932), pp. 744–45.

25 Ibid., pp. 747–48.

26 Ibid., p. 746.

27 Ibid., pp. 751–54.

28 Ibid., pp. 745–49.

29 Schlesinger, *The Crisis of the Old Order*, p. 426.

30 *Public Papers, FDR* (1928–1932), pp. 748, 750.

31 Ibid., p. 751.

Chapter 4: The Parade

1   All following citations are from Edmund Wilson, "Inaugural Parade," *New Republic*, March 22, 1933, reprinted in *Travels in Two Democracies* (New York: Harcourt, Brace, 1936), pp. 43–49.

2   Samuel I. Rosenman, *Working with Roosevelt* (New York: Harper and Row, 1952), pp. 89–90.

3   James MacGregor Burns, *Roosevelt: The Lion and the Fox* (New York: Harcourt, Brace, 1956), p. 161.

4   Raymond Moley, *The First New Deal* (New York: Harcourt, Brace, 1966), pp. 99ff.

5   Ibid., p. 98.

6   *The Life and Writings of Abraham Lincoln*, ed. Philip Van Doren Stern (New York: Modern Library, 1940), p. 656.

7   *Public Papers and Addresses of Franklin D. Roosevelt*, 13 vols. (New York: Macmillan, 1938), (1933), pp. 11–16.

8   Ibid., p. 16.

9   William Lemke to Farmers Union Convention (1933), in William Leuchtenburg, *Franklin D. Roosevelt and the New Deal* (New York: Harper and Row, 1965), p. 44.

10 Arthur Ekirch, Jr., *Ideologies and Utopias: The Impact of the New Deal on American Thought* (Chicago: University of Chicago Press, 1969), chap. 2.

11 Gary Wills, *Inventing America* (Garden City, N.Y.: Doubleday, 1978).

12 Hannah Arendt, *On Revolution* (New York: Viking, 1965), p. 238.

13 George Santayana, *Dominations and Powers* (New York: Scribner's, 1951), p. 311.

14 Ralph Waldo Emerson, "Experience," in *Ralph Waldo Emerson: Selected Prose and Poetry*, ed. Reginald L. Cook (New York: Holt, Rinehart and Winston, 1950), p. 253.

15 Robert N. Bellah et al., *Habits of the Heart* (New York: Harper and Row, 1985), pp. 292ff.

16 Herbert Croly, *The Promise of American Life* (New York: Capricorn, 1964), pp. 22, 42–43.

17 See chapter 9 in this volume for more discussion of this point.

18 *Public Papers, FDR* (1933), p. 518.

19 Ibid., p. 418.

20 Ibid., p. 342.

21 Ibid., p. 380.

22 Ibid., p. 491.

23 Ibid., p. 342.

24 Ibid., pp. 418–19.

25 T. V. Smith, "The New Deal as a Cultural Phenomenon," in *Ideological Differences and World Order* (New Haven: Yale University Press, 1949), p. 209.

26 *Public Papers, FDR* (1933), p. 342.

27 Walter Lippmann, "On Planned Planning," April 26, 1934, in *Interpretations: 1933–1935* (New York: Macmillan, 1936), pp. 253–55.

Chapter 5: Oh, Shade of Jefferson

1 James MacGregor Burns, *Roosevelt: The Lion and the Fox* (New York: Harcourt, Brace, 1956), p. 402; Howard Zinn, "The Grateful Society," *Columbia University Forum* 10 (Spring 1967): 28–32. Also see Paul K. Conkin's more complex assessment, *The New Deal* (New York: Crowell, 1967), pp. 7–21.

2 For example, see Herbert Agar, *The Peoples' Choice* (Boston: Houghton Mifflin, 1933) and *The Pursuit of Happiness* (Boston: Houghton Mifflin, 1938); Heywood Broun, "Shades of Jefferson," *New Republic*, July 29, 1938; Charles Beard, "Jefferson in America Now," *Yale Review* 25 (July 1935); Broadus Mitchell, "Jefferson and Hamilton Today," *Virginia Quarterly Review* 10 (July 1934). Jefferson, of course, provided the exemplar of criticism of the New Deal as well; see Samuel B. Pettingill, *Jefferson: The Forgotten Man* (New York: America's Future, 1938) and Alpheus T. Mason's review of Liberty League ideology in "Business Organized as Power: The New Imperium as Imperio," *American Political Science Review* 44 (June 1950). For a valuable general discussion see Peterson, *The Jeffersonian Image in the American Mind* (New York: Oxford University Press, 1960), pp. 355–76. Communist interpretations of Jefferson are discussed below.

3 Robert K. Gooch, "Reconciling Jeffersonian Principles with the New Deal," *Southwestern Social Science Quarterly* 16 (June 1935): 4.

4 Herbert Hoover, *Addresses Upon the American Road: 1933–1938* (New York: Scribner's, 1938), pp. 122–23.

5 Hannah Arendt, *On Revolution* (New York: Viking, 1965), p. 235.

6 Ibid., p. 238.

7 Ibid., pp. 258–59.

8 William E. Leuchtenburg, *Franklin D. Roosevelt and the New Deal* (New York: Harper and Row, 1963), p. 122.

9 Robert Sherwood, *Roosevelt and Hopkins* (New York: Harper, 1948), p. 57.

10 William E. Leuchtenburg, "The Achievement of the New Deal," in *Fifty Years Later: The New Deal Evaluated,* ed. Harvard Sitkoff (Philadelphia: Temple University Press, 1985), p. 165.

11 Ibid., pp. 163–64; Jane De Hart Mathews, "Arts and the People: The New Deal Quest for Cultural Democracy," *Journal of American History* 62 (September 1975): 319–20; Jerre Mangione, *The Dream and the Deal: The Federal Writers Project, 1935–1943* (Boston: Little, Brown, 1972).

12 Sherwood, *Roosevelt and Hopkins,* p. 60.

13 Studs Terkel, *Hard Times* (New York: Random House, 1970), pp. 435, 450–51. It is useful to compare these accounts with the passivity of the unemployed as revealed in depression studies. For example, Paul F. Lazarfeld, Marie Jahoda, and Hans Zeisel's description of Marienthal as "die müde Gemeinschaft" (the weary community) could have been applied cross-nationally (*Marienthal: The Sociography of an Unemployed Community* [Chicago: University of Chicago Press, 1971]). See John A. Garraty, *Unemployment in History* (New York: Harper and Row, 1978), pp. 172–87, for a review.

14 Sherwood, *Roosevelt and Hopkins,* p. 57. Hopkins, of course, could be more expansive in terms of goals in other contexts; Mathews, "Art for the People," p. 324.

15 Mathews, "Art for the People," pp. 322; Hallie Flanagan, "Testimony before HUAC," in *Thirty Years of Treason,* ed. Eric Bentley (New York: Viking, 1971), pp. 3–47; "American Resources in the Arts," in *Art for the Millions,* ed. Francis O'Connor (Greenwich, Conn.: New York Graphic Society, 1973), pp. 43–44. The prints were destroyed or auctioned off in 1941; the largest buyer was Thomas J. Watson of IBM. While "ownership" by the artist of his work might have been said to suggest the "old" conception of the activity, there were signs of new forms of artistic alienation: a concern with production quotas and time-punching rules and some indifference by bureaucrats to the product itself; see O'Connor, *Art for the Millions,* p. 18. When Audrey McMahon later asked easel and graphic artists what became of their works, the frequent reply was, "I was never told" (*The New Deal Art Projects: An Anthology of Memoirs,* ed. Francis O'Connor [Washington, D.C.: Smithsonian Institution Press, 1972], p. 322).

16 Some regarded the Index work as employment for the less talented, a complaint about the programs in general by critics. But Francis Pollock's comment ("I am so eager to have the Index approved since it offers a catch-all for a large number of artists not suitable and useful for any other purpose") while blunt is nonetheless utilitarian; see Lincoln Rothchild, "The Index of American Design of the WPA/FAP," in O'Connor, *The New Deal Art Projects,* p. 179.

17 Walter Quirt, "On Mural Painting," in O'Connor, *Art for the Millions,* p. 79.

18 I rely here upon the reproductions of murals generally from Marlene Park

and Gerald E. Markowitz, eds., *Democratic Vistas: Post Offices and Public Art in the New Deal* (Philadelphia: Temple University Press, 1984).

19 *Public Papers and Addresses of Franklin D. Roosevelt,* 13 vols. (New York: Macmillan, 1938), (1933), p. 419.

20 Stuart Davis, "American Artists' Congress," in O'Connor, *Art for the Millions,* pp. 249–52. Also see the essays by Chet La More, Robert Jay Wolf, Einar Heiberg, Lincoln Rothchild, Hugo Gilbert, and E. Herndon Smith on artists' organizations in the same volume.

21 Elizabeth Olds, "Prints for the Millions," in O'Connor, *Art for the Millions,* pp. 143–44; Holger Cahill, *New Horizons in American Art* (New York: Museum of Modern Art, 1936), pp. 11–12.

22 Paul K. Conkin, *Tomorrow a New World: The New Deal Community Program* (Ithaca: Cornell University Press, 1959), p. 305.

23 Daniel R. Fusfield, *The Economic Thought of Franklin D. Roosevelt and the Origins of the New Deal* (New York: Columbia University Press, 1956), pp. 123–34.

24 Rexford Tugwell, "The Sources of New Deal Reformism," *Ethics* 44 (1954): 276; Franklin D. Roosevelt, "Back to the Land," *American Review of Reviews* 84 (October 1931): 64.

25 See Conkin, *Tomorrow a New World,* pp. 33–34 for congressional reactions. Conkin also cites doubters, one of the most bitter of whom was Congressman John C. Schafer, who asked: "Are you going to take these poor unemployed city people with their little children, and put them out on the farms where it is sometimes 22 degrees below zero and where the snow is as high as 10 feet deep, and then say that you are going to save them?" (p. 34).

26 Edward S. Shapiro, "Decentralist Intellectuals and the New Deal," *Journal of American History* 58 (1972): 938–57.

27 M. L. Wilson, "New Land-Use Idea: The Place of Subsistence Homesteads," *Journal of Land and Public Utility Economics* 10 (1934): 3–9; "The Place of Subsistence Households in Our National Economy," *Journal of Home Economics* 27 (1935): 227.

28 Rexford Tugwell, quoted in Sidney Baldwin, *Poverty and Politics* (Chapel Hill: University of North Carolina Press, 1968), p. 88.

29 M. L. Wilson, quoted in Schlesinger, *The Coming of the New Deal,* p. 371.

30 Conkin, *Tomorrow a New World,* pp. 305–7.

31 Tugwell, *The Democratic Roosevelt,* pp. 423–24.

32 Conkin, *Tomorrow a New World,* p. 186.

33 Harold Ware and Webster Powell, "Planning for Permanent Poverty: What Subsistence Farming Really Stands For," *Harper's* 170 (1934): 522; Louis Hacker, "Plowing the Farmer Under," *Harper's* 169 (1934): 73.

34 Terkel, *Hard Times,* p. 290.

35 Leuchtenburg, *Franklin D. Roosevelt and the New Deal,* pp. 344–45.

36 David E. Lilienthal, *TVA: Democracy on the March* (New York: Harper and

Row, 1944), pp. 1, 2; Rexford Tugwell, *The Battle for Democracy* (New York, 1935), p. 22; Norman Thomas, quoted in Schlesinger, *The Politics of Upheaval*, p. 180; *Public Papers, FDR* (1933), p. 123.

37 Paul K. Conkin, "Intellectual and Political Roots," in *TVA: Fifty Years of Grass Roots Democracy*, ed. Erwin C. Hargrove and Paul K. Conkin (Urbana: University of Illinois Press, 1983), pp. 3–34. For evidence of FDR's early interest see Frank Freidel, *Franklin D. Roosevelt: Launching the New Deal* (Boston: Little, Brown, 1973), pp. 351–54.

38 Lewis Mumford in *The New Yorker*, June 1941, p. 58.

39 Max Lerner, "Propaganda's Golden Age," *The Nation*, November 11, 1939, pp. 522–24.

41 For a review see Thomas K. McGraw, *Morgan vs. Lilienthal: The Feud within the TVA* (Chicago: Loyola University Press, 1970); also see Davidson's own assessment of the bureaucratic battle and a critique, *The Tennessee*, 2 vols. (New York: Rinehart, 1948), vol. 2, chap. 18.

41 Arthur Morgan, quoted in Erwin C. Hargrove, "The Task of Leadership," in Hargrove and Conkin, *TVA: Fifty Years*, p. 93.

42 Jonathan Mitchell, "Utopia Tennessee Style," *New Republic*, October 18, 1933, p. 272.

43 *Public Papers, FDR* (1934), p. 466. Also see FDR's speeches during his 1934 inspection tour of the valley, especially his remarks at Harrodsburg, Kentucky, addressed to "my fellow pioneers" (ibid., pp. 456–64). For Arthur Morgan's continued support of FDR see Hargrove, "The Task of Leadership," pp. 92–93. Morgan defends his ideas on a script economy in his *The Making of the TVA* (Buffalo, N.Y.: Prometheus, 1974), pp. 58–59; see also his *The Long Road* (Washington: National Home Library, 1936) on the importance of a "new man" for his conception of the TVA.

44 Harcourt Morgan, quoted in Hargrove, "The Task of Leadership," p. 96.

45 Harcourt Morgan, quoted in Philip Selznick, *TVA and the Grass Roots* (Berkeley: University of California Press, 1949), p. 43.

46 Harcourt Morgan, quoted in Hargrove, "The Task of Leadership," p. 97.

47 The "Unofficial Observer," who could be caustic in his portraits of selected New Deal apparatchik, described Lilienthal as "calm, charming, quiet voiced and very disarming in his mode of speech." He was a "terrific worker" who could "couch firm, and even bold, proposals in conciliatory language" (*The New Dealers* [New York: Simon and Schuster, 1934], p. 194). But Arthur Morgan had another view. His dispute with Lilienthal involved a disagreement not between two conceptions of the public interest but "between the public interest and a private interest concealed in the trappings of public interest" (*The Making of the TVA*, p. 171).

48 *The Journals of David E. Lilienthal* (New York: Harper and Row, 1964), pp. 106–7.

49 Lilienthal, *TVA: Democracy*, pp. 2–3.

50 Ibid., p. 27.

51 Ibid., p. 142

52 Ibid., p. 140.

53 Ibid., pp. 147–48; 143–44.

54 Ibid., pp. 144, 81, 87.

55 Ibid., pp. 90–91.

56 Ibid., p. 90.

57 Excerpts from speech (1934), Arthur Morgan, *The Making of the TVA*, pp. 157–58.

58 Davidson, *The Tennessee*, 2: 238.

59 Ibid., p. 256.

60 Ibid., p. 292.

61 Ibid., p. 305.

62 Ibid., pp. 224, 313, 322–33.

63 Hugh S. Johnson, *The Blue Eagle from Egg to Earth* (1935; reprint, New York: Greenwood Press, 1968), p. 316.

64 Frances Perkins, *The Roosevelt I Knew* (New York: Viking, 1946), p. 240.

65 Ibid., p. 206. For a compelling examination of the NRA and its fascist counterparts, see John A. Garraty, "The New Deal, National Socialism and the Great Depression," *American Historical Review* 78 (1973): 907–45.

66 *Public Papers, FDR* (1933), p. 301.

67 Johnson, *The Blue Eagle*, p. 264.

68 Perkins, *The Roosevelt I Knew*, p. 213.

69 Robert H. Zieger, *American Workers, American Unions, 1920–1985* (Baltimore: Johns Hopkins University Press, 1986), pp. 30–31, 26.

70 Peter H. Irons, *The New Deal Lawyers* (Princeton: Princeton University Press, 1982), chap. 10.

71 Zieger, *American Workers*, pp. 40–41.

72 Broadus Mitchell, *Depression Decade* (New York: Harper and Row, 1947), p. 282.

73 Irving Bernstein, *Turbulent Years* (Boston: Houghton Mifflin, 1970), pp. 496–97.

74 See Sidney Fine, *Sitdown: The General Motors Strike of 1936–1937* (Ann Arbor: University of Michigan Press, 1969).

75 Perkins, *The Roosevelt I Knew*, pp. 321–22, also see p. 307. FDR's public statement reveals this same approach; see: *Public Papers, FDR* (1938), pp. 34–36.

76 John Locke, *Two Treatises on Government*, ed. Peter Laslett (New York: New American Library, 1965), p. 312.

77 Perkins, *The Roosevelt I Knew*, p. 325.

78 Harvey Klehr, *The Heyday of American Communism* (New York: Basic Books, 1984), p. 49. Also see James Ford's assertion that "Jeffersonianism"

had been "continued and brought to higher levels in Marxism-Leninism" (p. 211).

79 Irving Howe, *Socialism in America* (New York: Harcourt Brace Jovanovich, 1985).

80 Earl Latham, *The Communist Controversy in Washington* (New York: Atheneum, 1969), p. 74.

81 Nathaniel Weyl, *Treason* (Washington, D.C.: Public Affairs Press, 1950), p. 425. Also see Whittaker Chambers on this point in *Witness* (New York: Random House, 1952), p. 269. Chambers described Hiss as "American as ham and eggs and as indistinguishable as everybody else" in the Ware group (p. 332). Ironically, it was the Communist Party's own popular-front claim that they were "no different" from other Americans that fired the paranoia of the 1940s and 1950s. For if you couldn't tell who was a communist, then the danger seemed all the more great. Of course, the anti-communist investigators knew that the communists really were not like "everybody else."

82 Latham, *Communist Controversy*, pp. 95, 122.

83 Herbert Fuchs: "it seems to me that there is an advantage to the Communists and this is the trap of communism in their own illegality, because as they are a conspiracy and secret, then every member is involved in a kind of trap, potentially a blackmail trap or perhaps only a trap with respect to his sentimental desire not to involve other people in trouble. As soon as he has engaged in one or more violations of the law, he is in a hostage to this conspiracy to which he perhaps altruistically lent himself in the first instance." Quoted in Latham, *Communist Controversy*, p. 146. Elizabeth Bentley, a star congressional witness before Chambers's revelations, told an espionage story part Hollywood and part soap opera in *Out of Bondage* (New York: Devin-Adair, 1951). Remmington seems to have psychologically disintegrated from the masks required for the spy, see Murray Kempton, *Out of Our Time* (New York: Simon and Schuster, 1955), pp. 230, 223–24.

84 Browder estimated that there were 500,000 people in the fronts in 1934; see Klehr, *Heyday*, p. 165. Benjamin Gitlow placed the number at one million in *The Whole of Our Lives* (Boston: Americanist Library, 1948), p. 292.

85 Klehr, *Heyday*, pp. 104–5.

86 Ibid., p. 110. In another and unintended sense the Communist Party was tethered to the Tocquevillian rule concerning voluntary association in America. Given the length of time recruits spent in the Party (Browder complained that in order to get a net gain of twenty-five, one hundred people needed to be added), perhaps Americans did regard the Party in Tocquevillian terms.

87 Ibid., pp. 105, 106.

88 Ibid., p. 105; also see Schlesinger's comments on "demi-intellectuals" in *The Politics of Upheaval*, pp. 165–66.

89 Sara Gordon quoted in Vivian Gornick, *The Romance of American Communism* (New York: Basic Books, 1977), p. 110. Also see Gitlow, *The Whole of Our Lives*, pp. 239–41.

90 On the "independence" of the rank and file, see Steve Nelson, *The Autobiography of Steve Nelson* (Pittsburgh: University of Pittsburgh Press, 1986); Mark Naison, "Harlem Communists and the Politics of Black Protest," *Marxist Perspectives* 1 (Fall 1978): 20–51; Roger Keeran, *The Communists and the Auto Workers Unions* (Bloomington: Indiana University Press, 1980). But also see Richard Wright's account in *American Hunger* (New York: Harper and Row, 1977).

91 Zieger, *American Workers*, p. 55.

92 For the Hickok and FDR comments see: Schlesinger, *The Coming of the New Deal*, pp. 272, 460. Although he was clearly out of his element during this minievent (he was an Indiana educator), Wirt was more prescient than the Hearst papers' predictions about a soviet America. Hearst saw the New Deal as communist; Wirt perceived that there were (submerged) communists in the New Deal.

93 Susan Ware, *Beyond Suffrage: Women in the New Deal* (Cambridge: Harvard University Press, 1981), chap. 1.

94 Harvard Sitkoff, "The New Deal and Race Relations," in Sitkoff, *Fifty Years Later*, p. 111. Also see John B. Kirbey, *Black Americans in the Roosevelt Era* (Knoxville: University of Tennessee Press, 1980).

95 See Alan Brinkley, *Voices of Protest* (New York: Random House, 1982), esp. chap. 8. Gerald L. K. Smith, a peripatetic lieutenant in each of these movements, describes the process of chapter formation, exquisite in its simplicity and characteristic of American ad hoc communities from the antislavery society to the Tupperware party: "An individual would hear a speech on the radio by Huey Long and write him a letter. Long would send him a broadside circular . . ." and "urged [him] to form a local 'Share the Wealth' Society with the understanding that it could meet in the home and not have a treasury . . . this encouraged small organizations, too small to trade off the organization and too small to trade off the enterprise to a political foe." See Smith, "The Huey Long Movement," in *As We Saw the Thirties*, ed. Rita James Simon (Urbana: University of Illinois Press, 1967), p. 64. Also see Philip Abbott, *Seeking New Inventions* (Knoxville: University of Tennessee Press, 1987), on organizational structures of movement groups in general.

Chapter 6: The Jacksonian Turn

1 Basil Rauch, *The History of the New Deal, 1933–1938* (New York: Creative Age Press, 1944), p. 156; Arthur Schlesinger, Jr., *The Politics of Upheaval* (Boston: Houghton Mifflin, 1960), p. 291; Raymond Moley, *After Seven*

Years (New York: Harper, 1939), pp. 332ff; Rexford Tugwell, *The Democratic Roosevelt* (Baltimore: Penguin, 1957), p. 326; James MacGregor Burns, *Roosevelt: The Lion and the Fox* (New York: Harcourt Brace, 1956), pp. 270–71.

2   Tugwell, *The Democratic Roosevelt*, p. 328.

3   Alan Brinkley, *Voices of Protest* (New York: Knopf, 1982), p. 147.

4   Ibid., p. 155.

5   Louis Hartz, *The Liberal Tradition in America* (New York: Harcourt, Brace, 1955), p. 262.

6   *Public Papers and Addresses of Franklin D. Roosevelt*, 13 vols. (New York: Macmillan, 1938) (1935), pp. 16–17.

7   Schlesinger, *The Politics of Upheaval*, p. 291; *Public Papers, FDR* (1935), p. 272.

8   Moley, *After Seven Years*, p. 330.

9   *Public Papers, FDR* (1936), pp. 9, 14, 16.

10   Ibid., pp. 16, 17.

11   Ibid., p. 44. In late 1934 FDR had written to Garner after a visit to the Hermitage: "The more I learn about Andy Jackson the more I love him!" Burns, *Roosevelt: The Lion and the Fox*, p. 208.

12   *Public Papers, FDR* (1935), pp. 41–42.

13   Ibid., p. 198–99.

14   *Public Papers, FDR* (1936), pp. 383–84, 566–73.

15   Ibid., pp. 385, 403, 438, 486.

16   Ibid., p. 570.

17   Ibid., p. 568.

18   Tugwell, *The Democratic Roosevelt*, pp. 413–14.

19   Moley, *After Seven Years*, p. 350; *Public Papers, FDR* (1936), p. 40.

20   Herbert Croly, *The Promise of American Life* (New York: Capricorn, 1964), p. 59.

21   *Public Papers, FDR* (1936), pp. 459, 460.

22   Marvin Meyers, *The Jacksonian Persuasion* (Stanford: Stanford University Press, 1957), pp. 33–34. Alexis de Tocqueville, *Democracy in America*, ed. J. P. Mayer (Garden City, N.Y.: Doubleday, 1969), pp. 531–32.

23   *Public Papers, FDR* (1936), pp. 573–74; *Public Papers, FDR* (1933), p. 340.

24   *Public Papers, FDR* (1936), p. 574.

25   Morton Frisch, *Franklin D. Roosevelt* (Boston: Twayne, 1975), p. 114.

26   *Public Papers, FDR* (1935), p. 237.

27   *Public Papers, FDR* (1936), pp. 341–42.

28   Ibid., pp. 345–48.

29   *Public Papers, FDR* (1938), p. 430.

30   Donald R. McCoy, *Landon of Kansas* (Lincoln: University of Nebraska Press, 1966), chap. 11. See also, Francis W. Schruben, *Kansas in Turmoil*,

1930–1936 (Columbia: University of Missouri Press, 1969), for an account of Landon as a governor in the progressive tradition.

31 McCoy, *Landon of Kansas*, p. 272.

32 Ibid., p. 273.

33 *New York Times*, October 30, 1936.

34 McCoy; *Landon of Kansas*, p. 330.

35 Ibid.

36 Ibid., p. 283.

Chapter 7: They Have Retired into the Judiciary

1 *Public Papers and Addresses of Franklin D. Roosevelt*, 13 vols. (New York: Macmillan, 1941) (1937), pp. 1–2.

2 Ibid., pp. 4–5. Samuel I. Rosenman reports that summation, "I see one-third of a nation ill-housed, ill-clad, ill-nourished," was added by the president in the second draft (*Working with Roosevelt* [New York: Harper and Row, 1952], p. 143).

3 *Public Papers, FDR* (1937), pp. 3–5. The Exodus metaphor, though only implied here, is, of course, a staple of American political rhetoric; see Conrad Cherry, ed., *God's New Israel: Religious Interpretations of American Destiny* (Englewood Cliffs, N.J.: Prentice-Hall, 1971).

4 Rexford Tugwell, *The Democratic Roosevelt* (Baltimore: Penguin, 1957), p. 400.

5 All these aspects are emphasized in Joseph Alsop and Turner Catledge, *The 168 Days* (Garden City, N.Y.: Doubleday, Doran, 1938). Jim Farley spoke of the defeat by a "one two punch" (the resignation of Van Devanter and the death of Robinson) (*Jim Farley's Story* [New York: McGraw-Hill, 1948], p. 82). William E. Leuchtenburg, "Franklin D. Roosevelt's Supreme Court 'Packing' Plan," in *Essays on the New Deal*, ed. Harold Hollingsworth (Austin: University of Texas Press, 1969), admits that FDR gained judicial "legitimization for the New Deal" but paid a "fearful price" (p. 115); also see Rosenman's catalog of "mistakes," *Working With Roosevelt*, p. 161, and for a more recent account emphasizing the success of the Court's tactics, see Gregory A. Caldeira, "Public Opinion and the Supreme Court: FDR's Court-Packing Plan," *American Political Science Review* 81 (December 1987): 1139–53.

6 Tugwell, *The Democratic Roosevelt*, pp. 389, 395; Harold Ickes to William Allen and Donald Richberg to Ray Clapper White in Leuchtenburg, "Roosevelt's Supreme Court 'Packing' Plan," p. 82; *Public Papers, FDR* (1937), p. lxv.

7 *Public Papers, FDR* (1935), pp. 201, 209.

8 Ibid., pp. 206–7.

9 Alsop and Catledge, *The 168 Days*, p. 35.

10 *Public Papers, FDR* (1937), p. 126.

11 Railroad Retirement Board v. Alton Railroad Co. 295 US 330 (1935).

12 National Labor Relations Board v. Jones and Laughlin Steel Corp. 301 US 1 (1937).

13 Lochner v. New York 198 US 45 (1905); Adkins v. Children's Hospital 261 US 525 (1923); West Coast Hotel v. Parrish, 300 US 379 (1937). Monrad Paulson relates the continued use of *Lochner* ("The Persistence of Substantive Due Process in the States," *Minnesota Law Review* 91 [1950]). For a more recent and broader review of the use of substantive due process at the state level, see Susan P. Fino, "Remnants of the Past: Economic Due Process in the States," in *Economic Due Process*, ed. Stanley Friedelbaum (Westport, Conn.: Greenwood Press, 1987).

14 Nebbia v. New York 291 US 54 (1934). Also see Sutherland's pointed dissent in *West Coast Hotel* arguing that precedents for upholding regulation were available within the boundaries of substantive due process: West Coast Hotel v. Parrish 300 US 379 (1937). Also see Hughes's position that the Court, overall, sustained progressive legislation, Charles Evans Hughes, *The Supreme Court of the United States* (New York: Columbia University Press, 1928), pp. 95–96.

15 West Coast Hotel v. Parrish.

16 *Public Papers, FDR* (1937), p. 116.

17 Ibid., p. lxvii, 55; (1935), p. 4.

18 *Public Papers, FDR*, (1937), pp. 124–25, 126.

19 Ibid., pp. 127–29. Also see Robert H. Jackson, solicitor general and attorney general under FDR, *The Struggle for Judicial Supremacy* (New York: Knopf, 1941). Jackson argues that only at the "threshold of the New Deal" had the Court "established itself as a Supreme Censor of legislation" (p. 70).

20 Edward S. Corwin, *Court Over Constitution* (Gloucester, Mass.: Peter Smith, 1957), chap. 1; Charles S. Hyneman, *The Supreme Court on Trial* (New York: Atherton Press, 1963), chaps. 6, 7; Alexander Bickel, *The Least Dangerous Branch* (Indianapolis: Bobbs-Merrill, 1962), chap. 1.

21 Herbert J. Storing, *What the Anti-Federalists Were For* (Chicago: University of Chicago Press, 1981), p. 50.

22 *The Federalist Papers*, ed. Clinton Rossiter (New York: New American Library, 1961), pp. 464–70.

23 Thomas Jefferson, Letter to John Dickinson, 1801.

24 Andrew Jackson, in *Messages and Papers of the Presidents*, ed. James D. Richardson, 20 vols. (New York: Bureau of National Literature, 1896), 2: 82.

25 Abraham Lincoln in ibid., 6:9.

26 Michael Kammen, *A Machine That Would Go of Itself: The Constitution in American Culture* (New York: Knopf, 1986), p. 201. Kammen is speaking here of the 1911–12 crisis. He notes as well that the "controversies of 1814–15, 1857–65, 1870–73 (the Legal Tender cases), and 1882–83 (the Civil Rights cases) undermine any meaningful notion of a nineteenth century consensus" (p. 185).

27 Ibid., pp. 203–4. Also see John Milton Cooper, *The Warrior and the Priest* (Cambridge: Harvard University Press, 1983), pp. 150–51.

28 The 1924 Progressive Party platform also called for the election of all federal judges.

29 U.S. Senate, Committee on Judiciary, 75th Congress, first session, Report 711.

30 Leuchtenburg, *Franklin D. Roosevelt and the New Deal*, p. 255; Leuchtenburg, "Roosevelt's Supreme Court 'Packing' Plan," pp. 86–88; *The New Republic*, March 31, 1937, p. 225.

31 Robert Dahl, "Decision-Making in a Democracy: The Supreme Court as a National Policy-Maker," *Journal of Public Law* 6 (1957): 280–81.

32 *Public Papers, FDR* (1937), pp. 365, 366.

33 *Public Papers, FDR* (1938), p. xxix. These lines, written in 1941, borrowed upon Nazi tactics to describe the Court battle. The opposition had organized a "strong 'putsch'" against the president in 1937 and since 1933, opposition to his reforms had "developed into 'blitzkreig' proportions" (pp. xxii, xxvii).

34 Ibid., p. 398. On the development of the use of the word *liberal* by FDR, see Ronald D. Rotunda, *The Politics of Language* (Iowa City: University of Iowa Press, 1986), pp. 52–87.

35 *Public Papers, FDR* (1938), pp. 430, 453, 447.

36 *New York Times*, August, 22 and 23, 1938. For FDR's remarks on feudalism and the South see *Public Papers, FDR* (1938), p. 475.

37 Leuchtenburg, *FDR and the New Deal*, pp. 272, 274.

38 *Public Papers, FDR* (1939), p. 61.

Chapter 8: Black Easter and Other Lincolns

1 *New Republic*, August 18, 1937, p. 46.

2 Cited in David Donald, *Lincoln Reconsidered* (New York: Vintage Books, 1967), p. 153. The "Black Easter" tradition is also discussed in Stephen B. Oates, *Abraham Lincoln: The Man Behind the Myths* (New York: Harper and Row, 1984), pp. 3–17; Lloyd Lewis, *Myths after Lincoln* (New York: Harcourt, Brace, 1929); Roy P. Basler, *The Lincoln Legend* (Boston: Houghton Mifflin, 1935); Richard N. Current, *The Lincoln Nobody Knows* (New York: McGraw-Hill, 1958), pp. 282–87.

3 *The Life and Writings of Abraham Lincoln*, ed. Philip Van Doren Stern (New

York: Modern Library, 1940), p. 224; Richard Hofstadter, *The American Political Tradition* (New York: Knopf, 1948), p. 100.

4 *Herndon's Lincoln,* ed. David Freeman Hawke (Indianapolis: Bobbs-Merrill, 1970), pp. 3–7, 112, 122. Also see David Donald's biography of Herndon, *Lincoln's Herndon* (New York, 1948).

5 Edgar DeWitt Jones, *Lincoln and the Preachers* (New York: Harper and Row, 1920); William J. Wolf, *The Almost Chosen People* (Garden City, N.Y.: Doubleday, 1959).

6 Michael Davis, *The Image of Lincoln in the South* (Knoxville: University of Tennessee Press, 1971), pp. 119.

7 Ibid., p. 125.

8 Edgar Lee Masters, *Lincoln the Man* (New York: Dodd, Mead, 1931), pp. 15, 9.

9 Carl Sandburg, *Abraham Lincoln: The Prairie Years* (New York, 1926), p. 12.

10 Masters, *Lincoln the Man,* pp. 491, 494, 497. Noteworthy on this point is M. E. Bradford's contemporary critique of Lincolnian rhetoric, *Remembering Who We Are* (Athens: University of Georgia Press, 1985), p. 155.

11 Sandburg, *Abraham Lincoln: The Prairie Years,* p. 11; Masters, *Lincoln the Man,* pp. 273, 275.

12 Sandburg, *Abraham Lincoln,* p. 92.

13 *Public Papers and Addresses of Franklin D. Roosevelt,* 20 vols. (New York: Macmillan, 1938) (1936), p. 222; (1938), pp. 40–41.

14 Ibid. (1938), p. 520; (1940), pp. 26, 29.

15 Ibid. (1940), p. 30.

16 Rexford Tugwell, *The Democratic Roosevelt* (Baltimore: Penguin, 1957), p. 403.

17 *Public Papers, FDR* (1940), pp. 30, 436.

18 James MacGregor Burns, *Roosevelt: The Lion and the Fox* (New York: Harcourt, Brace, 1956), pp. 422–23.

19 Sandburg's speech is reprinted in *Home Front Memo* (New York: Harcourt, 1943), pp. 29–30. For FDR's use of Sherwood's and Sandburg's Lincoln as well as of the talents of both, see Alfred Haworth Jones, *Roosevelt's Image Brokers* (Port Washington, N.Y.: Kennikat, 1974).

20 *Newsweek,* June 19, 1939, p. 56; *New York Times,* February 14, 1939, p. 14, and October 19, 1940, p. 8; Max Lerner, "How Much of Lincoln Does Roosevelt Have in Him?" *Nation,* June 22, 1940, pp. 753–54; *Time,* January 5, 1942.

21 *Public Papers, FDR* (1940), p. 99.

22 For a discussion of this point see Robert A. Divine, *Roosevelt and World War II* (Baltimore: Penguin, 1969), pp. 21–23.

23 Robert E. Sherwood, *There Shall Be No Night* (New York: Scribner's, 1940), pp. xxii–xxiv.

24 *Public Papers, FDR* (1933), pp. 11–16.
25 Samuel I. Rosenman, *Working with Roosevelt* (New York: Harper, 1952), p. 259.
26 *The Life and Writings of Abraham Lincoln*, p. 349.
27 Ibid., p. 429.
28 *Public Papers, FDR* (1940), pp. 298–300.
29 Ibid., pp. 301–2.
30 *The Life and Writings of Abraham Lincoln*, p. 674.
31 *Public Papers, FDR* (1940), p. 302.
32 Ibid., p. 408.
33 Ibid., pp. 432–34.
34 Ibid., pp. 436, 439, 472.
35 For a review of opinion polls see William L. Langer and S. Everett Gleason, *The Challenge to Isolation*, 2 vols. (New York: Harper and Row, 1952), 1: 11–51.
36 Burns, *Roosevelt: The Lion and the Fox*, p. 433.
37 *New York Times*, September 17, 1940, p. 11; September 20, 1940, p. 1; and November 1, 1940, p. 18.
38 See the GOP complaint that FDR was not running against Willkie but against Hitler with the Republican candidate as a "poor third" (Steve Neal, *Dark Horse: A Biography of Wendell Willkie* [New York: Doubleday, 1984], p. 150).
39 *New York Times*, September 15, 1940.
40 For a full account of the Lewis speech and the complex reasons for his decision, see Robert Zieger, *John L. Lewis: Labor Leader* (Boston: Twayne, 1988), pp. 103–31.
41 *New York Times*, September 17, 1940, p. 10.
42 Ibid.
43 Ibid., September 15, 1940, p. 15.
44 Ibid., November 1, 1940, p. 18.
45 Rosenman, *Working with Roosevelt*, p. 236.
46 Ibid., p. 245.
47 *Public Papers, FDR* (1940), p. 532.
48 Ibid., pp. 531–32.
49 Both Rosenman and Sherwood admit that there was what we might call a brief Jacksonian return in October. Rosenman speaks of the Brooklyn and Cleveland speeches as a "glorious chance to turn the tables on his [FDR's] opponents" (*Working with Roosevelt*, p. 246). Sherwood notes that these were "strong words and one might call them unfair" but they were "at the time unanswerable, and this was the kind of fighting talk that the people want to hear" (*Roosevelt and Hopkins* [New York: Harper and Brothers, 1948], p. 194).

50 See Neal, *The Dark Horse*, pp. 161–65 for what Willkie complained was a "whispering campaign" against him.

51 *Public Papers, FDR* (1940), p. 551.

52 Ibid., p. 544.

53 Ibid., p. 640.

54 Ibid., pp. 634–36.

55 Ibid., pp. 665–66.

56 Ibid., p. 672.

57 James MacGregor Burns, *Roosevelt: The Soldier of Freedom, 1940–45* (New York: Harcourt, Brace, 1970), p. viii.

58 *Public Papers, FDR* (1940), p. 663; (1941), pp. 485–86.

59 *Public Papers, FDR* (1940), pp. 281–85.

60 Rosenman, *Working with Roosevelt*, p. 263.

61 *Public Papers, FDR* (1941), p. 3.

62 *The Life and Writings of Abraham Lincoln*, p. 240.

63 *Public Papers, FDR* (1941), p. 3.

64 See Charles B. Strozier, *Lincoln's Quest for Union* (New York: Basic Books, 1982), pp. 177–81.

65 *Public Papers, FDR* (1941), pp. 4–6.

66 Rosenman, *Working with Roosevelt*, p. 270.

67 *Public Papers, FDR* (1941), pp. 45, 666, 139, 184.

68 Ibid., pp. 455, 458–60, 462.

69 Ibid., pp. 62, 83, 138.

70 Ibid., pp. 328–29. The *New York Times* headline the following day read: "President Bids Nation Awake to Peril/Roosevelt Is Grim/Quotes Lincoln to Show a Parallel . . ." (p. 1).

71 *Public Papers, FDR* (1941), pp. 64, 65, 368, 46.

72 Ibid., p. 63.

Chapter 9: Which Roosevelt Do I Imitate?

1 Dwight Macdonald, *Politics Past* (New York: Viking, 1957), pp. 285–87.

2 William E. Leuchtenburg, *In the Shadow of FDR* (Ithaca: Cornell University Press, 1983), p. 237.

3 *Public Papers and Addresses of Franklin D. Roosevelt*, 20 vols. (New York: Macmillan, 1938) (1933), p. 628.

4 Robert V. Remini, *Andrew Jackson* (New York: Harper and Row, 1969), p. 170.

5 Ibid.

6 Al Smith, "I am an American before I am a Democrat," *Vital Speeches* 3 (1936): 18.

7 Eric Goldman, "The American Liberal," *Reporter*, June 23, 1953, p. 25;

Harry Girvetz, *The Evolution of Liberalism* (New York: Collier, 1963), p. 387.

8   Ellis Hawley, "The Corporate Ideal as Liberal Philosophy in the New Deal," in *The Roosevelt New Deal*, ed. Wilber J. Cohen (Richmond: Virginia Commonwealth University Press, 1986), pp. 85–103.

9   Henry Wallace, *New Frontiers* (New York: Reynal and Hithcock, 1934), pp. 38, 52.

10 Ibid., pp. 274–75, 283.

11 Speech of Henry Wallace, "Licking the Ghost of Alexander Hamilton" (May 1935), cited in Peter H. Irons, *The New Deal Lawyers* (Princeton: Princeton University Press, 1982), p. 181.

12 Harry Truman, *Memoirs*, 2 vols. (Garden City, N.Y.: Doubleday, 1955–56), 2:171. See also Robert J. Donovan, *Tumultous Years: The Presidency of Harry S Truman, 1949–1953* (New York: Norton, 1982), p. 17.

13 Thomas Sancton, "Second Chance for the New Deal," *Nation*, January 15, 1949, p. 61; Joseph Alsop and Stewart Alsop, "Candidate Truman's Magic Brew," *Saturday Evening Post*, December 31, 1949, p. 12.

14 Arthur Larson, *A Republican Looks at His Party* (New York: Harper and Row, 1956).

15 Leuchtenburg, *In the Shadow of FDR*, p. 99.

16 Arthur Schlesinger, Jr., *A Thousand Days* (Boston: Houghton Mifflin, 1965), pp. 210–12. See also Henry Pachter, "JFK as Equestrian Statue," *Salmagundi* 1 (1966) for a thoughtful analysis of Schlesinger's assertion that the Kennedy administration represented a "politics of modernity."

17 Schlesinger, *A Thousand Days*, p. 640.

18 *Public Papers of the Presidents of the United States: Lyndon Baines Johnson*, 10 vols. (Washington, D.C.: Office of the Federal Register) (1965), pp. 394–99.

19 Ray Price, *With Nixon* (New York: Viking, 1977), p. 45.

20 George Will, *Nixon Agonistes* (Boston: Houghton Mifflin, 1970), p. 86.

21 William Safire, *Before the Fall* (Garden City, N.Y.: Doubleday, 1975), p. 50.

22 Alonzo Hamby, *Liberalism and Its Challengers* (New York: Oxford University Press, 1985), p. 300.

23 Henry Adams, *History of the United States of America during the Administration of Thomas Jefferson* (1889; reprint, New York: Library of America, 1986), pp. 12–39.

24 Reagan selections are from "The Speech" in 1964 and the 1981 State of the Union message that focused upon the "troubles" caused by the "mass of regulations imposed upon the shopkeeper, the farmer, the craftsman, professionals" (*A Time for Choosing: The Speeches of Ronald Reagan, 1961–1982* [Chicago: Regnery, 1983]).

Index